The Politics of Money

D0878361

The Politics of Money

Towards Sustainability and Economic Democracy

Frances Hutchinson, Mary Mellor
and Wendy Olsen

Pluto  Press

LONDON • STERLING, VIRGINIA

First published 2002 by Pluto Press
345 Archway Road, London N6 5AA
and 22883 Quicksilver Drive,
Sterling, VA 20166–2012, USA

www.plutobooks.com

British Library Cataloguing in Publication Data
A catalogue record for this book is available from the British Library

ISBN 0 7453 1721 9 hardback
ISBN 0 7453 1720 0 paperback

Library of Congress Cataloging in Publication Data
applied for

10   9   8   7   6   5   4   3   2   1

Designed and produced for Pluto Press by
Chase Publishing Services, Fortescue, Sidmouth EX10 9QG
Typeset from disk by Stanford DTP Services, Towcester
Printed in the European Union by Antony Rowe, Chippenham, England

Contents

Preface

We wish to acknowledge all the resources and all the people known and unknown who have helped and sustained us in the writing of this book. We are particularly grateful to our families for their patience and support, especially Keith Hutchinson, Nigel Mellor, Terry Leyland and Corrie. Our special thanks also go to Dorothy Peart for the original conceptualisation and drawing of The Good Ship TINA.

In preparing this book we have considerably reduced the number of works originally cited, focusing on key texts which will themselves provide references for extended study. We hope that the reader will find the final Bibliography to be a valuable resource for further reading.

We are fully aware that our illustrative material and examples of contemporary debates are drawn predominantly, although not exclusively, from the UK. Since all three authors are currently resident in the UK we prefer to focus upon our geographical location rather than embrace the spurious universalism which is so central to global capitalism. We are confident that the country-specific material can be readily understood by readers from other countries. Furthermore, we have sought to move beyond the Anglo-American cultural context by citing research and examples from a substantial number of countries across the world.

Frances Hutchinson
Mary Mellor
Wendy Olsen

1 The Money Society

This book is about money, economics and economic democracy. Our starting point is that the current dominance of capitalist economic theory and practice is socially and ecologically destructive. New ways of theorising and organising economic systems are necessary if sustainable and equitable human societies are to be achieved. Our particular focus is the role that money has played in the development of capitalised market societies. However, there is a relative silence within conventional economic theory on this subject. This silence is not only one of omission, the assumption that the theory of money and credit is very much secondary to the study of economic systems, but also of exclusion, even exile, of dissident voices. Those who have sought to raise critical questions about the nature and role of money and the radical potential of money systems are dismissed as radicals or cranks. In this book we will explore those voices from the Marxian critique of the cash nexus in the nineteenth century through the institutionalists, guild socialists and social credit movements of the early twentieth century to the contemporary 'new economics' movements.

Central to our argument is the view that ecological sustainability and social equality cannot be separated from economic democracy. With the global dominance of the capitalist market and the large-scale incursion of money values into most aspects of social life, access to money and credit is vital. In market societies, where resources are privatised and production is capitalised, goods and services necessary for survival can only be accessed through a monetary exchange. The hopes of organising production and consumption within a collectivised state system have been severely undermined by the failures of the Soviet model. Even if there were a move back towards nationalisation or municipalisation of some services or industries there would be an expectation that a profit-based market will still remain fundamental to the allocation of resources. If this is the case, then the organisation and structuring of that market and the money system that funds it is a fundamental question for democracy.

Our overall aim is to reclaim models of economic democracy that can (re)establish social(ist) principles. We will not write this word in such a peculiar way again, but we want to stress that we are looking for a renewed radical politics through the recognition of economics as a social principle. In particular, we argue that the nature of money systems as access systems is a critical issue for socialists. In seeking to make a contribution to the development of economic democracy as a socialist strategy for the twenty-first century this book will draw on contemporary movements concerned with social approaches to economics. We will also explore interesting innovative contemporary economic experiments at the local level but we will argue that these can better contribute to a more comprehensive strategy if we understand them through the analysis and proposals of earlier movements. We look in particular at institutional views of money and proposals for the socialisation of money and credit.

We also seek to retain the energy of the political economy of Marx through incorporating the work of feminist and ecological economists into his critique of capitalism and his materialist view of the economy. This would add to Marx's analysis of the exploitative relations between capital and labour the marginalisation and exploitation of women's unpaid labour and the economic appropriation and degradation of natural resources. At the same time we join with those feminist, ecological and institutionalist economists in their questioning of the elevation and reification of 'the economy' as a distinct and dominant social domain.

Money and society

In capitalised market economies having money means belonging, particularly in the US and the UK. Lack of money brings real hardship and refusal of access to money is indicative of exclusion from citizenship. In Britain asylum seekers were initially stigmatised by the refusal of the state to give them benefits as money instead of vouchers tradeable at selected shops. In the US welfare recipients are given food stamps. Early in the industrial revolution wages were often paid in a company currency or scrip recognised only by the company store or truck shops. Legitimated access to money became a sign of citizenship, culminating in the Blairite notion of 'responsible' citizenship. Following on from the Thatcherite era, those in receipt of money benefits without 'earning' are seen as 'scrounging'. The UK Welfare to Work strategy is based on the argument that no-one is entitled to money for 'nothing'. Even being a parent does not qualify as being socially worthy, with single parents being urged to take paid work.

Everyone must be seen to make a contribution to 'society'. Making a money-rewarded contribution is central to the exercise of citizens' rights, regardless of the social or ecological impacts of the 'economic' activity. The 'taxpayer' is much more important than the voter in the mind of governments. The political focus of governments is on financial stability from the 'pound in your pocket' of Harold Wilson, to the 'sound money' of Margaret Thatcher and 'it's the economy, stupid' of Bill Clinton. Massive money incomes and particularly lucrative share options for company executives have been a feature of late capitalism. What in the 1970s was called the unacceptable face of capitalism by UK Conservative Prime Minister Edward Heath is now not only acceptable but applauded. Greed is good. By the end of the twentieth century, the rapidly increasing number of billionaires was led by Bill Gates with over $50 billion amassed through attaining a monopoly position in information technology until the collapse of internet stocks when he was overtaken by Sam Walton, head of the US hypermarket chain, Walmart. Cultural icons such as pop, film and sports stars also command huge incomes. Status is defined by consumption. Advertising urges the latest, improved, must-have items, with children as particular targets. The sophistication of advertising is such that trading is more around 'logo' than product (Klein, 2000).

Consumption is not just about having money; it is access to credit as people and countries consume far beyond their current wealth. In mid 2001 the US had a credit bill of $28 trillion, 300 per cent of GDP (*Guardian*, 15 October 2001). Much of this had gone into the ill-fated stock market boom. By the end of 2001 the US was in recession. The second half of the twentieth century saw a huge growth in personal credit, which is, of course, a charge on future earnings. In mid 2001 the UK population owed £700 billion representing 110 per cent of disposable income. On average each household owed £5,300 on top of mortgage debt (*Guardian*, 31 August 2001). Mortgage debt in the UK at the end of the twentieth century was £409,433 billion, an average of £38,400 per house (1996 figures; Rowbotham, 1998: 18). In the early 1990s a national random sample survey showed that 8 per cent of households with a mortgage declared that they had difficulties making their mortgage payments (Buck *et al.*, 1994: 143). In other western countries, particularly those who follow the UK/US model, similar levels of indebtedness are common, whilst in the southern and Asian regions of the world rapidly rising levels of consumer debt are also becoming widespread. This is additional to traditional levels of indebtedness. For instance, many Indian farmers are seriously in debt to local moneylenders whilst also being keen to receive bank credit. Sri Lankan farmers and emigrants are prepared to borrow at interest rates as high as 25 per cent (from banks) rising to 240 per cent (from moneylenders).

When major purchases are made, definitions of creditworthiness determine access to credit and therefore to goods. A catch-22 for many people seeking credit is that one of the main ways to gain creditworthiness is already to have had credit. For the poor, and particularly for many women, access to credit or even banking is effectively denied. Whole communities are cut off from financial services, banks, insurance, loan facilities and so on, either because of their personal situation or because there are no facilities in their locality. In the UK 1.5 million households use no financial services and 10 per cent of households have no bank account. In the absence of high street banking facilities, around 3 million households rely on local credit agencies often paying at least 50 per cent interest and often much higher.

Apart from their centrality to contemporary society, financial services are also a major employer, outstripping both farming and engineering in the UK. In 1996 and 1997 financial services counted for one-third of UK growth. In 1999 it was responsible for half of all output growth. The assumption that the money train would go on forever led Britain under the Thatcherite experiment to think that primary production and manufactures were no longer necessary. Britain would trade its way to prosperity via the value of its currency and its intangible services, particularly its financial services. This has left the UK very exposed to a collapse in the banking 'industry'. While Britain gained from the 20-year-long boom, it is now exceptionally exposed to a bear market. The superficial growth of financial services has also been undermined by doubts about the financial probity of some of its activities, including the mis-selling of pensions, endowments and other products.

Money/credit has also become electronic, so its physical existence has largely disappeared. Future archaeologists will have little idea how the twenty-first century economy worked. There will be no hoards of coin buried in fields, books of accounts or hieroglyphs carved into stone. The intangibility of money has allowed a huge fluidity in money/credit and severe problems with financial regulation, particularly after the so-called Big Bang reforms in 1986. The financial system has been riven by financial scandals and spectacular collapses. In December 2001 Enron, the world's largest energy trader, collapsed with losses that some commentators estimated could be up to $40 billion (*Observer*, 2 December 2001). This was a company that had been engaged in humble gas pipe-laying before the lure of the money market called. In 1991 in the UK the Bank of Commerce and Credit International collapsed owing £20 billion. In 1995 the 28-year-old trader Nick Leeson lost £800 million and destroyed Barings Bank. In 1998 the US hedge fund ironically named Long Term Capital Management collapsed owing $4.3 billion. This one was deemed 'too big to fail' (or small enough to save?) and a rescue was mounted by a consortium of banks and financial agencies (Lowenstein, 2001). The intangible nature of money has generally created a looseness in the financial system that undermines claims to 'sound money'. Banks, credit card companies and internet traders face fraud on a massive scale, but the holes in accounts are quietly closed electronically to keep 'confidence' in the financial system. How long this can continue is, however, another question.

Globalisation and finance

The finance industry lies at the heart of globalisation. Of the total international transactions of a trillion or so dollars each day, 95 per cent are purely financial. Globalisation is not about trade: it is about money. For Gibson-Graham (1996: 136) 'financial gamesmanship' has led to money being traded for money in such a way that even the exchange of physical commodities is more concerned with future monetary transactions than meeting real needs for goods and services. As McEwan points out, global trade as a percentage of national output is very little different to what it was at the end of the nineteenth century – around 40 per cent (1999). Investors no longer put their money into factories or merchant ships but, instead, into a plethora of overlapping 'financial products' such as futures, derivatives, hedge funds or currency speculation. Even a small rise or fall in the value of a currency can make a fortune for large-scale investors, while a larger rise or fall, caused by those same investment practices, could destroy a national economy. Value in money terms has become ephemeral and, as we will argue, always was. What was valuable yesterday becomes valueless today, and vice versa. Within the global economy the relevant performance or efficiency of business is much less important than the value of currency. Wages are cheap, partly because workers are relatively less well paid, but also because they are also paid in a less valued currency (Hines, 2000). Currency imbalance also fuels a mass tourist trade as the wages of workers in high-value currencies can buy services and resources at seemingly minimal prices in low-value countries.

Another source of devastation wrought by the inequality in the value of currencies is the huge transfer of wealth from South to North through the loan shark system of North–South debt. We do not here enter into the debate on the relationship between international debt, trade and cash cropping on the one hand and the spread of famine and the degradation of the land on the other (see, e.g., Shiva, 1988). The scandal of the debt crisis has been told many times (see, e.g., George, 1988). Globalisation has been a disaster for poorer countries, with minority elites fighting for power both militarily and economically through the sale of minerals, cash crops and cheap labour to the developed world (Chossudovsky, 1997). Research by the Worldwatch Institute shows that UN figures indicate that by the end of the twentieth century the 20 per cent of countries at the top end of scale earned 86 times more than the 20 per cent of countries at the bottom end. In 1997 the difference was 74 times; in the 1960s it was 'only' 30 times. Between 1950 and 2000 global trade grew by 17 times – but Africa's share of trade has fallen from 8 per cent to 2 per cent and Latin America's from 11 per cent to 5 per cent (report in *Guardian*, 14 April 2000). At the dawn of the twenty-first century, one-sixth of the world's population had 80 per cent of world income averaging $70 dollars a day, while 57 per cent of the world population in the 63 poorest countries had only 6 per cent of world income averaging $2 per day. There are 1.6 billion people living on under $1, a figure that has not changed since 1987, while 1.2 billion are overnourished, or badly nourished, to the point of obesity (Worldwatch, 2000). As we demonstrate in these pages, however, the money value of an income is a poor indicator of well-being.

While money value can provide some measure of inequality, the relationship between money and livelihood has greater significance. Around 30 per cent of the world population still lives on or near the land, a figure which overlaps with the proportion of the world that has very little money (under $2 a day). For this group of people what is critical is access to sufficient fertile land to sustain the continued existence of subsistence livelihoods. Around 25 per cent of the world population live in highly commodified economies with a high standard of living and rely almost entirely on the market for their sustenance. In 1939 the UK supplied over 95 per cent of its food regionally, but by 1999 the position was entirely reversed. For the remainder of the world's people, rapidly becoming the majority, their livelihoods are uncertain as they gradually coalesce into the burgeoning cities as land is commodified and depopulated. Within those cities the problem of how to make a living becomes predominant as the dynamism of most city economies depends on money investment and circulation.

The limits of money

The merry-go-round of the global money economy appears to be faltering at the beginning of the twenty-first century. By the 1990s Japan, a leading trading nation in the 1970s and 1980s, was caught in a depression brought on by the collapse of a bubble in land prices. For the last ten years of the twentieth century it was unable to get money to circulate, even with interest rates at zero. Equally, many communities in the old industrial economies have become becalmed, left behind, even abandoned by the global economy. Those still swinging around at the centre of the global financial economy are beginning to be troubled by overcommitment to the 'bottom line'. Rich populations seem not much happier than poor ones, certainly not as happy as their relative wealth would indicate. Caring, friendship, love cannot be bought. Women have pointed to the huge amount of caring and domestic work that lies beyond the world of money and credit (Himmelweit, 2000). The limits to money can be seen most clearly in the areas of health, happiness and the environment. Money may buy cosmetic surgery but it cannot buy contentment, spiritual growth or ultimately defy death itself.

Interference in natural processes through the billions of pounds spent in biotechnology causes increasing public concern, giving rise to distrust, as in the case of GM foods in the UK. This distrust appears justified given the reports from Mexico that GM contaminated seeds have travelled 60 miles and infected indigenous species despite the fact that GM production ceased in 1998 (*Guardian*, 30 November 2001). Britain has also faced several crises around food security: the BSE scandal, and the foot-and-mouth disease that appears to have been spread by letting purely financial calculations determine animal feed and movement. More generally, the claim of the global market economy that it can increase world prosperity through an increase in material wealth, measured in money terms, is coming face to face with the limits of environmental damage. The collateral damage of the 'development' process became clear only ten years after the US President Truman made his famous 'underdevelopment' speech in 1949. In 1960 Rachel Carson raised doubts about the environmental safety of the new technologies with her vision of a 'Silent Spring' as pesticides continued to enter the food chain in escalating numbers. By the 1990s the environmental messages on a global scale could no longer be ignored, with fossil-fuel-induced climate change heading the global agenda.

The very security of the financial system itself is coming into question. Within market societies money is security, money is the future. Caught in a welter of personal finance, mortgages, endowments, and insurances, individuals and households juggle with financial products in a quest for control over their finances. During the late-twentieth-century financial boom many were tricked into thinking that the stock market was an ever-rising escalator for their future security (Dordoy and Mellor, 2000). As social mechanisms of security such as welfare states and mutual societies disappear, people are increasingly putting their faith and hopes in money and stock values particularly in the Anglo-Saxon economies (US, UK). In the US the late-twentieth-century stock market boom made people feel so safe that they even borrowed money to invest. The old mechanisms of savings and loans for working people were cast aside as savings banks and mutual societies were tossed onto the funeral pyre of the global stock market. In the UK the government began forcing more elements of social security into the money system, in particular stakeholder pensions based on a financial 'pot' of savings. However, as with all money systems, the crucial question is the long-term value of those savings. This is particularly critical when many companies are closing final salary pension schemes in favour of money purchase based on financial investment.

Anthony Giddens, one of the architects of the 'Third Way', admits that in the future there will be effectively no automatic retirement for the present generation of young people in the UK and US (Giddens, 1998), a situation previously associated with impoverished economies. What this means is that the transfer of resources between generations ceases to be a social system at the level of the whole society and returns to a transfer within single families or single lifetimes. The spread of risk that was inherent in the social/mutual systems is lost. All future security depends on the health and success of the particular family or individual. We could ask, has the whole of the industrialisation process just been for this, to return to the insecurities of the past? Families, and women in particular, are showing the reality of the situation as the birth rate tumbles down. Contemporary economies are family-unfriendly. The choice for women is (at best) secure, well-paid work and few or no children, or children and less income. As a result the late industrial societies are dying at the roots; they face a future of insecure money incomes and a contracting pool of labour.

In Britain the hopes of a rapprochement with capitalism in the political economy of the Third Way has been exposed as a false rhetoric masking social tensions. Exploration of the language and analysis used by its political leaders show how their discourse is used to debase and deny class conflict (Fairclough, 2000). One of the core concepts the Third Way embraces, 'social capital', which is central to Third Way thinking, is rooted firmly in a false, ill-fitting, rational-choice model of individualistic human action (Fine, 2001). We go beyond Fine's critique of 'rational economic man' and Fairclough's deconstruction of Third Way discourse by offering constructive ways forward for practical action as well as for theory. We also argue that if there was to be a Third Way it would not be compatible with the global market and its capitalised money systems. This is particularly critical in the face of the world crisis that emerged after the 11 September bombings and the further evidence of financial instability in the collapse of the Argentinian economy.

This book does not aim to address current world economic issues directly. Rather it seeks to go back to reclaim lost arguments and lost histories and join them with new ideas and agendas. This is necessary because so many good ideas have been abandoned. Given the upsurge of Islamic ideas, our book may also be seen as culturally limited. We do not address, for example, Islamic banking. Also, we do not pass judgement on such issues as the adoption by Britain of the euro. Our aim is the very specific one of looking at the role that money/credit has played in the emergence of capitalism and the way that mainstream economic theory legitimises contemporary economic systems by denying even the conceptualisation of alternatives.

Money and economics

Despite the centrality of money and money access in contemporary societies, very little attention is paid in economic thought to what money actually *is*, how it comes into existence and how it mediates the relationships between resources, products and people. Most economists follow a convention of regarding money as merely one commodity among many, although with special properties which make its use desirable. It is common practice to argue that what is actually traded is material goods and services. Economists study the things that 'really matter'. The study of money is a matter for (mere) accountants. Although banking, and the different forms that money can take, may appear in economics textbooks, discussion of its role is mainly limited to its ability to facilitate exchange of 'other' commodities, including labour. In the absence of serious attention to the phenomenon of money by economists, the field has been left to geographers, anthropologists, historians, sociologists and people from a range of backgrounds who have critically and/or lovingly excavated the subject. We will draw gratefully on these works in this book. We also draw mainly on what would be seen from a mainstream perspective as maverick economists and economic commentators.

It was Schumpeter who identified perhaps the most recognised metaphor for money within conventional economics, when he described it as a mere

> 'garb or veil' of the things that really matter, both to households or firms in their everyday practice and to the analyst who observes them. Not only *can* it be discarded whenever we are analyzing the fundamental features of the economic process but it *must* be discarded just as a veil must be drawn aside if we are to see the face behind it. (Schumpeter, 1954: 277. Emphasis in the original)

From this perspective, the really important issue 'behind' money prices is the relationship between commodities. Hence, income formation is really an exchange of labour and the physical means of subsistence. Saving and investment really means the saving of some tangible factors of production and their conversion into real capital goods. It is these physical capital goods that are 'really' lent when an industrial borrower arranges for a loan. As Schumpeter explains, it is a convention of economists to assume:

that all the essential phenomena of economic life are capable of being described in terms of (real) goods and services, of decisions about them, and of relations between them. Money enters the picture only in the modest role of a technical device that has been adopted in order to facilitate transactions. (Schumpeter, 1954: 277)

There is also a theoretical assumption that economic activity is organised within a circular flow. People sell their resources (labour, land capital) so that tangible goods and services can be produced. They receive money in exchange. They take the money to the market place and buy the goods and services they require. This completes the circle. Certain assumptions are made about this circle. The first and main one is that people behave rationally and calculate their economic choices in commensurate terms: that is, that each activity or economic choice can be judged within a common scheme of measurement. The second is that the circle is complete in itself, that it fully embraces all the necessary economic calculations. The third is that, left to itself, the circle will meet all economic needs; no-one will produce more than can be sold, no-one will be left without. Although market failure is acknowledged, this does not lead economists to challenge the efficacy of the money/market system. From time to time, a malfunction may occur, causing inflation and involuntary unemployment or deflation and under-consumption. If it is out of order, the money balance of the economy may need to be corrected – that is money and interest rates are adjusted in such a way that the quantity of money does not exceed the quantity of goods available for exchange. However, as long as it functions normally, money is considered to have no effect on the economic process, which is seen as operating on a barter principle, i.e. guns exchange for cabbages according to the operation of supply and demand in the market.

For mainstream theory, then, money is said to have four functions:

1 *medium of exchange*: the chief function of money is to operate as a universally acceptable medium of exchange. Money is anything, from shells, beads, precious metals and paper to blips on computer screens. Money is anything universally recognised as acceptable in exchange for goods and services, and in the settlement of debts within a given market.

2 *unit of account*: for exchange to take place it is useful to have a standard measure of value so that a pile of cabbages can be traded against a bicycle. The pile of cabbages can be traded for a fair quantity of money, or 'price'. It can easily be seen whether or not the quantity of money exchanged for the cabbages is sufficient to buy the bicycle or any other desired item(s).

3 *store of value*: when a quantity of money received in exchange for goods or services is insufficient to purchase goods and services immediately, or otherwise not required, the value can be 'stored' in the form of money until it is sufficient or required at a later time.

4 *standard for deferred payments*: as a unit of account, money can be used to record debts incurred so that payments can be made in instalments and/or at a later time.

For functions 3 and 4, money must be durable. It must retain its value over time: hence its traditional association with precious metals such as silver and gold. Metallic money is widely acceptable, easily divided into measurable units by weight and does not corrupt or corrode quickly. It therefore fulfils all the functions required of money. Unlike modern forms of coinage, paper and 'plastic' money, metallic money is also a commodity, desired for use or consumption in its own right as ornamentation.

Next, economists go on to distinguish between wants backed by money (effective demand) and needs which may exist but do not register as economic 'facts'. From this standpoint the 'facts' registered as economically relevant through statistical analysis are almost exclusively money prices. These prices include wages which are seen as the sole indicator of human work effort, and interest rates which are seen as the sole indicator of the value of credit. What economists, therefore, study as the economy is the sphere of production, distribution and exchange *for money*. If a thing has no money price, or cannot be accorded a money price or assigned a commensurate metrical value, it does not exist in the discipline of the orthodox economist. Economics is therefore caught in a tautological position. What is of value is measured in money terms, but that money has no value itself, which leaves no mechanism to record the value of the original object. Money value measures money value not the object.

Economists also tend to assume that money prices have a natural equilibrium. Several examples illustrate this tendency among orthodox economics: the idea of an equilibrium exchange rate versus 'overvaluation'; the idea of the equilibrium interest rate; and the 'law of one price' which states that commodities sold in wider markets will reach their equilibrium price whereas those sold in fragmented markets will be traded at a range of non-equilibrium prices. These assumptions idealise the notion of equilibrium and give it centre stage in an idealised world that is easily modelled but does not readily fit more complex reality. Exchange rates overshoot and jump around, interest rates are diverse in actual money markets, depending on the terms and conditions of borrowing and commodity prices vary far more than the law of one price would suggest.

As we will show in this book, money is much more than a neutral facility that enables the 'real' economy to work. Once it ceases to exist in its metallic commodity form, i.e. having value in its own right (with even that value operating merely, and primarily, as a changeable social construct), money is an entirely social form relying on the authority and legitimation of the institutions that support it. Access to money or its future existence through credit is a profoundly social question that determines wealth and well-being. We argue that in many senses money is the 'real' economy, given the way that we have been led to understand what an economy is within mainstream economic thinking. Certainly money value is the 'bottom line' that is generally accepted as validating economic decisions. That bottom line is, in turn, determined by an assumption that economic activity only takes place within a capitalised market system and on market values. This leads to another tautology: what is 'economic' is defined by the economy itself. Orthodox economics is a closed system.

Vogon economic theory

We share with John Adams the view that contemporary economic thinking espouses 'Vogon economics'. Adams derived the term 'Vogon economics' from *The Hitchhiker's Guide to the Galaxy*, a novel by Douglas Adams in which the Earth is to be destroyed to make way for a hyperspace 'express route'. For John Adams, Vogon economics describes the way in which the *raison d'être* of capitalist economic theory justifies socially irresponsible and ecologically destructive economic activity. He notes that cost–benefit analysis is used by planners *after* a decision has been made, in order to justify or support it. Plans to build a new bypass, for example, can be justified on the grounds that the benefits outweighed the costs. However, winners do not bear or share the costs suffered by the losers. Loss of home, community and beauty of environment cannot be recompensed with a money reward. Economists are even employed by the Inter-governmental Panel on Climate Change in order to provide a 'rational' assessment of the costs and benefits of global climate change expressed in monetary terms (Adams, 1995: 170–3). It is the conversion of all decision-making to monetary terms that gives economic theorising its apparent strength.

As Karl Marx noted, capitalism can be distinguished from previous forms of social organisation through its use of money and exchange value to initiate its reproductive circuit. Previously, production was based upon use value. People made the houses, clothes and tools they needed for everyday use, and grew or collected the food they needed. Although trade has existed throughout human history, the traded goods were bought by merchants *after* they had been produced, to be exchanged in different markets for a higher price. Traders were performing the services of transportation, storage and risk, for which they received payment. Capitalism emerged as money came to initiate production. As capitalists purchased the factors of production (land, labour and capital) they came to control the productive processes involved in producing use values. Capitalists acquired ownership of the land and its natural resources, human labour and the instruments of production, enabling them to determine what was produced, how it should be produced, and how it would be distributed. As McMurtry, drawing on Marx, noted, once the 'money-investors' had gained ownership and control over human work and the means of production, mechanisation could be rapidly intensified 'with no internal limit to the treatment of human lives or environmental resources used as components in the system' (1999: 102). For this reason in this book we will draw a distinction between the means of production and the means of provisioning.

Mainstream economic theory in effect operates as a system of rules, procedures and assumptions that justifies elite appropriation and manipulation of the material, social and intellectual resources of society through the institutions of the formal economy: property, finance and markets. The internal logic of economic theory only possesses an elegance in so far as it is detached from the wider reality, that it is seen as a distinct 'economic' system. For this, it is necessary to ignore the fact that the people who operate the formal economy and the materials they use originate outside the economic process, including the non-economic social institutions of the family, the common cultural inheritance of skills and knowledge, the educational, religious and other cultural institutions of society. Mainstream economic theory ignores the prior existence of a natural world and the aeons of time it took to form and evolve. It also largely ignores damage to the ecosystem. To the extent that the money economy places a money value on the resources and activities of any of these institutions and the natural world in which they are embedded, these are drawn into its service as productive or consumer agents, giving rise to the misapprehension that their availability is dependent upon the existence of money. This ignores the fact that, while human societies and the natural world can thrive, and have thrived, in the absence of a money economy, contemporary economies would cease to exist if human societies or the ecosystem collapsed.

This view of the disembedded economy has been challenged by institutional theorists such as Veblen and Polanyi and by feminist and ecological economists. Institutional theorists point to the centrality of society, feminists to women's unpaid work and partial exclusion from economic activity, while ecologists see the source of all economic activity as underpinned by the natural environment. Sometimes these are described as the social and natural economies, but it is necessary to be clear what meaning of economics is being adopted here. As we have pointed out, money/market economics is a closed system. Although it appears to study the processes of the combination of factors of production (land, labour and capital) in the creation of wealth, the subject of study in economics is limited to *the money values* (prices) of tangible resources and claims to those resources. Economists do not study the social fabric which houses economic activity, still less the natural environment from which all economic resources are drawn. They assume that economic agents can take whatever they want *from* society and from the natural world in a linear fashion, owing no responsibility to elements outside the sphere of money exchange. The continued existence of the social and environmental base of the economy is taken on blind faith, a childlike trust (see Feiner, 1999). In short, the study of economics is limited to the study of the (unsustainable) capitalist economy.

Mainstream economic theory has been associated with the political assertion that there is no alternative to the present globalising money/market system. As James Buchan has argued, since the time of Adam Smith there has been an 'ominous pairing of liberty and money profit' (Buchan, 1997: 59). What we have effectively been presented with is 'economism', a view that not only is there no economic alternative, there is also no alternative way of thinking. According to the *Collins English Dictionary*, 'economism' is a '*political* theory that regards economics as the main factor in society, ignoring or reducing to simplistic economic terms other factors such as culture, nationality, etc' (Collins, 1986, our italics).

Within the economistic perspective, the formal economy operates according to a closed system of accounting based upon money values. 'The economic' can be interpreted as a plane of existence to be viewed and treated as distinct from other societal dimensions of reality such as the cultural, the political and the social. This allows the territory of 'the economy' to be identified in technical terms, addressed by 'administrative concepts' such as 'unemployment' and 'balance of payments', and made measurable through skills like statistics. A specific range of activities are defined as 'commercial' through laws and regulations, and a 'body of experts ... come to speak in the name of the economy and to seek to optimise its forces' (Walters, 1999: 314). Those who do not support the economistic canon are deemed beyond the pale, by definition not economists, effectively 'economic exiles' (King, 1988).

Wider solutions for specific problems

Gibson-Graham describes mainstream economic theorising as embracing 'capitalocentric discourse'. Capitalocentric theorising is linear, the discourse of a single directional progress from technologically primitive past to sophisticated future (1996: 41). Linear theorising assumes there can be no going back and no need to change direction. If society is plunging out of control, destroying its institutional fabric and life-support resource base, this must be accepted as the inevitable price of progress. It is seen as inevitable that there will be losers from social and historical change. Hence, symptoms of injustice and malaise are tackled as 'single issue problems', and the search for solutions to isolated symptoms replaces any attempt to locate common underlying causes of malaise. For mainstream theorists capitalism is here to stay.

Gibson-Graham argues that linear thinking has been the hallmark of socio-economic theorising throughout the twentieth century (including Marxism) which has supported the 'development' discourse. Although there may be disagreement about individual examples of rights and wrongs, both mainstream and 'radical' theorists adopt an 'essentialist' view of capitalism which sees capitalism as driving the global economy. It is the motivating force, the powerful, dynamic, creative mechanism steering social change onwards and upwards into an all-embracing unity. Where capitalism meets other cultures it sweeps them aside because they lack efficiency, dynamism and productivity in money/market terms. This, thinks Gibson-Graham, gives far too much credence to capitalism and ignores other types of economy – domestic, subsistence, co-operative – and the 'transformative spaces' associated with them. It creates capitalism as an essentialist hegemonic notion rather than looking for a 'space of economic diversity' (1996: 5). Lawson also argues that the economic system must be perceived as open, organic, malleable, and self-transforming (1997). This new conception of an evolving economy empowers people to see themselves as agents of change. While we have sympathy with this view and one of us has written elsewhere on the subject (Langley and Mellor, 2002), we feel that the money-centrism of the capitalist economy must also be confronted.

As the old story goes, a city tourist asks directions from a local farmer. 'Well,' replies the farmer, 'if I was going *there*, I wouldn't set out from *here*.' The would-be reformer of capitalism might well receive a similar reply if asked to chart the route towards a socially just and environmentally sustainable economy. In order to understand the present *political* economy it is necessary to trace the course of events which gave rise to the evolution of the institutions comprising the economy and the theories purporting to enhance our understanding of economic affairs. Only then will it become possible to chart a sound course towards a sustainable future.

Mapping a way forward

Despite the huge inequalities that have emerged in capitalised, market-driven societies, radical social thinking is still very much in the doldrums. Socialism is a word that hardly dare speak its name. At every turn social criticism is rebuffed by the retort 'but who is going to pay?', 'where is the money to come from?' As a result it is getting increasingly difficult to argue for economic rights as human rights. To claim that there is an alternative way of creating wealth or that money is not a source of liberation for the individual is seen as misguided at best and heresy at worst. Money and access to money is symbolic of freedom, money talks, money ignores difference, the colour of money is more important than the colour of skin. There is truth in this as Marx himself acknowledged. Labour became 'free' to be exploited and the money wage is the source of that freedom as well as the mechanism of exploitation. People are free to labour or to purchase but not to control the means of their own livelihood.

We consider this a fundamental question for democracy. Do people have control over their own means of existence? The right to livelihood which is not expressed by the more limited demand of the right to work is at the heart of what we would see as economic democracy. Within capitalist market society the right to a livelihood is not a right of citizenship but a by-product of the money/market system. Access to money and credit therefore represents access to livelihood; it is a matter of social justice which, we argue, makes it a fundamental issue for socialists. Those without independent access to money in contemporary economies are the focus of charity from those deemed to be full members of society, that is, the 'wealth-creator' (money-maker) and the taxpayer (who pass over some of that money). As welfare states are rolled back there is increasing emphasis on the charitable sector, the voluntary donation of money. It is ironic therefore that the poor give more generously than the rich as proportion of income (Egan, 2001).

Outline of the book

Our task in this book is to retrace the history and theory of capitalised money in order to discover where we are and how we got here. This will be done by tracing the history of economic thought as it accompanied the evolution of the institutions governing economic activity. By comparing and contrasting alternative perspectives we seek common ground with a view to establishing a basis for viable holistic alternatives to capitalist political economy. Throughout this work we have sought to minimise the use of technical jargon with a view to increasing the accessibility to the general reader. Within each discipline in the social sciences, and political economy is no exception, different terminologies have created barriers to understanding and hence to joined-up thinking. Throughout the text we draw upon the works of a wide variety of thinkers, both mainstream and radical, heterodox and orthodox, revitalising material which may have lain dormant for over a century.

In Chapter 2 we describe several mainstream schools of economic thought and their approach to money. Taking neo-classical thought as an exemplar of contemporary thinking, we critique its key theoretical assumptions, in particular, the circular flow model. We briefly introduce a range of alternative perspectives which are elaborated in later chapters. In Chapter 3 we look at the history of money and banking. We draw out money's historical role in order to explain why money/credit is so dominant in contemporary economies. Chapter 4 looks at the particular development of capitalism and the capitalised market. As well as looking at the Marxian critique of the cash nexus we look also at more recent explorations of the way in which subsistence economies have been undermined by the imposition of money as access to livelihood. This involves looking at the history of enclosure, the destruction of subsistence and the necessity of engaging in wage labour.

From Chapter 5 onwards we begin to build the basis for alternatives to money-credit capitalism. In Chapter 5 we start chronologically with the earliest critics from the institutionalist perspective, most notably Veblen, but also still drawing on Marx. In Chapter 6 we look at guild socialist and social credit thought in some detail. The specific proposals made by writers in this tradition develop schemes that relate to the use of money to achieve social goals and indeed socialism. In Chapter 7 we show that the de-linking of credit from profit-oriented enterprise and the ability of political bodies to issue money credit for social purposes creates a space within which real economic democracy can thrive.

In Chapters 8 and 9 we look mainly at contemporary movements. In Chapter 8 we look at the critique of mainstream economics from the viewpoint of green and feminist economics. We go on to argue that a reassessment of food and farming requires a new form of economics, because within capitalism the food production system neither enhances human health nor sustains the ecological system upon which it depends. Our alternative view re-embeds the economy within the wider social framework of production.

In Chapter 9 we examine some historical and contemporary attempts to innovate in money systems, such as local money and exchange systems (LETS), micro-finance and basic income. We argue that unless there is a clear theoretical analysis alongside this often very worthwhile work, there is no basis upon which to launch a clear alternative to mainstream economic ideas. It is also possible that mainstream ideas will pervade these initiatives. Specifically, while recognising the genuine desire for collective empowerment that drives people into micro-finance and other initiatives at the grass roots all over the world, we question the usefulness of such initiatives if they are aimed at the growth of small enterprises operating within a capitalist money/market structure.

Finally, in the concluding chapter we evaluate a range of practical alternative approaches in order to establish the elements of an effective way forward towards economic democracy based upon the socialisation of money/credit. The central consideration is the vital necessity for money to be socially and locally administered. The administration of the money-creation process provides the key factor in the evolution of local production and distribution. Furthermore, a social money/credit system offers the potential for adapting the wage/salary labour system into a social system able to value human capabilities independently of any cash payments. In order to replace state-capitalism (Chomsky, 2002) with a more equitable and environmentally sustainable steady-state economy (Daly, 1973) it is necessary to revisit the alternative theorising of the twentieth century. By establishing links with contemporary green, social and feminist movements and ideas we demonstrate the feasibility of the socialisation of money/credit as a viable component of radical non-capitalist theorising. Such theorising is essential in the quest for a radical political economy.

2 Why is There No Alternative?

As we pointed out in the introduction, mainstream economics has seen money as a neutral and convenient element within economic systems. While there are schools that see monetary regulation and control as important, this is directed towards the functioning of the economic system. It is not a question related to economic democracy. Our argument is not that economists never address money and credit, since many do. In fact monetarist theory was in the ascendancy by the end of the twentieth century. Our issue is about the *way* economists address it. Money is seen as a universally acceptable medium within a given market that eliminates the 'high trading costs' of barter by removing the need for double coincidence of wants. For conventional classical and neo-classical economics money is merely one commodity among many, although with special properties which make its use desirable. It is a 'veil' behind which the real elements of the economy operate. It has its four technical functions as a medium of exchange, a unit of account, a store of value and a standard for deferred payments. Its form may have changed over time, but for conventional economists money plays a universal role. As we will discuss in the next chapter, both the form and function of money and credit have changed and this has played a major role in the emergence of the capitalist market economy.

In this chapter we explore the way in which the dominant schools of economic thought have hijacked our understanding of how 'the economy' works and have silenced alternative perspectives. Within current political circumstances we are told that there is only one effective model of 'the economy', the neo-liberal school of neo-classical economics. Even if that seems a little harsh, there is certainly no alternative to the capitalist market. All other models have been tried and found wanting. The market model may be flawed, but it is all we have, the best that can be hoped for is to iron out market failures, bring in marginalised people and communities and somehow get a fix on the environmental problem. It is hardly surprising that alternative perspectives can make little inroad into current economic theorising when the only schools to be given any serious attention and taught in depth as core subjects in Western universities are the neo-classical, Chicago and orthodox Keynesian schools. As a result, the research and teaching of the other schools, such as Marxist and institutional perspectives, let alone feminist and ecological economics, have been constrained by the necessity to be logically consistent with the mainstream schools. Even the Keynesian schools lie somewhere on the margins. In this chapter we are concerned with what we see as the orthodoxy of the core market model.

By the 1980s it was possible to plot the position of 'virtually the whole range of economists' within the neo-classical tradition. Its internal consistency appeared elegant and intellectually appealing. A student with a tidy and logical mind could put aside 'intuitive doubts' and master it with ease (Seers, 1983: 45). Seers recalls the celebrated British economist Joan Robinson once pointing out to him that the effort needed to understand the algebra in neo-classical analysis diverted the economic student's attention from the plausibility of its assumptions. After graduating, the student saw that any future career depended upon publishing analyses derived from those models, which in turn were passed on to the next generation. This legacy has impacted on economic policy. Despite the work of Keynes and that of Veblen, Galbraith, Heilbroner, Polanyi and a host of intellectuals, throughout the twentieth century 'the economy' has remained very much as classical economy defined it. The theories associated with it are now taught as standard in economics classrooms under the umbrella of orthodox economics. As we have pointed out, all attempts to diverge substantially from the orthodoxy tend to get marginalised, criticised, trivialised and discarded by proponents of mainstream economics.

Since the core assumptions of the orthodox schools are compatible, we do not in general distinguish between 'mainstream' and 'neo-classical' theory in the discussion below. Orthodox theory is based on key overarching assumptions. First, that 'the economy' is a natural system that is only amenable to social and political interventions at the margins, if at all. Secondly, that the economy is a self-sufficient phenomenon that is explainable by abstract and universal theoretical models. This approach sees economics as the 'queen' of the social sciences, although even the idea of being associated with the 'social' is anathema to most orthodox economists.

Economics as normal science

Orthodox economics has established itself in Kuhnian terms as a normal science. Sheila Dow sees the 1990s trend toward reinforcing the dominance of neo-classical economics in terms of a Kuhnian paradigm shift with its continual marginalisation of all divergent viewpoints (Dow, 2000). All constructive criticism is seen as epistemologically flawed or trivial. Meanwhile a range of differing heterodox positions (institutionalist, feminist and environmentalist), each generating interesting empirical work, are routinely ignored. Neo-classical economics is the disciplinary hub around which other perspectives must locate themselves. As with the pre-Copernican revolution critical perspectives do not challenge the geocentrism of the model. Failures in the model are addressed through theoretical epiphenomena. Those who are 'not economists' are dismissed as irrelevant. Those who challenge the heart of the theory are seen as heretics. It remains to be seen whether challenges to neo-classical theory can knock it off its pedestal, but in the UK at least neo-classical economists are not only theoretically but also practically and bureaucratically dominant. They exert power through their social networks and voluntary associations (such as the Royal Economic Society), through peer reviewing and through their domination of the mechanisms used by government to reward research.

Academic economists are judged by their publication in a 'Diamond list' seen as representing the *best* international journals constructed by Peter Diamond, an orthodox economist. The Diamond list concentrated on journals which espouse orthodoxy, such as the *Economic Journal* and omitted several important heterodox journals, such as the *Cambridge Journal of Economics*. It was a political act to make such a list, which belies the supposed value neutrality of the modelling exercises which neo-classical economists undertake. In the US there is evidence of a purge during the 1990s of non-neo-classical and non-mathematically oriented economists from university faculties. This has been described as a 'stalinization' of the profession with history of economic thought being particularly targeted. Although there is sizeable opposition to orthodoxy it is fragmented (*Post-Autistic Economics Newsletter* 1, September 2000). Despite this there is a growing debate raising the questions covered in this book. A damning indictment of the 'science' of economics was made by McCloskey (1994) and others have called for the 'end of economics' in the hope of evolving a 'more humane science of political economy' (Dupré and Gagnier, 1999).

Central to the definition of orthodox economics as a science is the assumption that it is studying a natural system. Within both classical and neo-classical economics there is the assumption that capitalism is the natural system that expresses 'economy'. Its essence is the money/market system. There may be imperfections, but it is only a matter of time and good (but minimal) management before these are resolved. There is no alternative, because the 'free' market is the only route to political freedom. The ideal is either a relatively egalitarian, property-owning democracy exchanging skills through the market place or a paternalistic system in which those who can best use economic resources exercise them on behalf of the rest of humanity. In the latter case the original allocation of property rights is not seen as an issue. The assumption of the naturalness and inevitability of capitalism masks its rather insecure history. It was not until the latter half of the nineteenth century that the model became secure in the UK through a combination of legislation and colonialism. By the early twentieth century it was undermined by a global recession only to re-emerge within the nursery of post-war reconstruction. By the 1960s and 1970s the cracks were showing once more. In the mid 1970s in the UK and the US an ideological coup was staged by neo-liberals largely through the Chicago School. That model is now under threat from anti-globalisation forces, the instability of stock market and currency values and the threat of global recession.

We would not underestimate the ideological domination of both mainstream economics and 'the economy' it represents or the very real impact of capitalist market forces on the lives of people and the ecology of the planet. However, we want in this book to identify a clear alternative. We begin with the dominance of the orthodox model in the development of economics as a discipline. Alternatives have existed but they have been silenced. It is our intention to reclaim those alternative views, but first we must look at how the orthodox model was constructed. This discussion will go back to first principles, partly because that is where our story begins, but also because those who are not economists need to know on what the TINA ideology is based. We are aware that there are many economists struggling with orthodoxy and we will discuss them where appropriate. However this book is not a debate *within* economics, it is a debate *with* economics. To put our cards on the table, we do not distinguish between economics and politics. We are not addressing the wealth of nations, or even the relations between the market and the state. We are addressing the relationship between the economy and the people and the role of money/credit in that relationship. In this chapter we want to look in more detail at the core assumptions of the orthodox model and introduce briefly some of the alternatives to it.

Classical and neo-classical schools of economic thought

The classical school

The classical school of Adam Smith, David Ricardo and James Mill based its economic theory on the potential of the industrial revolution. They celebrated what appeared to be an immense and unlimited source of wealth creation through industrial processes supported by monetary exchange. They saw the growth of factories and new technologies in which the division of labour could speed up and vastly increase production of 'wealth' as being of benefit to all. For Adam Smith the money economy represented natural liberty, although he assumed this would be within a social framework of 'moral sentiments'. The money economy would free people from economic bondage and would achieve through the circuit of production and exchange the well-being of the whole nation. As a natural system the 'hidden hand' of the market would meet all needs. Within the classical theory which underpins conservative macro-analysis of the self-sustaining economy, money is purely a measuring device having no influence upon economic outcomes. Commodities exchange for commodities, while money merely facilitates exchange. There are two key ideas within this view: first that money is neutral and without history – that is, it simply exists as a technical resource; secondly, a circular model of the economy.

The efficacy of the circular economy lies at the heart of orthodox economics and was most clearly set out by Jean-Baptiste Say (1767–1832). Say was a practical businessman who moved into the teaching of economics. Although there is some doubt about what his teachings actually meant, there is no doubt that his conceptualisation of the 'circular flow' has permeated economic thought throughout the past two centuries. In his model businesses sell their output on the market and generate incomes in the form of wages, rent, interest and profits. Households receive the incomes and use them to consume and invest. Since any supply of goods calls forth its own demand, aggregate supply equals aggregate demand. Every purchase constitutes a sale, while every sale converts into a money income. There can be no excess supply of goods, and no involuntary unemployment. Within a free enterprise economy there may be temporary dislocation, but no long-term depression. Left to itself, the capitalist economy will automatically return to full employment at stable prices. Say's teaching continues to inform the monetarist view that, since unemployment is both temporary and voluntary, no government interference is necessary or desirable.

While the early classical economists produced the positive concept of the natural market and a macro-economic view of a system that maximised economic benefit through always attaining an equilibrium of maximum efficiency, micro-economists fleshed out what had been implicit in the classical system, the rational economic actor to drive the self-interest that lies at the heart of modern economic thought. As Hunt and Sherman argue:

> Say's law and the policies that follow from it are not merely a historical curiosity. Modern conservatives, such as the monetarist school led by Milton Friedman, still believe in Say's law and therefore advocate no government action to cure unemployment, no matter how severe it is. In fact, all neo-classical economists begin their analysis with the preferences of individuals and ordinarily assume all economic activities are voluntary. (Hunt and Sherman, 1990: 441)

The neo-classical school

The neo-classical school is primarily a micro-economic school, that derives from the marginalist revolution of the 1870s. The 'marginalist revolution' flowed from Bentham's concept of 'hedonism' and the pleasure-seeking individual. Rejecting the study of the community as a whole, the utilitarian approach focuses on the individual 'rational economic man' and the individual firm. It sees economic choice as resting on the pleasure–pain principle: hence the 'marginalists' study the point of change of pleasure or pain. Study at the 'margin', the increase/decrease over a very small unit of time, has enabled neo-classical economists to describe the balancing act known as 'equilibrium' with mathematical elegance. Money as we have seen is only an expression of this process. Another micro-economic school, the Austrian School, also derives from the 1870s marginalist revolution, and traces the exchange relationships between individuals. It regards state intervention in economic activity as counterproductive. Individuals should be free to rely upon the market for the information necessary for decision-taking. The school studies the processes whereby self-interested individuals come to their decisions. Money again plays a purely functional role. The neo-classical and marginalist schools have added to the classical view of the integrated and self-sufficient model of the market an individual actor to populate that market, who is also amenable to abstraction and modelling. As a recent critic argues, 'if current neo-classical macro-economics is the ideology for economic policies, micro-economics is the hard core theology of contemporary orthodoxy' (Joseph Halevi, *Post-Autistic Economics Newsletter* issue 6, 5 June 2001, p. 6).

The neo-classical school has two major concerns. First, to explore the mathematical conditions for a hypothetical general equilibrium in the allocation of resources by rational, fully informed economic agents. Secondly, to explore the mathematical conditions under which economic harmony in the form of Pareto optimality might occur in a real-life market economy. This process is based upon the adoption of a series of assumptions, one of which is the non-occurrence of the unexpected. The cell unit of neo-classical theory is the commodity. Accordingly, labour is a commodity to be exchanged alongside other 'goods', and money is a commodity, albeit with special properties. Money is assumed to be a mere facilitator of exchange, with no influence over policy relating to production and distribution.

The Chicago School

The political assumptions underpinning the classical and neo-classical view have been brought together in the Chicago School. This macro-economic school approaches exchange relationships from a right-wing and libertarian perspective. It rejects government intervention and fiscal policy. The Chicago School was particularly influential in the United States and Britain in the latter part of the twentieth century. Government policy was to be based on the right of the individual to make (and keep) as much money as possible. Reduction of tax on earnings was central to public policy. The leading thinker of the period was Milton Friedman, who argued that the supply of money in an economy was important and was a matter for public policy but that its location and circulation was not. However, how money entered an economy or where it accumulated was a matter for the functioning of the economy itself. Money was still only a neutral instrument responding to economic forces and to interfere would be to disrupt the efficacy of the economic process. Nothing must stand in the way of the exercise of economic initiative. Hence, state intervention in the form of taxation, subsidies and social expenditure must be minimised. As for classical political economy the focus was on 'national income', based on the argument that economic growth will benefit the poor, the so-called 'trickle down' theory. It is this version of neo-liberalism that underpins the thrust towards a globalised macro-economy. Global economic enterprise must be allowed unfettered freedom so that world poverty can be overcome through expansion of the world economy.

Basic assumptions of orthodox economics

General free-market equilibrium

The core theoretical premise of classical political economy is that the natural state of all economies is to be at, or working towards, long-run equilibrium in some timeless continuum. Relative prices, working through the market, ensure that goods supplied and goods demanded are equated. The market clears, so avoiding over-supply (wastage) or under-supply (scarcity). Both micro- and macro-economics conceptualise the economy as a 'circular flow'. Economic agents (people, the general public) take employment in primary, secondary or tertiary production. They may 'work' as labour, landlords or investors, providing the factors of production necessary to create 'utilities', i.e. goods and services which are to be made available for exchange. In return for their efforts, providers of the factors of production receive money from the firms which employ them. Economic agents then move into the sphere of exchange. Each economic agent goes to the producing firms (and their retail outlets) to obtain a basket of goods and services that yields personal utility/satisfaction. As the goods are destroyed by consumption, the economic agent returns to work for the next cycle. The system operates in perpetual motion but with each cycle being complete in itself (already a logical impossibility). The supply of utilities calls forth its own demand because the production of all utilities is paid for in each cycle. Consequently, the money paid out in employment of the factors of production should be sufficient to purchase the products of that cycle. If left to the free play of market forces, over-production, under-consumption and unemployment will not occur over the long run, because there will be constant adjustment when minor imperfections occur in the workings of the system of supply, demand and price.

Methodological individualism

Despite the existence of macro-economic perspectives, orthodox economic thinking is reductive. Economic activity is seen ultimately as an aggregate of utility-maximising economic agents whether they be firms or individuals. Firms are motivated by maximisation of profit. Individuals are motivated by maximisation of 'utility' (satisfaction) and minimisation of 'disutility'. Price is 'the only, and the only necessary, form of communication' (Nelson, 1993). The agent's actions are based on rational deliberation in full knowledge of all relevant factors, with the aim of maximising personal utility. Hence, it is the task of the mainstream economist to predict and model individual responses and aggregate them to explain economy-wide behaviour. Therefore, all understanding of economic systems must be directed at the level of the actors engaged within the market. Competition between individual economic actors, the existence of large numbers of buyers and sellers in the market, allows the invisible hand to guide private interest in the service of public welfare. Private action produces the most efficient outcome.

In its extreme form, pure neo-classical theory argues that the economy can and should function entirely without any social or political interference. The myriad of individual choices must be allowed to interact according to the model of perfect competition. In practice government-sanctioned collective action does take place, but orthodox economics would limit its use to the following circumstances – although even many of these would be disputed:

1. The legal enforcement of property rights, providing an institutional basis for economic activity.
2. Provision of public goods, e.g. transport systems, and the regulation of private monopolies.
3. Manipulation of fiscal policy to maintain aggregate demand on a true course between inflation and unemployment.
4. Minimal social welfare provision to avoid destitution.
5. Correction of 'externalities' which occur when voluntary exchanges between two individuals have important effects on third parties.

6. Under globalisation the direction of government policy to open up local markets and withdraw collective provision, i.e. government interference to 'activate' the market under structural adjustment policies

Methodological individualism rests on a scientific abstraction, the rational economic actor. The actor may be a firm, but as an individual he is deeply gendered, Rational Economic Man (REM). This core concept of orthodox economic theory has been heavily criticised by feminist economists. We will return to these criticisms in Chapters 8–10.

The abstraction of economic systems

As we have seen, orthodox economics is greatly reliant on economic modelling, which in turn rests on an essentialist assumption that economies are 'natural'. Local variance and complexities are therefore noise which disrupts the purity of the theoretical framework. This does not mean that orthodox theory is not aware of complexities, but there is sometimes the suspicion that, as with the pre-Copernican epi-theorists, unfortunate facts must be twisted to the theory, rather than the other way around. The elements of economic modelling demand a static *a priori* framework if economics is to achieve its desired status as a universal and not an historical science (Hodgson, 2001). As a science, orthodox economics would claim to be value-free, but the first premise of the neo-classical school is a value judgement that existing social patterns and the institutional framework of the economy be taken as given. The economy as a process must have no history and not be specific to a culture or geographic location. The existing distribution of ownership of resources within society is not relevant to the study of economics. Thus Pareto optimality is concerned with the efficiency of allocation of resources on the prior assumption that the distribution of property is given. The outcome of this level of abstraction is a feat of technical sophistication and theoretical elegance which masks its inability to provide a meaningful analysis of social relations and institutional structures which constitute the real-life economy. The abstraction of economic function disembeds the economy theoretically not only from its social milieux but also from its physical base within the wider environment. This approach has real consequences as ecosystem use and damage is treated as external to the economic cycle. This will be central to our later discussion.

A critical problem of the abstracted economic model is that there is no history involved in its emergence. Although modern economies are seen to have evolved in a linear direction from 'primitive' barterers to the sophistication of industrial money/market economies, there is no explanation of how this occurred other than a naturalist teleology. This is the way it was meant to be. From this perspective, the transition from a non-capitalist to a capitalist economy requires no explanation. From the neo-classical standpoint rational, marginalist, optimising behaviour occurs in all societies. Hence 'the same analysis can apply to neolithic cave dwellers, Egyptian pharaohs, feudal nobility in France, and modern English financiers' (Sherman, 1993: 303). Universalist, ahistorical economics can analyse *any* system of production, distribution and exchange regardless of historical or cultural context. So

> a gang of Aleutian Islanders slushing about in the wrack and surf with rakes and magical incantations for the capture of shell-fish are held, in point of taxonomic reality, to be engaged on a feat of hedonistic equilibration in rent, wages and interest. (Veblen, 1990: 193)

Polanyi (1944) makes a similar point.

What is perhaps of most concern is the colonising nature of economic thinking where non-market forms of human interaction within an established capitalist economy are interpreted through economic models (Becker, 1976; Cameron, 1995). Public and social policy is filtered through accounting principles, subject to utility or cost–benefit analysis. People are seen as utility-maximisers in all aspects of their life. What is effectively happening is that the politics is being taken out of politics and replaced by economics. The irony is that economics itself is what the futurist Hazel Henderson (1988) has aptly named 'politics in disguise'.

The role of money in the circular flow

For orthodox economics money is merely a convenient medium within the circular flow of production and exchange. Nevertheless, as Marx argued, the exchange of goods *for money* is what the capitalist market is all about. The capitalist economy does not operate as a barter system enabled and veiled by money. As Freeman and Carchedi explain, if goods did not exchange for money the orthodox economic model would not hold. For example, if a builder was prepared to build a house and was prepared to accept a car in return, we would not be living under the same economic system. In money exchange, unlike barter, there are *three* parties, not two. If I have a sweet and need a biscuit, I will sell to a sweet-lover first, and then exchange with the biscuit-seller. Economic theory is about selling *for money*: supply, demand and price exist in terms of money. Furthermore, the institutions governing the supply and circulation of money play anything but a neutral role within the political economy.

Since goods exchange for money, goods can remain unsold: aggregate supply does not necessarily equal aggregate demand. As Alan Freeman explains:

> If agents are allowed to accumulate money in exchange then *any* set of price rations are compatible with *any* required distribution of product. If I have a sweet and you have a biscuit, and we want to strike a deal, then under barter we can only exchange at the rate of one sweet to one biscuit. But if money can change hands, you can sell me the biscuit for £2, buy the sweet for £1, and end up £1 the richer. ... If, therefore, we require prices to be determined by the set of exchanges they are to effect, we cannot allow money as a store of value, to play any operational role. (Freeman and Carchedi, 1996: 21)

If goods did not exchange for money, economic activity under capitalism would cease. Say's 'law' (that every sale is a purchase and that therefore markets clear) and the general notion of free market equilibrium, occur in a fictional world, uninhabited by the real-life reality of finance and its institutions. It is true that if there were a small, local economy, where barter was common and money transactions rare, Say's law might hold. However, there is little evidence that local barter economies ever existed as most people until comparatively recently were largely self-provisioning and trade was used for exotics (Ingham, 2000). The capitalist market is not a surrogate for barter; under capitalism production is initiated for private financial profit. It ceases if there is no expectation of financial profit. Output is not bought by the producers (i.e. by the people who made it, in barter-like exchange). It is sold on the market for profit. When money is a key factor in the operation of the economy, the role of money requires considerable explanation.

If money exists as anything but a pure measuring device, its existence creates insuperable problems for the comprehensibility of neo-classical theory. In the real-life economy a commodity (a good or service) registers its existence as an economic fact as and when it is exchanged for *money*. The converse, however, does *not* hold. Money does *not* have to exchange for real goods and services in order to maintain its identity as money: money can be exchanged for money and still register as an increase in GNP. Meanwhile, voluntary work (e.g. caring work in the home and community) does not register as an increase in GNP unless artificially construed to do so (Waring, 1989). If people can accumulate money, the circular flow is no longer meaningful. Money ebbs and flows within the economy. People do not always spend. Hoarding is a perfectly rational economic choice. Foreign trade moves goods and money, affecting outcomes, and the government has considerable influence over economic functioning as it makes up a substantial proportion of gross domestic product in most states.

A fundamental question we will address is how does money enter the economy? In the following chapters we explore the appearance (and disappearance) of money over time.

The elimination of time in the circular flow model

Within a pure circular flow model time is erased. Yet as a store of value and as a standard of deferred payment money facilitates trade and exchange *over time*. As financial capital it plays a crucial role in determining production, distribution and exchange within the material, real-world formal economy. Mainstream practice has focused on the necessity for money to retain its value over time, yet the passage of time is not accounted within the neo-classical analytical framework. Central to neo-classical modelling is the notion of static equilibrium, in which relative prices are determined mutually rather than consecutively in a sequential train of causation. When chronological time is eliminated, capitalists buy today's inputs at tomorrow's prices, income and output prices being the same. The theoretical solution to the economy operating as a simultaneous system is a set of price ratios which are determined by the necessity that goods exchange for goods, in a stylised form of barter, in which values remain constant and unchanging. However, money *prices* remain inexplicable and sophisticated financial institutions appear as an unaccountable mystery. In the real-life economy purchase and sale are separate acts, mediated by money.

People go to work to produce things, taking the money so earned to spend on consumption goods arising from the productive process. However, in the real-life economy present actions are very largely determined by past events. Hence people operate as economic agents in much the same fashion from one economic period to another. Custom and habit formed over past periods enable the farmer supplying distant urban markets to know likely prices of inputs and outputs, quantities of labour and the means and methods of production necessary to achieve desired outputs. Individuals operate within a maze of contacts, networks and information flows which change only very gradually under pressure of circumstances. The producers of the present live on goods produced in the past period: they do not consume the goods they have produced in the *same* economic period in which they produce them (Schumpeter, 1934: 6–7; Douglas, 1920: 21–4). This point will become central to our analysis in Chapter 6.

To say that the circular flow model discounts time does not mean that time is not important for economics. Much of present-day money trading is obsessed with time. If there were no time there would not be futures, hedge funds or speculation of any sort. A transparent and contemporary market would destroy most of what passes for wealth creation which is, in fact, gambling or money inflation. This does not undermine our criticism of the inadequacy of theory.

Capital's non-existence in the circular flow

The non-existence of time is directly related to the non-existence of capital within the circular flow model. The study of economics postulates three physical factors of production: land, labour and capital. The owners of each factor receive a money reward (rent, wages or interest) for the 'disutility' of allowing the factor to be consumed in the production process. Within the circular flow model land and labour (real physical resources) produce commodities for sale and purchase. Abstinence, the failure to consume, normally considered the source of physical capital (plant, tools, machinery) as a factor of production, is a logical impossibility. Once the circular flow is established, the productive forces of land and labour sell in exchange for consumption goods. Whether the goods produced are 'producers' goods' or 'consumers' goods' is immaterial. In each period the real services of labour and land are exchanged for consumption goods produced in the previous period. Each good sees two economic periods, the one in which it is produced, and the one in which it is consumed. 'Capital' cannot be stored up because there are no gaps in the continuity between the process of production and the process of consumption. Counting abstinence as a legitimate cost would involve counting the same item twice (Schumpeter, 1934: 38). The implications of the logical non-existence of capital in equilibrium theory, coupled with the distinction between physical and financial capital, is pursued in greater detail in subsequent chapters.

Whether a firm makes producer or consumer goods for the future period, it exchanges its productive services directly for present consumption goods produced in the past period. Once the system is up and running, there is neither 'fund' accumulated from the past, nor debt owed in the future. The system maintains itself. Land and labour produce the stream of goods and services required by the economy, creating just as many consumption goods as are necessary to meet effective demand, equating wants with the means for their satisfaction. Labour and land create, and by rights share, the whole 'national dividend' (Schumpeter, 1934: 44–6). As owners of produced means of production, capitalists would merely be producers employed in the same market as other producers, part of the continuous flow of production. Once established, the stream of production flows continuously from one period to the next. However, the question then arises as to how the system came into existence, and how it changes its pattern, as it manifestly does from time to time. On this question, neo-classical theory has no answers.

Alternatives and variants

We have pointed to problems in the orthodox view of economic systems, in particular the assumptions underpinning the equilibrium circular flow model. What are the alternatives? Such is the hold of general free-market equilibrium theory over the discipline of economics that even theoreticians questioning the basic assumptions of the circular flow have been forced into conformity with its basic assumptions. Keynes has been challenged on the grounds that 'it works in practice, but not in theory', while Marx has been misrepresented entirely.

J.M. Keynes (1883–1946) and the Liberal view

John Maynard Keynes rocked the academic establishment by relating theory to fact, noting that equilibrium could occur at less than full employment, due to the possibility of hoarding money. His concern was triggered by the existence of widespread involuntary unemployment during the 1920s and 1930s. Observing that the market system does not necessarily result in a full-employment equilibrium, Keynes suggested that government had a role to play in influencing aggregate demand through the use of public investment to create effective demand. Taking the basic notion of the circular flow, through which business pays the national income to households, and households spend incomes to buy goods from businesses, he explored the relationship between planned aggregate demand and planned aggregate supply at current prices.

Aggregate supply (total £ output produced and offered for sale) may equal aggregate demand (total £ amount of final goods and services that consumers, investors, government and foreign overseas sales plan to buy from firms) so long as all saved income (in aggregate) is invested. Equilibrium may result if total saving equals total investment demand plus hoarding or dis-hoarding. However, disequilibrium can occur where the hoarding of saved income is in excess of dis-hoarding, and the total money available for all goods is less than the total value of goods at present prices. As stocks of goods rise, capitalists lose money, production is cut and workers are sacked. A new lower level of supply results in involuntary unemployment. Government intervention may be necessary to secure investment so that production will provide employment incomes to be spent into the economy. Shocking though Keynes' revelations were (and are in some quarters), his theory remained within the basic paradigm of the 'circular flow' general equilibrium theory: businesses allocate incomes on the basis of productive 'work' done. The purposes for which investment finance is made available remains on a theoretically neutral 'profitability' basis. In reality, as we will demonstrate, the process of allocation of finance to new investment cannot be regarded as benign or politically neutral.

Karl Marx (1818–1883) and radical economics

According to Alan Freeman (1995) throughout the twentieth century Marxists have followed the orthodox path of erasing finance from the study of economics. The unfortunate result is to obscure the nature of capitalist power over the means of production. For Freeman, capitalist power stems from the *financially* based institutional constructs of legally enforced contract and sale. Ownership of the physical means of production, itself a matter of financial contracts based upon debt and credit, forms only a proportion of capitalist economic power. Unfortunately, Marx's labour theory of value has been interpreted from the neo-classical simultaneous methodological standpoint, in which the profit rate is 'everywhere actually equal, technology does not change, the market always clears during each act of circulation, and money is a pure *numéraire*' (Freeman, 1995: 49). In this equilibrium analysis money and time do not exist.

Throughout the twentieth century it has largely been assumed that Marx had a 'transformation problem', and that his economics was flawed. We follow Freeman in drawing a distinction between Marx's original 'sequential and nondualistic' economics and subsequent attempts by Marxist and non-Marxist economists alike to interpret Marx's economics from a general free-market equilibrium perspective (Freeman, 1995). Hence the explanation of the existence of involuntary unemployment (or inflation), i.e. of recurrent crises, has been presented as if it relied upon neo-classical equilibrating assumptions. Although, as Freeman and others have shown, this was not the case (Freeman, 1995; Freeman and Carchedi, 1996), the dominant Marxist analysis of macro-economics throughout the twentieth century assumes that wage income includes all wages from hourly paid work and piecework, including salaries, while property income includes all unearned income deriving from the ownership of property. Therefore, the national income comprises total wage income plus total property income. Workers tend to spend the whole of their incomes on consumption, i.e. on the purchase of basic needs. Therefore, in aggregate, total wage income equals total workers' consumption. Capitalists, on the other hand, have sufficient income to save some of it. Hence, total property income equals total capitalist consumption plus total capitalist saving. Capitalists may hoard or invest their savings. If saving is greater than planned investment, unemployment results. If saving is less than planned investment, inflation results. Disequilibrium is caused by the unequal distribution of income under capitalism coupled with capitalist profit-seeking.

The institutional/evolutionary school

Such has been the over-arching dominance of neo-classical, neo-liberal theorising that the term 'institutional' has been adopted by 'new institutional economists' (NIE) pursuing the theory of the firm. It is therefore important to distinguish between NIE which remains within the framework of orthodox economics and the 'old institutional economists' (OIE) such as Thorstein Veblen (1857–1929). The old institutional school rejects the concept of a global science of economics. It takes a holistic and evolutionary view of the economy, which it sees as determining, and in part being determined by, the institutions of society. For example, it does not follow the neo-classical practice of taking wants as 'given'. Rather, it sees wants as a function of the social, political and power relationships which determine individual actions. Nevertheless, throughout the twentieth century OIE has been constrained by the dominant paradigm in economics. In Veblen's day it was still possible to recognise that economics could be the study of *political* economy. In 1898, Veblen observed that the emerging neo-classical economic theory of that time was rooted in 'symmetry and system-making' bearing little relationship to the economic facts of life (Veblen, 1990: 68). Unfortunately, over one hundred years later it remains true that

> the economic life process [is] still in great measure awaiting theoretical formulation. The active material in which the economic process goes on is the human material of the industrial community. For the purpose of economic science, the process of cumulative change that is to be accounted for is the sequence of change in the methods of doing things, the methods of dealing with the material means of life. (Veblen, 1990: 70–1)

As Veblen anticipated, the combination of economic jargon and statistical methodology has dominated the study of economics, enabling economists to talk with each other on, and offer policy advice about, money, wages or land ownership with only occasional reference to concrete practicalities. Throughout the course of the twentieth century economics has remained little more than 'taxonomy for taxonomy's sake' (Veblen, 1990: 69).

Rather than build models of economic systems, old institutionalist economists (OIEs) use case studies to record the evolution of particular institutions within particular cultures. Their methodology is interdisciplinary and inductive, being concerned with policy in the real-life economy. They do not assume that the consumer is sovereign, endowed with wants which spring from fixed personal characteristics. Rather, they observe that tastes are affected by technological change, social status and power, and the ability of firms to manipulate tastes through advertising. The market itself is an interconnected series of evolutionary institutions, and does not operate as a neutral and allocatively efficient mechanism as assumed by neoclassicals. In this book our approach will draw heavily on the work of the old institutional *economists*, Marx, Veblen and Douglas.

The flawed logic of orthodox approaches

The critique of neo-classical economics from an institutional perspective is joined by contemporary critiques from a realist perspective (Lawson, 1997; Sayer, 1992). In both cases the nature of the criticism is the same: neo-classical economics relies upon flawed logic and an incoherent ontology. The neo-classical paradigm is seen in utility-maximisation models and is typically methodological individualist so that even if a 'firm' is the maximiser that firm acts just like a person. No supra-individual secondary agents are relevant. The paradigm is generally atomistic and sees each individual actor as isolated, calculating, rational, and not linked to other actors. Any and all co-operation must be rational for self-interested actors, and thus rests upon cynical use of others for one's own purposes. Variants on utility-maximisation models include profit-maximisation models, income-maximisation among farmers, and satisfaction-maximisation among consumers.

Symbolic of the neo-classical approach is the idea of the marginal utility of money, which is treated like any other good in economic theory. Here it is assumed that the utility of money falls as the money's owner becomes richer. This model tries to show that money somehow means more to poor people than to rich people, asking empirical questions such as, 'is a 1 per cent rise in income going to have lower marginal utility to the wealthier than to the poorer households?' In other words to a neo-classical economist the question of the absolute fall in the marginal utility of money is self-explanatory, but it might be interesting to enquire about a relative fall in the marginal utility of money. Here we see evidence of the neo-classical tendency to metricate everything, to decontextualise the issues, to ignore the difference between a person and a household, to atomise the person and to ignore the use values while paying attention only to the realm of exchange values. In the words of Tony Lawson, such an approach is idealist (1997); it exaggerates the importance of idealised models and implicitly ignores empirical realities and the diversity of contexts within which money is obtained. The supposed strength of the neo-classical approach is that it can be applied anytime, anywhere but this can be seen as a weakness if economists are trained to ignore social and historical details. The debate about analysing reality has been a wide-ranging one over the last decade. The ontological critique of neo-classical economics is that it has a quite literally unrealistic view of what an economy is and its logical problem is that its criterion on proof is internal to the theoretical framework. As philosophers of science have shown, 'proofs' are not an appropriate part of the scientific method when they are obtained within a framework in which assumptions, axioms, and corollaries of the theory come first. It was shown in the philosophical debate about positivism that if researchers simply try to verify their own theories, they may be blinkered to evidence that would falsify the theories (Smith, 1998 reviews this debate). Verification is not the best epistemological stance. Within our alternative paradigm theoretically and ontologically people come first. Differentiated, thriving, living, capable people: not homogenous, calculating, lazy, selfish people. We argue that people should use research as a way to learn progressively and cumulatively about the real economy. Science should unmask that which is hidden by ordinary social life and everyday discourses. Economics as a science should be a network of arguing, communicative experts who know a lot about actual economies while being wary of simple models. Verifying and sustaining one model should not be the aim. Improving the real economy through changing, competing, alternative frameworks is more realistic because it is more fallible.

The problem of growth

For green thinkers a key problem of orthodox economics is its assumption of the perpetuation of economic circulation. Growth is seen to be ecologically destructive and increasingly socially inequitable (see *New Internationalist*, issue 334).

As Daly and Cobb explain, the systems which form the subject-matter of economics as a discipline are those committed 'to large-scale, factory-style energy and capital-intensive, specialised production units that are hierarchically managed. They also rely heavily on non-renewable resources and tend to exploit renewable resources and waste absorption capacities at non-sustainable rates' (Daly and Cobb, 1990: 13). The goal of economic activity is assumed to be the production of a growing quantity of goods and services. Growth is built in for two reasons. First the role of credit and capital which demands a reward in the process of circulation builds in an expansionary element. Secondly, if the trickle-down effect is to be achieved eventually, the model must expand to meet the needs of all those within the potential economic community. This continues the assumption of Adam Smith that industrial production was designed to increase wealth and bring all out of poverty through the invisible hand of the market.

However as Herman Daly points out in terms of the drive for growth there is a contradiction between micro- and macro-economics. While micro-economics has a concept of optimal behaviour, conventional macro-economics has no theoretical means of halting its expansion although there is clearly a point at which 'uneconomic growth' exists, i.e. when any perceived benefits are far outweighed by social and ecological dis-utilities (2001a: 22–3). Daly also identifies a 'futility' level of growth where the market is so satiated that no further satisfaction is possible at any price. Arguably the level of advertising at present indicates that the affluent west is very near that position, if not over it. Daly's main concern is that catastrophic environmental collapse (which could happen quite suddenly) will be reached before growth becomes uneconomic in market terms. Our logic would indicate that this is the most likely scenario where every incentive leads to the destruction of natural resources in order to turn them into money-as-capital and/or money-as-livelihood. As we will point out using Marx's theory, money must destroy value as utility without itself ever attaining any real value. We return to the ecological question in Chapter 8.

Chrematistics or oikonomics? Production or provisioning?

The model produced by orthodox economics fuses and confuses wealth production with money making. Within a capitalist economy production would not occur if there was not a profit. Exchange would not occur unless there was a monetary benefit. The starting point for establishing an alternative framework must be to question that connection. Such a challenge would separate wealth creation as money value from wealth creation as the meeting of human needs (provisioning). By the same token it would see poverty defined not just by a lack of money within a money system, but as the lack of access to real resources and provisioning processes. This will be central to our approach and is very much part of emerging radical perspectives drawn from feminism, ecology and sufficiency-based perspectives. Separating production from wealth creation follows a very old tradition that can be traced back to Aristotle. Daly and Cobb define chrematistics as

> the branch of political economy relating to the manipulation of property and wealth so as to maximize short-term monetary exchange value to the owner.

By contrast, oikonomia (from which our term 'economics' is derived) is

> the management of the household so as to increase its use value to all members of the household over the long run. If we expand the scope of household to include the larger community of the land, of shared values, resources, biomes, institutions, language, and history, then we have a good definition of economics for community. (Daly and Cobb, 1990: 138)

Mainstream/neo-classical economics has not only fused chrematistics and oikonomia; it has concentrated on the former to the exclusion of the latter. Recognition of the distinction between chrematistics and oikonomia facilitates clarification of the relationship between the money economy and the social resources and natural resources economies which are essential to its survival. These resources would include the unpaid work of women and the resilience of the ecosystem. The concept of oikonomics as the economics of the household has been taken up strongly by feminist economists who have developed the concept of provisioning (Nelson, 1993). For Nelson mainstream economics is losing touch with what should be its focus and 'has come to be defined not by its subject matter but by a particular way of looking at the world' (1993: 25). Instead she argues 'economics could be about how we live in our house, the earth' (ibid: 33). Drawing on Adam Smith's view of economics as being about the 'necessaries and conveniences of life',

Nelson argues that economics should be about provisioning. This is echoed by Geoffrey Hodgson:

> Economics broadly defined, should be the study of the social structures and institutions governing the production, distribution and exchange of the requisites of human life. In other words economics should be the study of all provisioning institutions. (2001: 346)

In the following chapters we will seek to undermine the dominance of chrematistics and explore an alternative theoretical framework that would support oikonomics.

There is an alternative

We have argued in this chapter that mainstream theorising has focused upon a limited range of phenomena occurring within the formal economy as defined by an abstracted economic model. Any theories and methodologies that sought to broaden this agenda have been marginalised or consigned to heretical oblivion. We have sought to question the 'there is no alternative' assumptions that underpin orthodox economic theory. Much of this stems from the fallacy of 'misplaced concreteness' evident in economics. Like other disciplines in which there is a high level of abstraction, practitioners socialised to think in these abstractions 'apply their conclusions to the real world without recognising the degree of abstraction involved' (Daly and Cobb, 1990: 25). The fossilisation of economic thought renders economists increasingly incapable of offering coherent explanations of economic phenomena. As Paul Ekins and Manfred Max-Neef argued a decade ago, economic theorising in its mainstream neo-classical form

> is failing to provide an intellectually coherent explanation of economic reality, especially with regard to such issues as the nature of markets, environmental degradation, persistent poverty and household production. (Ekins and Max-Neef (eds), 1992: xviii)

It would appear that the aim of neo-liberal economic theory is to dominate all other theories, just as the aim of market capitalism has been to eclipse all value systems beyond those of the money economy. Loyalty to any other cause, however 'worthwhile', is seen as sectional, and therefore theoretically untenable, i.e. 'not scientific'. As we have argued, although alternatives to neo-classical theorising have circulated outside and on the margins of orthodoxy ever since its inception, the strength of the claim that 'there is no alternative' lies in the successful way in which these voices have been silenced. However, the gap between the promise of conventional economic theory and the reality of delivery is getting ever wider. It could also be argued that such a restriction of other perspectives, particularly represented within the economic establishment and its policing of orthodoxy, is not a sign of strength, but of weakness. As Sandra Harding argues:

> the tensions we long to repress, to hide, to ignore, are the dangerous ones. They are the ones to which we give the power to capture and enthral us, to lead us to actions and justificatory strategies for which we can see no reasonable alternatives. (Harding, 1986: 243)

In our view economics, like all traditional scientific discourses, is

> full of such damaging tensions. They encourage us to support coercive scientific claims and practices, and claims *about* science, that are historically mystifying and epistemologically and politically regressive. (Harding, 1986: 243. Emphasis original)

Evidence that repressed reality had begun to surface within the economic fraternity emerged in France in June 2000. Economics students at one of France's leading institutions, the École Normale Supérieure, circulated a petition protesting against the lack of pluralism and excessive mathematical formalisation in economics. It called for a return to concrete realities. The petition argued that economics had become autistic and schizophrenic through the way in which modelling was cutting economics off from reality and called for a public debate and a national conference to discuss the issue. It gained 800 signatures and made the national press (*Le Monde*, 21 June 2000; *L'Humanité*) and radio and TV – even the Education Minister was forced to give a response. The students were joined by more than 140 economists including leading thinkers such as Robert Boyer, André Orléan, Michel Aglietta, Jean-Paul Fitoussi and Daniel Cohen. A government report on university economics teaching had reached conclusions similar to those of the students.

The report admitted that 'under the guise of being scientific' economics had cultivated an anti-scientific environment 'which leaves no room for reflection and debate' (*Les Echos*, 23 June 2000). The theme was taken up by radical economists. *Le Nouvel Economiste* declared that economics had succumbed to a 'pathological taste for *a priori* ideologies and mathematical formalisation disconnected from reality'. Economics, it continued, should give up its false emulation of physics and 'should instead look to the human sciences' (30 June 2000). *Alternatives Economiques* carried an article entitled 'The Revolt of the Students' which noted that French Nobel Prize winner, Maurice Allais, had, despite his mathematical approach, come to conclusions similar to those of the students (*Post-Autistic Economics Newsletter*, 1 September 2000). The critique was circulated as a *Post-Autistic Economics Newsletter* through the internet and was taken up by other students including 27 PhD students at Cambridge University in the UK who issued their own public letter.

Through the *Post-Autistic Economics Newsletter*, the US feminist economist Susan Feiner argued:

> every major tenet of neo-classical economics has been roundly challenged, on grounds of theoretical incoherence and/or empirical inadequacy, and yet the set of ideas which make up the core of the paradigm are gospel to a stunningly large number of people who in other respects are astute observers of the world. The concepts of false consciousness and ideology will only get us so far in explaining the enduring legacy of a bunch of third rate 19th century social commentators, bigots and fascists (J.B. Say, J. Bentham, V. Pareto, I. Fisher and the marginal triumvirate). There are for sure real interests at stake in the struggle over economics for whom and to what ends, but the continued silence in the profession on all these questions is as curious to me as the incredible acceptance of these ideas among non-economists.

She sees orthodox economics as equivalent to a religious belief:

> The stories of mainstream economics appropriate and rely upon key biblical tropes, to show that neo-classical economics – despite its scientific pretensions – is but one more attempt to tame the future by holding out the promise of life ever after in the eternal Eden of equilibrium. (10 September 2000)

A similar comment was made on the orthodoxy of the WTO suggesting that its adherents are in thrall to some 'obscure religious belief' (David Ransom, *New Internationalist*, May 2001: 8).

These obscure beliefs are being challenged by movements around the globe. We want to support these movements by recovering those voices who have been silenced or marginalised by orthodoxy and, together with contemporary radical thinking, build a real alternative.

3   Money, Banking and Credit

The love of money is the root of all evil
(The Second Epistle of Paul to Timothy)

Money makes the world go round (Traditional)

These two quotations sum up the dilemma of money. The first puts the onus on the coveter of money but not necessarily on money itself. The second sees money as the oil in the mechanism of society. From this we would assume that money is beneficial unless squandered, coveted, exploited or otherwise misused. Unfortunately, the history of money is that it has been squandered, coveted, exploited or otherwise misused. Mainstream theorists of the economy have seen the misuse of money as an aberration rather than as a typical act, and by looking at things this way they condone the present system.

Far from seeing money as a veil that hides the 'real' economy, we argue that money is a crucial social form in its own right. It has been left to anthropologists, geographers, historians and the curious from a range of backgrounds to explore money, banking and credit in their historical and social contexts (Davies, 1994; Vilar, 1991; Dodd, 1994; Rowe, 1997; Buchan, 1997; Lietaer, 2001; Ramage and Croaddock, 2001). The concept of 'money' appears so familiar that it hardly seems to require explanation. Neither money, banking nor credit is new. Each has a long history.

Money in history

Evidence of the use of money dates back to 3000 BC (Davies, 1994) and the earliest writings were statements of accounts. In biblical times money could buy food (Isaiah 55: 1) and the services of casual labour (Matthew 20). There is evidence that communal grain stores were used as a banking resource in ancient Egypt with what were effectively cheques exchanged between the depositors. However, until modern times the use of money to settle everyday social obligations and meet basic needs was virtually unknown. Money was used in exceptional circumstances, in times of famine, hard times generally, for travel and for warfare. What is new is a society driven by money, banking and credit. Fundamental to our discussion of economic democracy will be the role of money in acquiring the means of sustenance. With Marx, we argue that this is *the* critical feature of modernity. It therefore seems odd that 'modern' economists should marginalise the study of this aspect of the economy. As Marx pointed out money is not a medium for the exchange of use values, in fact it destroys utility (see Chapter 4). Goods and services are exchanged in order to facilitate the circulation of money and thereby the accumulation of wealth as financial capital. Marx was a profound critic of the cash nexus, creating an analysis of money and credit that has been inherited and interpreted by some of the radical theorists discussed in later chapters.

It is generally accepted that the first money was a commodity valued in its own right. Most societies seem to have had some objects prized for their use as currency whether it be beads, tobacco or stones. The assumption is that such money held an intrinsic value, as in the case of gold or silver. Indeed such precious metals moved between acting as money for exchange activities and possessing other decorative and valued uses. However, there is no basis on which such an intrinsic value could be calculated, except if it were in terms of another commodity acting as money. As Marx argued, the money form cannot be valued in terms of anything else (as that then becomes money) and cannot be valued in terms of itself. The search for an intrinsic value of money (as in the use of gold and silver) is a vain one.

An early use of money seems to have been as tribute, for temple offerings. It was probably this type of money that might have incensed the historical Jesus when he threw the moneychangers out of the temple. The changers were probably turning exchangeable money into especially purified money which would be a temple offering. It has been argued that the priests may have used the exchangeable money to attain a luxurious lifestyle thereby exciting popular resentment (Channel 4, *Son Of God*, 8 April 2001). Concern about usury in the Old Testament also shows that the idea of lending money for interest is very old and religious laws against this practice were carried into both Christianity and Islam. Usury is still against Islamic law.

The Lydians of Greek Asia Minor are credited with the invention of money as coin. In the seventh century BC they were striking coins from electrum, a gold–silver alloy that occurred naturally near their capital Sardis (Ramage and Croaddock, 2001). Their King Croesus has become a symbol of the accumulation of riches. Concern about the destructive power of money did not long follow its emergence. The distrust of money led to it being outlawed in Sparta. Aristotle had a low opinion of money-based wealth creation as a human activity and records the marginal status of bankers in Athens. For Aristotle money was unethical because it threatened to destroy art. Buchan agrees: 'Greek civilisation conspired in its own destruction … its great invention, coined money, undermined its other monuments of art and intellect' (1997: 34). Despite Aristotle's concern, Greek coinage was valued as much as an object of art as a medium of exchange. In the various battles for ascendancy would-be emperors and local potentates competed to achieve the most Alexander-like or Godlike countenance on their coinage.

Coins spread far and wide during the Roman empire with their value guaranteed by the authority of Rome, which forbade the use of coin as commodity. It is perhaps salutary to recall as we 'celebrate' economic globalisation, that an economic system enabled by coin that had an imperial range for hundreds of years could collapse and its currency fall into disuse. Britain was the only country actually to abandon coin as money (although not as gifts) after the Romans left in the fourth century. The use of money was revived in the seventh century. By the eighth century there was a money standard across Europe and coinage supported international trade, which puts the current acrimonious debate about the euro into an historical perspective. For standards of value, weight measures based on silver became the standard: twelve denarii = one shilling (shaving); twenty shillings = one pound/lira. Paper money was first used in ninth-century China during the Hein Tsung period 806–821 (Davies, 1994) and some coinage held remarkable value sometimes for more than a thousand years – the Chinese copper quian (cash) and the Greek drachma. The empire of Kubla Khan (1260–1294) had its paper money recognised from China to the Baltic.

For Buchan, coins, Christianity and monarchy travelled together in the history of Europe (1997). Exchangeable money was important for the consolidation of monarchy. Feudal armies had to be rewarded in land, but later Kings could pay in coin and maintain a standing army. This reflected a general movement to gold and silver as coin from their use decoratively in private houses or as ecclesiastical plate. From the twelfth century onwards the balance between decorative uses and money shifts in the direction of money as 'treasure'. Money is circulated as working capital and plate increasingly turned to coin. At least one of the anti-Muslim crusades was financed by mortgages arranged by rich abbeys acting as bankers. The big surge of money coining and use in Europe was in the thirteenth century. Even so, the expansion of trade in the early Italian cities was also accompanied by a high level of indebtedness. The cities of North Italy saw a massive growth in trade and the use of large coin, florins, ducats, sequins, genovines. Double-entry bookkeeping was well entrenched by 1340 in Genoa when Luca codified it. Genoa also had paper money. Nevertheless, the level of trade led to a constant shortage of currency and the need to use debased coin or paper. When money was not available, the Dutch East India company paid its dividends in pepper, mace and nutmegs.

Europe had run out of gold by the fifteenth century but the shortage was (temporarily) relieved by Columbus's rape of the Americas. For the Incas skill in design was a symbol of wealth and they did not use gold as money at all but as decoration. The Spanish cleaned them out in three years. According to Buchan gold worth $5 trillion came into Spain, but most of it rapidly left again. By 1724 only £100 million worth remained as coin, ecclesiastical plate or in households. The gold that had cost so many lives in the Americas was mainly spent on war or exotic luxuries. There was also remarkably little of it. In 1905 the French statistician Foville calculated that the total amount of gold mined until that date would only form a block 10 m cubed (Vilar, 1991). Its attraction through history was its rarity, beauty and malleability. It is an interesting reflection on all those who died in pursuit of gold, that it is now so relatively valueless that on coming to power in 1997 the UK Labour Chancellor of the Exchequer, Gordon Brown, sold half the country's reserves.

Far from benefiting the Spanish economy, the discovery of gold undermined its productive capacity. As one contemporary commentator explained:

The scarcity of things in Spain proceeds ... from the neglect of Husbandry, Trades, Business and Commerce; the People, even the meanest of them, being so excessive proud, that they can't be content with what Lot Nature has given them, but aspire to something greater, loathing those Employments which are not agreeable to their affect'd Grandeur. (Don Diego Saavedra Faxardo in 1700, quoted in Buchan, 1997: 82)

Although early European coins had a value based on weight in a precious metal, the demand for money very quickly outstripped the supply of gold or silver. Also, it was difficult to keep currency value in line with gold or silver values and coin was often turned back into bullion or ornaments. In particular, kings, princes and emperors wanted more goods and services than the weight of their precious metal would allow, and gradually the aims of power led to the debasement of coin by those who had a monopoly over their minting. Henry VIII made £1 million by debasing the currency. Ordinary traders also found ways of shaving (shilling) the coins until milling technology produced a serrated edge. As debasement grew, the only guarantee of the worth of the coin became the face or signature of the promissary: that is, the form of the money has no exchangeable or usable value itself as in the case of commodity money such as gold or silver. From this stage money begins to take two forms: promissory money that related to a commodity held by the issuer, and fiat money guaranteed by an authority. Promissory money emerged through goldsmiths' practice of offering paper promises-to-pay in place of actual gold. Fiat money, the second form, was issued as legal tender, guaranteed by the authority of the state, a Lord of the Manor, City office-holder or other authority source. Once these two interlinked (both are ultimately backed by the authority of the state) forms of money creation took place on a regular basis, the character and properties of money as a social phenomenon could be distinguished from notions of 'natural' wealth or intrinsic value.

Does money have a natural value?

As Dorothy Rowe argues 'with fiat money, money leaves the realm of tangible objects and enters the realm of ideas' (1997: 56). Lietaer agrees but argues that money has always existed in the realm of ideas:

> Ultimately money is trust, which lives and dies only in human hearts and minds. Money systems, including our current one, are mechanisms and symbols that aim at keeping that trust alive. Historically, entire civilisations have been built on trust, because it is at the core of the self-confidence required for a civilization to grow

> or even survive. On the negative side, when a society loses confidence in its money, it loses confidence in itself. (2001: 331)

Money is necessarily social in the sense that value itself is social. To accept any kind of token in place of something that is immediately useful, consumable or for one's labour must imply a trust that the 'money' object will be exchangeable in the future. It is true that some objects have attained nearly universal value, most notably gold and silver. However, we know now that gold and silver do not have a fixed value and we also know that, try as hard as they may, governments have not been able to fix permanently the value of their money in terms of gold, silver or anything else. Given that money is a purely social construct it is of concern that 'money displaces other values like a cuckoo in the nest' (Buchan, 1997: 94). For Buchan 'the key point is that trust in money can act as a substitute for trust in people. Gradually, as we shall see, it will displace trust in all human relations except those of the inner family' (1997: 29). This is the victory of money that Margaret Thatcher infamously celebrated when she said there was no such thing as society, only individuals and their families.

In terms of both economic theory and economic policy there is a schizophrenia about the value of money. Sometimes it is seen only as a measure of worth and at other times it is deemed to have real value as in Margaret Thatcher's aim of 'sound money'. Commodity-backed money appeared to have a value, that of gold and silver or some other precious commodity. However, such commodity money only pushes the problem back one stage to the value of gold and silver themselves. Even where the commodity money does have a value (and sometimes a residual use), that value is still arbitrary. As Rowe argues, 'cowrie shell, lumps of metal, bits of paper and numbers on a computer screen do not have an essential, immutable value' (1997: 13).

As we have seen, when money began circulating in Europe from the eighth century it was made of valuable metals such as silver. This meant that at times the coins were worth more as silver than as money and disappeared from circulation (Mayhew, 2000). When gold appeared the British currency was linked to both gold and silver, but silver coin still disappeared. In 1695 the secretary to the treasury argued that the existing silver coins should be reduced in size to their relative value, but the philosopher John Locke argued that the values of silver and gold were fixed by natural law and that they should not be altered. Locke argued for an enduring value for currency, and in 1717 Isaac Newton devised the gold standard by stipulating the gold value of the pound. As a result, Britain entered the industrial revolution committed to the 'natural' worth of a currency that was in grave shortage. The lack of currency meant that several parallel currencies circulated and national currencies in general were not established until the nineteenth century (Helleiner, 1999). A shortage of small denomination coin was a particular problem for poor people, particularly those who had no other source of livelihood than the money economy.

The first British gold standard lasted until 1797 when once again more money was needed to fight the Napoleonic wars than the stores of precious metal would allow. The fixed value of money was restored after the war and by 1880 the gold standard was adopted by the major economies. In 1914 war once again destroyed the balance of money values but a return to the gold standard after the war became a shackle to economic expansion and helped to trigger the crash of 1929. Dorothy Rowe records her father asking in the Depression how digging gold ore out of the rock and burying it in Fort Knox could achieve anything, while good food was being dumped in the sea because it had 'no value' (1997: 16). Britain eventually left the gold standard in 1931, but the US did not abandon it until 1971. While the gold standard might have stabilised money it did not stabilise economies – there were booms and slumps during the whole period that 'natural' value prevailed.

The UN Monetary and Financial Conference at Bretton Woods in 1944 was an admission that the value of currencies is a political matter. Leyshon and Thrift describe Bretton Woods as 'the most ambitious attempt to develop economic order ... within the history of capitalism' (1997: 261). The leading economies decided to stabilise currencies relative to each other with a structure of 'international settlements' that lasted until 1973. However, Keynes' view of international settlements was very different from that of the US. Keynes argued that the settlement process should be used to smooth out international trade and suggested that interest should be paid on credit as well as debit balances. This was opposed by the US who ushered in the era of the International Monetary Fund (IMF) and the International Bank for Reconstruction and Development (World Bank). The General Agreement on Tariffs and Trade (GATT) followed later. By the end of the twentieth century the medicine of structural adjustment had been applied to a large proportion of the world's population. In early 2002 the IMF refused support to Argentina, which had tried to secure the value of its currency by attaching it to the dollar. When this failed after ten years it was forced to devalue and default on debt payments. Its external debt, running at $130 billion and 50 per cent of GDP, was not exceptional, but Argentina found itself raiding the pension funds of its citizens and freezing their bank accounts in an attempt to avoid devaluation. Considerable social unrest followed as people were reduced to selling or bartering their goods. It is hard to think that one hundred years before this Argentina had been a very rich country and that in resource terms it still is. One of the main triggers of the crisis had been citizens sending large amounts of money abroad in anticipation of a devaluation.

Following the oil crisis of 1973 inflation of money values (or devaluing of currency) galloped away, ushering in the attempt to secure money values by controlling the supply of money (monetarism). The whole experiment merely destroyed investment and circulation within the productive economy while drastically inflating the financial sector and property prices. However, we still live in a political world committed to 'natural' economies if not 'natural' money. The control of money is now ceded to reserve banks in the US, UK and Europe. These banks seek to stabilise their economies by a gnomic calculation of the likely future behaviour of economic actors. The 'economy' remains a theoretical island, politically separated from governments and most certainly from democratic control. While the idealised model of 'the economy' has been politically set free, in practice the actual economy is spiralling out of democratic or any other form of control (Frank, 2001).

The delusion of reserve banks that they control money volumes becomes irrelevant when we take account of the globalisation of money. As Larry Elliot of the *Guardian* argues: 'the unshackling of finance was a colossal error, since it made controlling the global economy as difficult as taming a man-eating tiger' (23 July 2001). Financial speculation now is huge and a major creator of 'wealth'. Lietaer has calculated it as directly or indirectly involved in 98 per cent of foreign currency exchange activity. Currency speculation is now beyond control. Writing in 2001 Lietaer calculated that $2 trillion were circulating per day whereas the total reserves of all the world's banks was only $1.3 trillion of which $340 billion was in gold (2001: 327). He points out that:

Foreign exchange transactions today dwarf the trading volume of all other asset classes, even of the entire global economy ... such volume amounts to over 150 times the total daily international trade of all commodities, all manufacture and all services worldwide. It is in the order of 100 times the daily trading of all equities in all the stock markets around the world. It is even 50 times greater than all the goods and services produced per day (GDP) by all the industrialized countries. (ibid: 312)

Financial speculation is also growing five times as fast as global trade and therefore the gap will widen. Lietaer argues that 'something very unusual is going on ... something that we have never experienced before' (ibid: 313). The irony is that currency speculation acts directly against the other aim of money management, the need for 'sound money'. It also exacerbates the conflict between industrial and finance capital where the 'profits' from finance capital and the liquidation of physical assets into money destroys productive capacity, a major feature of Thatcherite capitalism (Ingham, 1984).

Where money was used in the pre-modern era, its acceptability depended upon the desirable properties it possessed in its own right, as decorative beads, shells, stones or precious metals. Coins or bullion could be melted down to serve decorative purposes, and were therefore, at least in part, desired for their potential use value as a metal commodity. From this historical fact derives the enduring notion that money is a tangible commodity, and the common illusion that the sophistication of modern banking practice remains based upon the sure foundations of a metallist theory of money.

Origins of banking and credit

A bank is an institution offering financial services. Banking has evolved from ancient times when banks were used to store precious metals and other valuables in safe keeping, to lend money at interest and to exchange foreign currencies. These functions of banking continue to the present day. Nevertheless, since early modern times a primary function of banking has been the issue of credit money in the form of loans, and the cashing of bills of exchange and other credit instruments, which has provided the basis for the growth of the formal (money) economy. The charging of interest on credit became legal in Britain when Henry VIII overturned Catholic law against usury. The earliest state banks in Britain, Holland and France were associated with both trade and war, the earliest in Sweden in 1688. The Bank of England, for example, was set up to provide legal protection for the interests of a group of private individuals. In 1694 William III approached the London goldsmiths for a loan of £1.2 million to finance his war against King Louis of France. He needed the money to equip ships, provide arms and pay, feed and clothe soldiers. Fearing a repeat of the Stuarts' renegation on past loans which had ruined many goldsmiths, the goldsmiths refused to lend the money to the King. Instead, they proposed that the financing of wars should be taken out of the King's hands.

The Parliament Act which established the Bank of England allowed a small number of merchants, trading as private individuals, to provide the sum of £1.2 million for the King. The King promised to pay interest at 8 per cent to those who had subscribed the money. Taxes were imposed on beer, ale and vinegar, from which the sum of £100,000 was retained to pay the interest to the holders of the 'National Debt'. Since that date the national debt has remained a permanent feature of formal cash economies, serviced and financed by public taxation. Furthermore, the Bank of England, like later national banks, became the statutory instrument for regulation of the money supply which governs the formal cash economy. At first the influence of the Bank of England was limited to the London area, while many small banks continued to operate independently, issuing notes under their own names. In time, however, the Bank of England gained sole control over the issue of legal tender, the notes and coins of the realm. It became lender of last resort, able to control the reserve currency of the nation with a view to regulating profitable trade and production for exchange.

Buchan has argued that, where the issue of paper money is seen as the liability of a national bank, this is really a call on the wealth of the nation (1997: 137). This is particularly important when we recall that the Bank of England was set up to provide legal protection for the interests of private individuals. It was profitable for the goldsmiths to advance loans to the King in order to finance his wars, but only in so far as their claims to the money loaned (capital), and the interest charges, could be enforced. It was to the King's personal advantage to wage war to secure his power and position. Furthermore, it became profitable to produce warships, armaments, cloth (for uniforms) and the other commodities required for war. These activities were financed through taxation. The legal framework of the statutory financial system was therefore based upon private profiteering and power struggles, at the expense of, rather than for the benefit of, the common good. Only very incidentally was it concerned with the provisioning of necessities for the members of the wider community most of whom remained in the feudal or subsistence sector.

The emergence of modern banking and the role of credit/fiat money shows the very political role that money plays in society. It also shows that money does not stem from any particular value or source of value. What money does is enable things to happen. Money is not a neutral instrument within trade, it creates the very potential of trade. Control of, or access to, the creation of money is vital to social and political power. Evidence for this exists in the 'John Law' phenomenon, an aspect of economic history which James Buchan argues has been largely hidden from mainstream economics with its theory of the neutral role of money and finance. We will gratefully follow Buchan in his aim of bringing Law 'out from the shadows of the economists' (1997: 133).

John Law and banking as money creation

Law was the son of a goldsmith/banker from Edinburgh born in 1671. After a rakish youth (including killing someone in a duel) he tried in 1705 to get Scotland to issue paper money to get out of an economic crisis. Law argued that what was needed was 'stimulatory paper currency' (ibid: 138) He based the issue of paper money on the future productivity of land and rejected more traditional options such as exchange controls, coining plate, 'raising the Money' (devaluation), bank credit based on coin (viz. Amsterdam Wisselbank) or sovereign loan (viz. Bank of England).

Still with an English warrant on his head Law had to leave Scotland after the Act of Union in 1707 and continued to promote the idea of a 'bank of issue' in Paris. His ideas again fell on deaf ears and he was expelled from the city. Law's chance came to put his ideas into practice in Regency France which was bankrupt after years of war and court extravagance. In 1715 Law opened a private bank which operated with only one-sixteenth of its equity in coin. The bank's paper notes become highly valued and by 1717 were used to pay taxes. By 1718 the bank was effectively nationalised and was used to capitalise the state of Louisiana. As a result by 1719 the bank was linked to a national trading company. John Law effectively became Prime Minister and all national debt and credit was taken on by him personally. He converted *rentes* and *billets* into a national commercial venture and the entire liquid capital of the country flowed into his company. The word 'millionaire' was coined for him as he owned a lot of France and half of the present US. As Buchan points out effectively 'the whole Nation becomes a body of traders' (ibid: 143).

There is lot of commonality between Law's integration of national interest and commercial interest through the banking and investment system and the stock market booms of the late twentieth century. People became convinced that their prosperity would be assured by commercial investments. As in the Thatcher era the push of bourgeois values led to a collapse of prestige for the rentier class. Within Law's France social differences were undermined and the rentier class lost their social edge. Law proposed taxes to be raised on land at 1 per cent with nothing to be paid by the clergy, labourers or the poor, although this was not implemented. As in the stock-market boom of the late twentieth century, the collapse had to come. In many ways Law's speculative ventures would have been at home at the beginning of the twenty-first century. He tried to buy into the English Indies market by selling short, but the market carried on rising and he ended up paying £372,000 for stocks contracted at £180,000. In order to maintain liquidity he increased money supply; this led to inflation, which saw Law as 'the father of paper inflation' (ibid: 133). By 1720 it was all over and, in a final irony, London and Amsterdam crashed not long after with their own bubbles.

James Buchan takes a positive view of John Law and agrees with Marx's assessment that he was a mixture of swindler and prophet. Schumpeter certainly knew and appreciated Law's ideas: 'Manufacture of money! Credit as creator of money! Manifestly, this opens up other than theoretical vistas.' Schumpeter argued that the seventeenth-century 'cowboy' experimenter in banking, John Law, 'fully realized the business potentialities of the discovery that money – and hence capital in the monetary sense of the term – can be manufactured or created' (1954: 321). Although the experimental schemes failed because they were not part of the accepted institutional framework of money and finance, this did not, according to Schumpeter, negate the accuracy of the theory behind the experiments. As Buchan points out: 'value was revealed for what it is, mere will' (1997: 147).

For Schumpeter, when money has no intrinsic value it is possible to *manage* the quantity of money, paving the way for 'management of currency and credit as a means of managing the economic process'

(1954: 322). Recognition of this possibility destroys the theoretical foundations of the concept of the equilibrating circular flow. John Law observed that the use of a commodity as a means of circulation affects its value. Once a commodity like silver or gold is commonly circulated as money in the form of coinage, its value changes, i.e. the exchange value of the monetary commodity ceases to be explained by its exchange value as a commodity. So long as the commodity can move freely between its monetary and industrial uses, the value will be equal; but once a commodity like silver is used almost exclusively as money it can easily be replaced by one that has no commodity value at all, such as paper. Law saw money as 'pure function' and attacked the bullionists like John Locke who argued for a gold standard: 'Money is not the value *for* which Goods are exchanged, but the Value *by* which they are exchanged: the use of Money is to buy Goods, and Silver while Money is of no other use' (Buchan, 1997: 137. Italics in the original).

Buchan argues that Law also saw money in its social role: 'For Law, the chief purpose of money is to mobilise the energies of people and the riches of the natural world' (1997: 137). Buchan goes on to argue: 'Law believed money was a distillation of human relations and might be turned to purpose and custom – to create a prosperous and just society … [and] he damned near pulled it off' (ibid: 149).

From his analysis of the emergence of a money economy, Buchan argues that 'money offers freedom, but not equality' (ibid: 152). This is certainly the evidence of the early money economies. Despite Law's insights, which like him were short-lived, the actual experience of the money economies was the overthrow of the feudal economies as the people of 'brass' gained social and political power, but the mechanisms of harnessing those economies for social ends were problematic. Thereby lies an irony. While, as we have argued, money values are social, or at least relative rather than natural, the presumed 'naturalness' of the economy justifies extreme inequality even to the present day. It was this view of the inevitability of economic relations that Marx railed against in *Capital*. Today it is taken for granted that there is no *economic* basis upon which to question what 'the economy' is doing, whether it be making weapons, trafficking in women, enslaving children, using environmentally destructive production methods, laundering money or trading in pornography and drugs. All those questions are seen as political or moral. Democracy does not enter into economic reasoning. The will of the people can only be expressed through the cash register. Equally, the only way that nation-states see of allocating any money for social causes is if they tax the so-called wealth-creating (money-making) sector. What we argue is that this so-called wealth is not created in trade but in the money system itself. Money and therefore wealth is created through the banking/credit system. As Buchan points out: 'in a paper-money economy [the difference between money and credit] can barely be detected' (1997: 133). The question is who gets that credit/money and how? How does the allocation of control over credit issue affect the processes of production, distribution of incomes and exchange?

The evolution of the debt-based money economy

It was not technical innovation but the use of bills of exchange and other credit instruments which gave rise to agribusiness and large-scale manufacturing industry. If a manufacturer of woollen cloth received an order for cloth worth £1,000, there might not be enough money available to buy wool from the farmer and hire workers to make and transport the cloth to the merchant. Without the money, the manufacturing firm could not produce the cloth. However, with a bill of exchange from the purchaser in the form of a promise to pay an agreed amount on the date the goods were to be delivered – also known as a 'draft' – the manufacturer could exchange the bill for metallic money (gold or silver) or for paper promises to pay in gold. The goldsmith or banker discounting the bill was creating financial capital because it was financially profitable to do so. The finance so created was for the production of tradeable commodities, and not to produce the necessities of everyday life. The distinction is vital. Commodities were (and are) not traded primarily because they are socially useful or necessary for provisioning populations. Goods are produced for trade because they are expected to produce a profit for the trader. In turn, credit is advanced because of the likely profitability of the transaction to the financial institution. What is produced depends upon profitability to private institutions rather than serviceability to the community as a whole.

Through the acceptance of bills of exchange bankers initiated the practice of financing production for future exchange. At the same time they made present money incomes available to the workers through the employing firms. The money supplied for present incomes was created effectively as debt, or 'credit'. Bills of exchange formed the earliest form of credit, and remained central to international trade until the development of increasingly sophisticated forms of banking overdrafts in recent times (Davies, 1994: 339–40). All forms of credit creation remain the same in principle. In effect, the merchant commissions the production of cloth, armaments or any other commodity so that he can trade it, that is, buy in one market and sell in another, for financial profit. Money in this context is not a veil masking barter of real commodities in a circular flow model. It forms a distinct socio-economic function, an evolution of Aristotle's chrematistics against oikonomics, of Veblen's commercial 'sabotage' of industry and workmanship for profit. The entire system revolves around credibility and reputation purely in terms of ability to pay money. The central point at issue is the ability to deliver money on time. As financial institutions develop, the ability to deliver commodities becomes secondary to the mainte-nance of the institutions governing production for profitable trade. The social use value of the production for which incomes are allocated remains secondary to financial considerations. Hence, production of armaments takes precedence over food supplies for the starving, even where 'surplus' food is being destroyed. Money value takes precedence.

From the sixteenth century onwards production for exchange, rather than use value, was increasingly initiated by debt financing. Bills of exchange are usually thought to have been introduced merely to facilitate long-distance trade in times of uncertain com-munications and poor transport between urban centres. However, they were essential to the initiation of production and distribution of incomes associated with production for trade.

Money as debt/credit

The earliest economists were familiar with stock exchanges and money markets, banking, bills of exchange and other instruments of credit. However, the classical economists interpreted the operation of these financial institutions on the basis of a metallist theory of money, as if money was gold or some other commodity with a concrete material substance. Sales contracts providing for deferred payment seemed to them no more than a proper sale, and a loan of the money. Equally, a deposit of money (e.g. in a goldsmith's vault) transfered the ownership of the money to the receiver (the goldsmith) who now owned the gold and *owed* money to equivalent value. Also, if in the course of trade A became debtor of B, and at the same time B owed money to A, the debts could be said to cancel each other out, with only the difference to be settled. The principle could be extended, so that several dealers could settle their debts through a clearing-house system without the use of cash. As a result, it appeared that neither lending nor the giving or receiving of credit had anything to do with the working of the monetary system: 'these things involved the use of money, no doubt, but in no other sense than does buying for money or making a gift in money or paying taxes in money.'

> But this, of course, is not so. 'Credit' operations of whatever shape or kind do affect the working of the monetary system; more important, they do affect the working of the capital engine – so much so as to become an essential part of it without which the rest cannot be understood at all. (Schumpeter, 1954: 318)

Under capitalism, money does not operate like a commodity. Schumpeter explored the implications of two vital distinctions between a metallist theory of money and the practicalities of a debt-based money system. Under the latter system, creation of credit increases the quantity of money in circulation and creates the ability for currency to be managed.

Credit and the velocity of money

A strict identification of money as a commodity (a 'strictly metallist conception of money') makes it necessary to draw a sharp distinction between money, on the one hand, and legal claims to money and operations in money on the other. It then becomes necessary to devise some other theory to explain the existence of the latter. This can be done by extending the concept of velocity. In this view, when a banker issues notes in excess of the bank's cash holding, this is not creating money, but merely increasing the velocity of its circulation. The same applies even when some of the cash deposited is lent. In these terms, it appears that there is very little difference between a bank note and a cheque: both are promises to pay in coin at some time or other. Most phenomena going under the heading of credit could be described as a form of money. Even government paper money can be viewed as government debt.

In the early days of economics (pre-Adam Smith) it was assumed that bankers were intermediary lenders of other peoples' money.

However, even if a banker does pay out a percentage of creditors with metallic money, economic outcomes are affected when this sum is lent out again and again *'before the first borrower has been repaid'* (emphasis original). Even more clearly, when issuing bank notes and checking accounts as debts, the bank is creating 'a velocity [of circulation] so great that it enables a thing to be in different places at the same time' (Schumpeter, 1954: 320). It would be logically possible for a cloakroom attendant at a restaurant to hire out the coats of diners while they were eating. But it would be impossible for two people – the owner and the hirer – to wear the same coat at the same time. However, this is exactly what happens when a banker makes a fresh loan. The new loan does not diminish the depositor's ability to draw on their money. Note that this process does not increase the velocity of circulation of money at all, or cut down the time it takes for a unit of money to pass through several stations, or affect people's propensity to save what they perceive to be cash. It changes the quantity of money in existence.

Banks do not lend their deposits, or other peoples' money. Banks create deposits and bank notes. Money is not a commodity, like any other commodity, because with no other commodity can a *claim* to the commodity serve the same purpose as the thing itself: 'While I cannot ride on a claim to a horse, I can, under certain conditions, do exactly the same with claims to money as with money itself, namely buy' (Schumpeter, 1934: 97). Bank notes and cheque deposits (sight deposits) do what money does, and hence must be classed as money. Certain credit instruments (e.g. bills of exchange) may in some circumstances form part of the money supply in the money markets because they can be exchanged, more or less readily, for other forms of money. In short, the institutions of banking and finance create the money supply through a range of mechanisms ultimately endorsed by statutory authority.

How banks multiply money

Real goods and services are created by labour's use of the natural resources of the planet. Money, the defining element within the formal economy, is created by financial institutions. The formal economy only recognises demand *backed by money*. However:

> The process by which banks create money is so simple that the mind is repelled. Where something so important is involved, a deeper mystery seems only decent. (Galbraith, 1975: 29)

In the early days of 'fractional reserve banking' the goldsmiths created loans of non-existent gold by the same method as they transferred the ownership of gold held in their vaults between customers by the issue of a 'promise to pay the bearer'. These loans were normally offered to individuals with reputations for reliability, or were secured against property in land or buildings (see Rowbotham, 1998). They normally carried an interest charge, the reward to the goldsmith for the risk of non-repayment. However, the goldsmith could only create money to a certain prudent level. If all customers presented their paper promises-to-pay-gold at the same time, (in order to physically move the gold to another place of storage) the goldsmith would be ruined. Exactly the same *principle* applies today. Banks and financial institutions need to stay in business and the statutory framework is constantly adapted to take account of changing practice. However, with the development of off-shore financial havens (*not* tax havens), the legal loopholes are increasingly difficult to police, while international finance has become a law unto itself (see Warburton, 1999).

Fractional reserve banking

When a bank issues a loan, it needs reserves of some kind to guard against the whole value of its outstanding commitments being presented at the same time. These 'fractional reserves' may take the form of cash and coins held by the commercial bank, together with the bank's deposits with the central bank, e.g. the Bank of England. In theory, the government/statutory authority, through the central bank, can regulate the money supply by manipulating reserves and reserve requirements. In practice, as Christopher Niggle has demonstrated (see below), evolving financial practice is progressively endorsed by the statutory authority. To do otherwise would be to threaten the stability of the fragile financial system upon which the modern economy depends.

Hunt and Sherman explore the principles of fractional reserve banking (1990). They take the example of a banking system where each bank seeks to maintain its cash reserves and deposits with the central bank (e.g. the Bank of England, the 'lender of last resort') at 10 per cent (1: 10) of the total amount its customers *could* withdraw from it. Suppose, then, Bank A has a sum of £100 in cash lodged with it. In this event its cash reserves *and* its liabilities to its customers rise by the same amount. But the ratio of liabilities to cash reserves is no longer 1: 10. The bank has £90 too much cash. It *could* increase its liabilities to the normal amount by lending £900 to its customers in the usual way. But if it did so it would risk running into 'adverse clearing balances'. The new loans/overdrafts could be withdrawn as cash and spent on goods, with the cash being transferred (by the receiving businesses) through rival banks, which would then claim the full amount through the central bank. The bank's liability would then be greater than 10: 1, an unviable situation.

Instead, Bank A, the original bank, will retain £10 of the original deposit, and create new loans to the value of £90, maintaining its own cash/reserve ratio. However, when received by Bank B, the £90 will represent £90 in new (excess) reserves. Bank B can retain 10 per cent as new reserves, and make new loans to the value of the remaining 90 per cent. The process continues throughout the banking system as a whole, until the original new deposit of £100 cash has resulted in new loans created *by the banking system as a whole* to a total value of £900 (see Hunt and Sherman, 1990: 505–8). The original deposit has allowed the banks to increase their loans to the public, and hence the money supply, by £1,000. Notice that the total amount a bank's customers could withdraw is not limited to the savings they may have deposited with the bank, but includes any loans and overdraft facilities the bank may have granted to its customers which they have not yet drawn. Across the system as a whole these amounts, together with notes and coins, form the nation's money supply (traditionally defined as M0/M4), i.e. its 'cash'.

Textbook theory on macro-analysis assumes central bank control over bank reserves and rigid reserve–deposit ratios. Furthermore, although the banking system as a whole creates 97 per cent of new money as loans, it was, until very recently, assumed that the money creation process was regulated by a central banking authority through its ability to regulate the issue of notes and coins. However, the money created by banks is not the same as notes and coins, which have a tangible existence. We could call the former 'bookkeeping money' and the latter 'pocket money'. Bookkeeping money is used by industrialists and retailers, and for transactions with them. Pocket money, when used by ordinary people for their everyday transactions, is normally regarded as real, tangible money, 'as good as gold'. A sharp distinction can be drawn between the two types of money. Notes and coins in the pocket can be physically transferred to another pocket or placed in a bank. Bookkeeping money has no existence outside a bank or financial institution. To use bookkeeping money one needs a bank account. Huber and Robertson (c.2000) calculate that 97 per cent of money in the economy is merely bookkeeping or electronic money, with only 3 per cent being legal tender such as cash and notes. As the level of bookkeeping money increases or decreases, the amount of pocket money in a country increases or decreases, i.e. bookkeeping money determines the quantity of cash in the economy.

Since the 1980s in the UK and US money has increasingly been issued into the economy through credit card borrowing, giving rise to 'credit card capitalism'. Credit cards were originally issued as a company currency. The first Diner's Club Card of 1949 was issued by oil companies to create brand loyalty and a symbol of creditworthiness. VISA issued by Bank of America in 1958 is now a network of 20,000 banks and the largest mutual company in the world with up to 600 million card-holders. The most important change with the widespread use of credit cards is that responsibility for the issuing of debt money into the economy and thereby for ensuring its vitality now rests with consumers. Arguably, at one level this creates a form of economic democracy as the consumer's choice will prevail (demand-led), but this ignores the role of advertising and the problems of those burdened with consumer debts. Furthermore, creditworthiness becomes the basis of participation in the consumer economy.

Credit cards also make a mockery of the idea of any control of money issue in an economy where nearly every store now has its own credit card. Far from limiting indebtedness, profligate expenditure is encouraged. Store-based cards can also lend money direct. One of the authors' children, an impecunious student, was sent an unsolicited cheque for £150 drawn on a reputable bank by a store-card company. On deposit the student had £150 cash and a whopping credit charge. It is clear that the credit issuing system is not only beyond control but is desperate to expand business. Financial services to the consumer is now much bigger business for the banks than services to business and industry. In order to avoid economic chaos, evolving practice is continually being endorsed by statutory measures. Stephen Tominey, a former hedge-fund manager writing in the *Guardian* newspaper, argued that the US stock-market boom had been largely funded by a credit bubble. However, the party has come to an end and there are no more eager investors willing to borrow to join the game. As Tominey points out:

The non-bank financial markets have their own deposit base, money market funds, that can be lent repeatedly (multiplied) without limit ... Lending to the financial sector – up 40% since 1998 is a turbo-charged credit machine into financial assets and corporate balance sheets. (*Guardian*, 15 October 2001)

The evolution of the money creation process

The following very stylised account of the evolution of banking practices is derived from Christopher Niggle (1990). Although it is not historically specific, it provides a valuable overview of the money creation process.

Stage 1: The economy has a commodity money (e.g. gold or silver) or a convertible paper currency with strict metallic backing. In such an economy the quantity of money is determined outside the financial and industrial sectors. It is dependent upon overseas trade flows, foreign investment, gold production or piracy, as in Britain before Ricardo's era. In this stage goldsmiths receive gold for safe-keeping and issue receipts. These receipts are promises to pay the gold in future. In these circumstances, money is a commodity, operating like any other commodity except that it stores well, can be easily divided and measured, and retains its value over time (it does not go off like a lump of old cheese). Furthermore, as we have seen in the case of the founding of the Bank of England, it can be used as a standard of deferred payment, i.e. to advance a loan.

Stage 2: Goldsmiths now introduce 'fractional reserve banking'. They issue convertible paper money in excess of their gold deposits. In the absence of a legal reserve requirement, the money supply becomes 'somewhat elastic'. The money supply is determined by the demand for credit, loan repayments and the prudence of individual bankers. Now to some extent the money supply is endogenously determined within the financial and industrial system. To the extent that receipts are offered by goldsmiths in excess of the gold they hold, they are *creating new money as debt*. A debt-based money system has come into existence, functioning on belief, trust, *credit*.

Stage 3: The introduction of some type of central monetary authority such as a central bank can impose reserve requirements on the money-creating institutions, the 'banks'. The practice of issuing loan-based 'money' is ratified by the legal system in order to harmonise economic activity at national and international levels. Using open market operations, or a discount window, the central bank can now adjust bank reserves to enhance its power over the money supply. The central bank can impose reserve requirements on commercial banks, and adjust their reserves by discounting eligible paper at discount rates intended to encourage or discourage borrowing or lending by the banks. In the early days of central banking, economists came to assume central bank control over bank reserves and rigid reserve–deposit ratios. It seemed plausible, therefore, to assume that the money supply was exogenously determined: it did not appear to be determined by the financial and commercial system.

Stage 4: Stage 3 places constraints upon financial entrepreneurs. They are limited in the extent to which they can expand their highly profitable lending activities. They therefore find ways around the restrictions, for example, through forms of inter-bank lending, which can increase the speed with which lending and money-creation respond to changes in reserves. More significantly, they find access to funds not covered by reserves, enabling them to make loans on demand and cover their reserve position later. Furthermore, banks are able to issue new lines of credit, including mortgages, overdrafts and credit facilities. They can even create new *banks*, as when supermarkets offer financial 'services'. Most bank loans are made under previous commitments: hence the extension of net bank credit results in money creation. The money supply is largely determined endogenously, i.e. within the financial and industrial system.

Stage 5: The monetary authority (the central bank under the legal auspices of the state) exists to prevent financial instability. As lender of last resort for the whole system, it has to recognise that, as banks make loans on demand, inadequate reserves system-wide will cause interest rates to rise and the value of fixed securities to fall. It has no option but to stabilise the financial markets by accommodating the banks' need for reserves to cover their 'loan-created deposits'.

In practice, Stages 4 and 5 often occur simultaneously. The money supply is determined by the financial system in conjunction with the commercial/industrial system to which it makes loans. The supply of money is determined by and within the economy itself. Both the supply of money and the commercial system are open to flows over the national borders. While the principle of endogenous organic growth of money remains central to theory, evolving practice is merely endorsed by the statutory authorities.

In a capitalist economy, where there are markets in land, labour and capital, money is necessary to set in motion the use of the 'real credit' – land, capital, raw materials and labour – which creates productive wealth. However, wealth as production fuelled by money and for money is not the same as wealth as provisioning/livelihood. The formal economy of capitalism depends upon a mix of legal, military, and social institutions to enforce claims. In the case of international finance these structures are shedding even the vestiges of democratic control (see Chossudovsky, 1997). The system of money and banking regulates production for distribution and exchange on a global scale. Bills of exchange formed the earliest form of credit, and remained central to international trade until the development of more sophisticated forms of credit in recent times. In effect, the merchant commissions the *production* of a commodity so that it can be *traded* (bought in one market and sold in another) for financial profit. Money is anything *but* a veil, a neutral facilitator of exchange masking barter of real commodities.

In common usage, people go to 'work' or into business, in order to 'make money'. In terms of meeting human need, wealth results from the combination of natural resources and labour. A farmer, for example, may take land (already available), tools (a spade) and saved seed potatoes from last year's crop. Using her/his own labour, the farmer can plant the field, tend the crops and in due course harvest the crop. Real wealth (goods) has been produced without money entering into the system. If the farmer places some potatoes in a sack and sells them to a neighbour for £5, has s/he *made* £5? No. The money pre-existed. If no other money exists in the economy, no further trade can take place until the farmer spends all or part of the £5. The farmer's production may have increased the *value of the money which exists*, but that is a different thing from *increasing the money*: that is done by financial institutions under statutory authority. The process whereby money became central to determining social outcomes in practice while being simultaneously eliminated from theory is explored in the next chapter.

4 Capitalism – The Elimination of Alternatives

Economic orthodoxy is the celebration of a particular model of human relationships centred upon the capitalist market, the market society. Globalisation at present involves the spread of capitalist market logic and its underlying mode of production to human relationships worldwide. Towards the end of the twentieth century and particularly after the fall of the Berlin wall, it seemed as if the western model had triumphed. It was even celebrated as the 'end of history' (Fukuyama, 1992). Thomas Frank has argued that during this period the market came to be associated with the expression of democracy. Speaking of the US context he claims that market populism came to imply that the capitalist market is somehow identified with the will of the people:

> Real democracy was only possible when the market was free to do its thing. Markets expressed popular will more adequately than elections – they were for the little guy. (Frank, 2001: x)

In the UK George Monbiot has argued that private corporations have made such inroads into political decision-making that they have managed to 'capture' the state (2000) and Korten has made a similar case in the global context (1995).

The position for capitalist corporations in the twenty-first century is less certain. Growing national and international inequality and the pressure of environmental limits on industrial expansion initially produced a backlash against the global market system in the form of a loose network of anti-globalisation campaigns. These were more than eclipsed by the terrorist attack on the US on 11 September 2001. While the vast majority of Muslims did not support fundamentalist terrorism, it was clear that western societies had largely ignored the response to the globalisation of capitalism and western values in the Islamic world. Even within western thought there was considerable sympathy with the view that the global market in general, and the US in particular, had gone too far in terms of world domination.

This chapter explores the characteristics of capitalism as a socio-economic system. It looks at the framework within which the money/market system developed to the extent that money and money debt became a dominant feature in economic life. These roots lie in the enclosure of land as property and the enclosure of people's time as wage labour. The money system has been central to the emergence of capitalism. Control of the productive life of the community through the imposition of capitalised money is very much a feature of political life today and is supported internationally through the World Trade Organisation and the IMF.

Characteristics of capitalism

In *The Origin of Capitalism* Ellen Meiksins Wood challenges the idea that capitalism is a maturation of pre-existing social forms. For Wood, capitalism, or 'commercial society', ruptures pre-existing institutional frameworks by offering the illusion of freedom, opportunity and choice. She argues that, although socialists may object to the commodification of labour power and class exploitation which capitalism entails, they often fail to recognise that the distinctive and dominant characteristic of the capitalist market is its compulsion. This is so in two senses:

> first, that material life and social reproduction in capitalism are universally mediated by the market, so that all individuals must, in one way or another enter into market relations in order to gain access to the means of life; and second, that the dictates of the capitalist market – its imperatives of competition, accumulation, profit maximization, and increasing labor productivity – regulate not only all economic transactions but social relations in general. (Wood, 1999: 7)

Presenting an account of the agrarian origins of finance capitalism, Wood describes capitalism as a unique social form originating in the evolution of markets in land, destroying pre-capitalist forms of land tenure, imposing market imperatives and environmental destruction as it expands across the globe. Corporate power has evolved from the forcible appropriation of the land and the statutory imposition of the basic institutions of capitalism, property, finance and the market. The distinctiveness lies in that fact that, whereas the peasantry in England and elsewhere had in past times 'availed themselves of market *opportunities*', they were now 'unique in their degree of subjection to market *imperatives*' (Wood, 1999: 53). Wood argues that the 'ethic of "improvement" in its original sense, in which production is inseparable from profit, is also the ethic of exploitation, poverty and homelessness' (1999: 118). Once market imperatives have replaced other social forms, even ownership of the means of production does not spell freedom from commercial compulsion.

Wood identifies four basic characteristics of capitalism:

1. Production of goods and services, including the most basic necessities of life, is undertaken for profitable exchange. Human labour power is itself a marketable commodity.
2. Since all economic actors are dependent on the market, the fundamental rules of life are governed by the requirements of competition and profit maximisation.
3. The capitalist rules of life dictate technological development to improve the productivity of labour.
4. The entire system is based upon the existence of propertyless labourers 'who are obliged to sell their labor power in exchange for a wage in order to gain access to the means of life' (Wood, 1999: 2).

It is the last point that is central to the issue of economic democracy as addressed in this book. Capitalism is a system based on commodity production for profitable exchange in which the majority of people are obliged to take part as waged labour if they want to survive. Capitalism is not concerned with supplying the *necessities* of life. Rather, it is based on institutions engaged in denial of access to the means of sustenance for the majority class, so that the minority class can pursue power and status through predatory competition. Capitalism can be defined as the private ownership of the resources for sustenance. It is lack of access to the means of sustenance that results in the phenomenon of 'employment'. To gain employment, 'free' labour offer themselves to those who command the 'means of production'. However it is important not to confuse the means of production with the means of sustenance. The means of production under capitalism do not necessarily make any contribution to human sustenance. That is why calls for the ownership and control of the means of production *as defined by capital* misses the point (Mellor, 2000a). For economic democracy what is important is that people have control over the resources necessary for their subsistence and the capacity to decide what form of productive activity will take place to meet social needs and desires.

The distinctive feature of capitalism is that it marshals and allocates labour in a historically unique way. In doing so it replaces all ancient socio-economic relationships. Many of these may have been harsh or exploitative, but many will also have been co-operative and convivial. What is certain is that most people historically will have had some direct access to the means of their own subsistence. Capitalism is not just about the exploitation of labour. There are many historical examples of hierarchical patterns of dominance based on forced or bonded labour. Many of those people would have been denied any resources other than through labour, but the important difference is that a large majority of the population would still have had direct links to sources of subsistence. People may have been heavily taxed or had their crops taken, but it is only within capitalism that resources are entirely removed from the majority of the people *and handed back to them only through the money system.*

The importance of the enclosure of land as private property is that many of the resources communities held would have been in the form of common land, or land based loosely on families or communities. Commons resources are those which have no deeds of ownership but are regularly used for farming or harnessing subsistence. Under these conditions most people would have gathered, hunted, gardened and herded, growing and preparing their own food. Much of this work would have been done by women (Boserup, 1970). The emergence of capitalist market society together with industrial patterns of resource use including agricultural production has broken down the direct relationship between people and the source of their subsistence for at least two-thirds of the world's population. Self-provisioning whether on a family or communal basis has been replaced by waged labour contractually engaged 'through a network of society-embracing markets' (Heilbroner, 1988: 89). In the process many traditional structures of husbandry have also been lost. It was this compulsion into waged labour, ironically described as 'free', which Marx argued made capitalism a unique form of exploitation. The two key elements of capitalism as identified by Marx are the institutions of property and the creation of the capitalised market system. As Marx pointed out 'in themselves money and commodities are no more capital than are the means of production and subsistence' (Vol. III: 737) but when capitalised they create a system in which the majority of people have no alternative but to participate as waged labour if they are to survive.

This process still continues. Research on exploitation in places like rural India show that many people feel compelled to migrate to find employment. To make matters worse, rural residents in many parts of India and its neighbouring countries often get indebted to their employer and 'bonded' into employment relationships. This can involve leaving home, migrating to a work camp or industrial zone, living in temporary accommodation without proper schools or access to health care, and every few months receiving whatever pay is left over after the current debts and interest is repaid to the 'master' (Olsen and Ramanamurthy, 1999). Such cases of bonded labour for landless people are not disappearing with capitalism, but rather are embedded within it, often funded by governments (Brass and Van der Linden, 1997). As one of the present authors has shown elsewhere, detailed analysis of the compulsions of capitalism within specific empirical contexts exposes the myth of 'free' labour under free-market ideology. While theoretically it may be argued that the compulsion to labour requires the active participation of workers, this can be achieved by paying people wages below the subsistence level (Olsen, 1998).

Property as enclosure

> The fault is great in man or woman
> Who steals a goose from off a common
> But what can plead that man's excuse
> Who steals a common from a goose?

> Anon. c1820.

In a passage towards the end of Vol. III of *Capital* Marx makes clear the importance of the institution of property in the process of enclosure to creation of the conditions for capital accumulation. For Marx, 'the process ... that clears the way for the capitalist system ... [is] the process which takes away from the labourer the possession of his means of production' with expropriation from the soil as 'the basis of the whole process'. The history of this expropriation is 'written in the annals of mankind in letters of blood and fire', a process of 'conquest, enslavement, robbery, murder'. The process of expropriation and the creation of private ownership can take place in different ways, most notably where 'great masses of men are suddenly and forcibly torn from their means of subsistence and hurled as free and 'unattached' proletarians on the labour market'.

The heart of the capitalist process lies in the two sides of this expropriation, the creation of private property as a basis of capitalisation and the creation of a mass population who have no means of livelihood of their own and therefore 'nothing to sell except their own skins'. For Marx the transformation of capital can only take place where the owners of money and the means of production and subsistence face the so-called 'free labourers', sellers of their labour power. At this point the process of capital accumulation proper can begin where 'money is changed into capital ... through capital surplus value is made, and from surplus value more capital' (Marx, 1974: 736–9).

Marx took the example of the particular situation of feudalism and enclosure in Britain, but acknowledged that this process could take place in many different ways.

Capitalism has evolved through progressive denial of customary rights of access to the means of life. The freedom to buy and sell land was founded upon the freedom of others to starve. It has been convincingly argued that capitalisation of land began in Britain in the era of 'high farming' (Wood, 1999; Friedmann, 2000). Capitalisation of the land occurs when it is expropriated from those who have historically occupied it and also when it becomes available for sale or as collateral for debt, i.e. mortmain to mortgage. The use of money in the expropriation of land is also important. When, it is claimed, Manhattan was bought from its inhabitants for a string of beads, that is expropriation through a money transaction. When people are trapped through taxes or debts into giving up their land, that too, is the use of money. However, the main way in which land was expropriated was the conversion of open or communal land to private hands whether by force, claimed ownership or monetary 'compensation'.

Enclosure, the fencing in of 'open fields', common and waste (meaning land not under cultivation) land, occurred on a wide scale in the English countryside during the sixteenth and seventeenth centuries. Around the time of the English Reformation commoners were often driven from their land as large landowners appropriated land for profitable sheep farming. The Elizabethan Poor Laws were enacted in reaction to the resultant flood of dispossessed 'vagabonds' roaming the countryside and threatening social disorder (Pinchbeck and Hewitt, 1969). The Reformation marked the first stage of creation of a capitalist class free from traditional customs and restraints. Massingham argued that the Commonwealth also undermined traditions of husbandry that protected the land (1942). Throughout the eighteenth and nineteenth centuries parliamentary acts endorsed enclosure of land and the extinction of traditional property rights by landlords seeking profitable investment (Wood, 1999: 83–4; see also Mabey, 1980; Thompson, 1991; and Hammond and Hammond, 1911, 1917, 1919).

Political theorists endorsed the theft by individuals of communal land in the early modern era on the basis that it was for the purpose of profitable exploitation. According to John Locke (1632–1704), although God gave the land to be held in common, it was the duty of individuals to improve (in the original meaning of make valuable) the land with their own labour. Where the land is made more productive and profitable, common possession must give way to private property. According to this theory, land has no value in itself. Hence when an individual encloses waste or common land, and labours to 'improve' it, they add to, rather than take away from, communal welfare. The privatisation (legally endorsed, forceful appropriation) of the land essential to the evolution of agrarian capitalism was justified by the peculiar Lockean notion of the 'social contract'. For Wood, Locke's idea that labour is the source of value and the basis of property does not stand up to rigorous examination 'because one man can appropriate the labour of another'. The right to property can be acquired by combining existing property with the labour of an employee. Apparently, 'the issue for Locke has less to do with the activity of labor as such than with its profitable use. ... The issue, in other words, is not the labour of a human being but the *productivity of property* and its application to commercial profit' (Wood 1999: 86. Emphasis original). The *'laissez-faire'* political economy of capitalism was founded upon the convenient but erroneous assumption that individuals in authority were authorised to act on behalf of the masses through the 'social contract'. By combining 'their' capital with the labour of employees, the capitalist class were making a unique contribution to the common good. Theorising on these lines will stand very little logical examination.

In short, 'enclosure' is the act whereby one individual nominates him/herself as the sole owner of an area formerly available to the whole community for the provision of the necessities of life. The purpose of individual appropriation of 'property' in land is not to provide more efficiently for the welfare of the dispossessed: it is to enhance the power and wealth of the individual free from traditional checks and balances relating to the conservation of the land and the provisioning of its people. Enclosure allowed 'improvements' to be made to the land. Such improvements enabled the individual (household or firm) to produce commodities for sale for money in distant markets. Techniques and technologies devoted to this end broke the relationship between the land and its people (Massingham, 1942; Carson, 1962). In the process it created the illusion that unsustainable practices could be escalated indefinitely. Natural resources could be mined and exploited with impunity, moving on when resources were exhausted to the next profitable location.

The process of absorbing the commons into the market system continues apace today (*Ecologist*, 1993; Goldman, 1998). Forest peoples in particular are struggling for the retention of the commons of tropical rainforests from Sarawak to the Amazon. Across the globe indigenous peoples and peasant farmers are launching anti-globalisation campaigns. For example, the Via Campesina movement led by MST, the Landless movement of Brazil, is demanding land redistribution and an end to the World Bank programme of market-led land reform. The Zapatista movement in Chiapas, Mexico emerged when the NAFTA agreement outlawed the common ownership of land. There are still some large commons systems surviving. Bennholdt-Thomsen and Mies point to the example of Papua New Guinea where in the mid 1990s 95 per cent of the land was still held in common (1999). Eighty-five per cent of the population lived on the land and a popular movement has arisen to defend traditional subsistence practices against an IMF-inspired land mobilisation programme. Structural adjustment programmes imposed by the World Bank/IMF often result in the registration, privatisation and enclosure of land. Common land has to be converted to 'income generation' to pay off debts. As in the past where people have remained within subsistence economies the logic of the market is to destroy their independence, in the name of 'improvement'. Bennholdt-Thomsen and Mies see the IMF/World Bank's aim as being to draw peasant farmers away from subsistence, to make them more productive (i.e.

to produce money incomes) or to use the agricultural labour of women in subsistence communities 'more productively'. By this is meant 'making them produce for the world market, not for their own subsistence' (1999: 144). Some authors argue that structural adjustment has been bad for women (Emeagwali, ed., 1995). Part of the reason is that structural adjustment involves a change from diverse livelihoods to monocropping and cash-cropping. Such a change away from sustainable provisioning creates risk-ridden lifestyles dependent on the money economy.

Bennholdt-Thomsen and Mies see a fundamental link between commons regimes and cultural diversity as people seek to retain and maintain their cultural heritages. Land rights have been a central issue for indigenous peoples across the world. Land rights campaigns are not always about the retention of the commons but over who gains the benefit from any commercialisation. The *Ecologist* sees defence of the commons as an issue of people's control over their own lives, and argues that it is a question of democracy as much as an issue of subsistence (1993). For those seeking profit or even the means of existence in the case of unemployed landless people, non-ownership can be seen as no ownership. The land is therefore up for grabs. There is also the problem that common land holders may want to convert their land to private ownership as it then becomes more 'valuable' in money terms. This is a particular problem where women farmers have historically had communal rights to land use while notional ownership lies in the hands of men (Sachs, 1996). However, from our perspective in this book the critical question is the move into the capitalist market regardless of the way in which this is achieved.

Property is a legally defined social relation which recognises the property holder as having rights over something of value. Thus, the property holder, whether an individual or a group, has a legally defined relationship with a benefit stream, or income, deriving from the property. In these terms property is not a material object, something to be held on to. Rather, it signifies a legally enforceable relationship between benefit streams, rights holders and duty bearers. Under capitalism, individuals (households and firms) are accorded the right to exploit the land and its people without corre-sponding obligations to replenish and repair. As we have argued, capital emerges as denial of access to the means of provisioning and distorts the productive process to socially divisive and environmen-tally destructive ends. As a result benefit streams may be more clearly defined than corresponding duties or obligations to maintain the social or ecological fabric. The rights and duties relating to private property are statutorily defined. In other words, they are designed by powerful interests in the elite class and guaranteed by the state. Private owners are the whistle blowers when the benefit streams from their properties are threatened. However, their duties to maintain the condition of their property, such as the fertility of the land for the benefit of future owners, is less clearly defined than in commons regimes (Bromley, 1991).

The statutory guarantees of rights (and duties) in property are vital to the economic process. Where property rights are not guaranteed in customary or statutory law, resources are open to being plundered and degraded by selfish individuals. Garrett Hardin is well known for his argument that without the controlling mechanism of private property ownership there would be nothing to stop everyone trying to add one more animal to the grazing herd (or from trying to fish the last fish) in commons systems (Hardin, 1973). The true 'tragedy' of the (so-called) 'commons' as outlined by Hardin is that such a 'commons' was *not* a commons, but an open access regime without community checks and balances. There are undoubtedly contemporary situations where commons such as the seas have been used as open access, where individuals, states or companies can take advantage of resources without obligation or co-operative interaction (see Hutchinson and Hutchinson, 1997). However, there is another view of commons regimes which are seen as *common property*, controlled and managed by a local community. The claims and duties of individuals and families are clearly defined, with rights being closely identified with obligations. The medieval English village, with its three-field system, commons and waste (unused) land is a classic example. It is this model of a commons regime that is being defended by indigenous peoples.

State property, if subject to the oversight of distant bureaucrats, may also fall (*de facto*) into the 'open access' category. In such an instance powerful individuals or groups appropriate benefit streams without incurring corresponding obligations. Equally, the state can guarantee the rights of the international, global capitalist elite class to plunder the social and ecological commons, placing the short-term profit of powerful individuals and corporations before the common good. In the eyes of many people organisations like the World Bank, IMF and the WTO are just that, agents of property regimes that seek to transfer all resources into capitalist corporate hands. In short, commons regimes confer rights *with responsibilities*. State, private and open access regimes reinforce or encourage destructive forms of exploitation of natural and communal resources.

Enclosing knowledge and skills

Capitalism is the enclosure not only of land but also tools and knowledge for the purpose of private financial gain. In the same way that land was once 'owned' by everybody or nobody, knowledge has also been captured for profit. As Veblen has argued, all invention is based upon the common cultural inheritance built up over countless generations. This point is central to our argument for economic democracy and for the social control of money-determined investment. Although the fencing of land is commonly portrayed as a means of securing opportunity to introduce more 'efficient' farming methods, it entailed far more than mere fencing. Loss of subsistence access through enclosure, exclusion or patenting leads to a loss of social inheritance and knowledge (Alier, 2000). Enclosure is the extinction of customary land use rights through which communities secured their livelihoods. It entails denial of access not only to cultivated land but also to 'wild' sources of foods, medicines and fuels and the knowledge of traditional usage.

Under industrial capitalism the employer owns not only the building, machinery and materials used by the workers but the knowledge and experience of the workers themselves. Intellectual 'property' is also 'privatised' through the patenting and copyrighting process. A patent is a government grant securing sole rights to make, use and sell a particular invention for a stated period. Ownership of a patent can enable an individual to deny others access to useful tools and processes. Moreover, firms can, and often do, buy up patents in order to *prevent* production of a desirable rival product or a more durable product. Obsolescence is essential to continual money growth. Intellectual property has now become an important aspect of world trade. The patenting of seed in particular is causing a loss of species as well as denying poorer people access to their traditional plants. Often this is because the seed has been hybridised and patented, but sometimes it is because competition from commercially more successful products has destroyed the financial viability of local species. What this might mean in the longer run is that hardy species developed over millennia such as grain that can resist salination, drought or low temperatures, or forage animals that can live in difficult terrain, will be lost for ever.

The capitalist market

The second major institution in the framework of capitalism is the supposedly free labour market. It is in the 'free market' that 'free' labourers exchange their labour power for money. Without independent access to the means of their own subsistence, people have no choice but to work for a wage, often making goods they neither need nor desire. At the time of writing the British government is proposing to grant an export licence for a £28 million, military traffic-control system for Tanzania, one of the poorest countries in the world. Despite widespread protest the deal is being justified on the basis that it will secure 250 jobs in the British aerospace industry. The deal is being backed by a commercial bank loan. Critics of the inappropriateness of such a deal to a heavily indebted country are silenced by the charge that they would not want to see people 'out of work'. To any sane person it would seem a long way round to secure the livelihood of 250 people. However, when employed by a commercial company these people are deemed wealth-creating (read money-making). If they were to make hospital equipment as aid to Tanzania, they would be a drain on the economy according to the logic of capitalised money/credit.

It is true that within a money/market economy many individuals may be able to find satisfying and/or useful employment, with certain sectors of the labour force gaining quite high money incomes, but this does not remove the issue of compunction. To live people must do paid work or find a source of money income. In Marx's terms waged labourers are alienated from their own labour power and from the products they produce.

For Marx, the key is the commodification of labour, and the conversion of it and everything else into a 'thing' to be bought and sold for money. When Marx (and others following him) spelled this out he was dismissed *as an economist* on the grounds that he had a 'transformation problem', that is, he could not explain how particular amounts of labour transferred into a particular price (see Freeman, 1996: 1). This would only be the case if Marx was working within Ricardo's labour theory of value which stated that 'the value of every commodity is (in perfect competition and at equilibrium) proportional to the quantity of labour embodied in it, providing this labour is used in accord with existing standards of productive efficiency (the socially necessary amount of labour)' (Burkitt, 1984: 54–5). As Freeman has argued, Marx was not working within the equilibrium framework of classical political economy. The key lies in the role of money as already indicated in the sweet and biscuit example presented in Chapter 2 (Freeman, 1996: 21).

The entire edifice of economic theorising has been built upon the false premise that *things* exchange for *things* and not for *money*. This is why Marx was outraged at the argument put forward by Jean Baptiste Say that in every sale there is a purchase, and in every purchase there is a sale, exactly as in barter. Marx is quite clear that money, not commodities, is the focus of the market economy:

> Money is not only 'the medium by which the exchange is effected' but at the same time the medium by which the exchange of product with product is divided into two acts, which are independent of each other in time and space. With Ricardo, however, this false conception of money is due to the fact that he concentrates exclusively on the *quantitative determination* of exchange-value, namely that it is equal to a definite quantity of labour time, forgetting on the other hand the *qualitative* characteristic, that individual labour must present itself as *abstract, general social* labour only through its alienation. (emphasis in the original. Marx *Theories of Surplus Value Part II*, quoted by Freeman, 1996: 28fn)

The term 'commodity fetishism' was invented by Marx to stress the error in logic that occurs when people focus too much on commodities as if they embodied value. Commodities are mainly symbols that give us hints of the reality of the social relations involved in their production. To see a product as having a price, and hence its 'value' indicated by that price, is to fetishise and over-emphasise the reality of prices. Instead of commodity fetishism, for Marx prices are epiphenomena. They are weak, shadowy reflections of the underlying reality. Prices and the things that get packaged as goods (which now include brand-name logo T-shirts, stylised mobile phone covers, and image-making cosmetics) do not exhaust the reality of the economy. Instead, goods reflect real social relations and in capitalism many typical relationships are unbalanced, exploitative, or oppressive. Marx did not foresee the prominence that consumers' lifestyles now have in capitalism, but no doubt would have added to commodity fetishism a cynical interpretation of consumerism as an attempt to reconstruct a meaningful life after the meaning of constructive work has been taken away. Certainly this was Veblen's interpretation.

Furthermore, according to Marx, the supply–demand approach creates and sustains illusions based on commodity fetishism.

> The conception ... that overproduction is not possible, or at least that no general glut of the market is possible, is based on the proposition that *products* are exchanged *against products*, or, as Mill put it, on the 'metaphysical equilibrium of sellers and buyers', and this led to the conclusion that demand is determined only by production, or also that demand and supply are identical. (emphasis in the original. Marx *Theories of Surplus Value*, quoted by Freeman, 1996: 28fn)

By 'capital' Marx means *money*-capital, the money claim to the means of production. In effect, the capitalist uses 'his' money to buy land, machinery/industrial plant/capital and labour and put them into production of anything he thinks he can sell for money. He rewards labour in money, enabling labour to buy back its own means of production/subsistence with the money given, but appropriating through the medium of money the so-called 'surplus' value generated through the process of production. Such abstraction of the product of labour by capitalism is only possible through the *denial* of access to the means of subsistence described in graphic detail by Marx in *Capital 1*. Abstract labour and its intrinsic connection with commodity fetishism has been discussed by a number of Marxists including De Angelis (1996).

Only if money is eliminated, is it possible to regard 'capital' as the *commodities* or 'things' comprising a necessary element in the productive process: hence the common misapprehension that ownership of the *physical*, rather than the *financial*, means of production is the key issue in the control and production of wealth. It is also possible to be drawn into the debate on booms, slumps, inflation, stagflation, unemployment and the general tendency for a falling rate of profit without challenging the conceptualisation of a formal economy which is assumed to be providing for universal welfare through the production of *things*. According to Freeman and his colleagues the study of economics which ignores the central role of money in the economy has also invaded Marxist economics:

All the 'simplifying' – in fact stultifying – assumptions which Walrasian economics has grafted on the Marxist stem should be left to wither in their chosen fashion. Economics must be situated in real time and the real world. The fiction of a uniform rate of profit and rate of exploitation, production without machines, capital without money and determination without time ... do not belong to a science of political economy. (Freeman and Carchedi, 1996: 26–7)

Marx's original analysis of the capitalist economy is revived and reviewed by Freeman and his colleagues in their reconceptualisation of political economy. They argue that the process of accumulation which now governs virtually all human life on the planet, sabotaging technical progress, engendering slavery to the machine, creating poverty amidst plenty, leaving environmental degradation in its wake, and leading to war and famine, does not take the form of produced goods put to use in production, i.e. physical capital, but in stocks of money value, i.e. financial capital (see Freeman and Carchedi, 1996: 264–5).

Demolishing capitalism by taking over the means of production is not therefore a radical solution. These are distorted production systems directed to the accumulation of capitalised and capitalising money. Money-credit secures access and ownership to resources and production systems and the money-based circulation process secures ever increasing accumulation. Capitalism has not merely appropriated the means of production, the land and machinery, leaving the labourer 'free' to accept or reject employment for a money wage. The whole structure of production and exchange is designed to increase money-based accumulation. It is not therefore a radical solution for the workers to 'reclaim' their rightful ownership of the means of production and return to business-as-usual production, distribution and exchange but on equitable terms under the ownership of the state. Nor is it a radical solution for workers to receive the full value of their product as wages. This is not what Marx was demanding. He wanted an end to the wage system and to the capitalist mode of production.

Marx, money and value

In *Capital 1*, Chapter 1 Marx distinguishes between the illusions about money created by 'bourgeois economy' and the 'purely social reality' of the value of commodities as expressed by money. Within bourgeois economics price value appears to be a natural phenomenon. However, for Marx value is a social construct and money is its symbol. Not content with criticising the economic system, Marx sets out to explain its inner workings, exploring first the relations of exchange followed later by those of production. A great deal of confusion has resulted from the persistence of generations of economists in following the illusions of 'bourgeois economists' while disregarding Marx's analysis of money, the key to his work as a whole.

Free-trader Vulgaris, the bourgeois economist (to use Marx's terms) ignores the vital difference between barter and the process of circulation of commodities through the medium of money. As we saw in Chapter 2, economics-as-we-know-it has continued to perpetuate the notion of the circular flow, the concept that commodities exchange for commodities, that supply and demand are equated through price settled via a hypothesised process of '*tatonnement*'. However, under capitalism '[w]hen one commodity replaces another, the money-commodity always sticks to the hands of some third person' (Marx, 1974: 114). Bourgeois economists, Marx argued, were determined to create the illusion that production creates wealth, that money is nothing but the neutral measure of that wealth, and that price is determined by the interplay of supply and demand. Yet Marx is crystal clear on the impossibility of constructing scientific theories about the operation of the capitalist economy while maintaining the fiction that money is a neutral arbiter of exchange. Alan Freeman succinctly interprets Marx on this point in his sweet and biscuit example previously cited. Although in the real-life economy money is the means whereby humans relate to each other, generations of economists have, from the time Marx was writing to the present, relentlessly, persistently and determinedly obscured the role of money in the economy.

According to Marx, commodification (the categorisation of 'things', including labour power, as exchangeable units of economic wealth) begins when people produce goods specifically for the market. Hence the

> division of a product into a useful thing and a value becomes practically important, only when exchange has acquired such an extension that useful articles are produced for the purpose of being

exchanged, and their character as values has therefore been taken into account, beforehand, during production. (Marx, 1974: 78)

The 'simple commodity form is the germ of the money form' (Marx, 1974: 75).

Marx's discussion of the process of exchange within the market shows clearly how money is both central to the construction of value-as-price but also to the destruction of value as anything other than price. To do this he makes a distinction between relative and equivalent values. The statement that 20 yards of linen =, or are 'worth', 1 coat establishes a relative value for linen expressed in terms of another commodity. Equally, the coat is the 'equivalent' of the value of the linen. The two poles – the relative and the equivalent – cannot be reversed. The coat might be worth 20 yards of linen, but then we are expressing the value of the coat in terms of the linen (Marx, 1974: 55–6), an entirely different operation. We cannot express the value of the linen in terms of linen, any more than we can express the value of the coat in terms of the coat, or money in terms of money. Following Aristotle, Marx notes that the expression '5 beds = 1 house ... is not to be distinguished from 5 beds = so much money' (Marx, 1974: 65).

It follows that we can 'expand' the relative form of value by considering that 20 yards of linen could be 'worth' 1 coat *or* 10 lb of tea *or* 2 oz gold *or* 1 ton of iron *or* ... *x* commodity A (Marx, 1974: 68). Marx argues that both the 'elementary' and 'expanded' forms of value merely express the value of a commodity in terms other than its use value or material substance. Where trade occurs, it may be barter (elementary) or some commodity, e.g. cattle may be commonly used in exchanges (expanded). In the latter instance, however, all other commodities cease to exchange for each other, but find their common expression of value in the single commodity, cattle. In both forms, production is for use value, not exchange.

It is now possible to move to the 'general' form of value, by expressing the value of all commodities (1 coat, 10 lbs of tea ... etc.) in terms of a single commodity, i.e. as = 20 yards of linen. This general form of value

results from the joint action of the whole world of commodities, and from that alone. A commodity can acquire a general expression of its value only by all other commodities, simultaneously with it, expressing their values in the same equivalent; and every new commodity must follow suit. It thus becomes evident that since the existence of commodities as values is purely social, this social existence can be expressed by the totality of their social relations alone, and consequently that form of their value must be a socially recognised form. (Marx, 1974: 71)

In this general form of value the single commodity (the linen) is given the characteristic of direct and universal exchangeability with every other commodity because this character is *denied* to every other commodity. All commodities are *not* directly exchangeable with each other, despite the persistence of so-called 'scientific' bourgeois economists in obscuring the issue by insisting that all commodities are directly and simultaneously exchangeable (Marx, 1974: 73). When a particular commodity is socially identified as the universal equivalent form of value in this way, it serves as money. 'It becomes the special social function of that commodity, and consequently its social monopoly, to play with the world of commodities the part of the universal equivalent' (Marx, 1974: 74). The money-commodity is now excluded from the relative value form because it would have to form its own equivalent: 20 yards of linen would equal 20 yards of linen.

If money is a purely social phenomenon, the question then arises, what is money 'worth'? We may know the price in terms of money, but what can we say about the *value* of money? Marx's introduction of the labour theory of value at this point obscures his sharp analysis of how the exchange value of money operates and gives rise to his so-called 'transformation' problem. However, it is clear that Marx sees labour value as emerging though the commodification process itself, not traceable back to the labourer: 'human labour power in motion or human labour creates value, but is not in itself value ... it becomes value only in its congealed state, when embodied in the form of some object' (Marx, 1974: 57). Marx criticised 'vulgar economists' for assuming that labour can be the measure of value, arguing that it cannot be differentiated. Exchange values by definition must be commensurate and must therefore work in abstracted value. For Marx labour value can only exist in its abstracted and generalised form.

Within bourgeois economics price value appears to be natural, but Marx argues that value is a social construct as is its symbol – money: 'a particular commodity cannot become the universal equivalent except by a social act ... thus it becomes – money' (Marx, 1974: 90).

Since Marx's overall aim is to challenge the 'naturalism' of classical economics and of the economic system it represents, he asks: 'Whence arose the illusions of the monetary system? To it gold and silver when serving as money, did not represent a social relation between producers, but were natural objects with strange properties' (Marx, 1974: 86). Marx certainly didn't think there is any inherent money value in gold and silver, but argued that they were very useful as money, although not both at once as we have already noted. Gold and silver are not useful as money if they have a commodity value, particularly in terms of each other, as there must be only one universal equivalent form of value because 'money itself has no price' (Marx, 1974: 98).

Since money itself has no value, then 'the value of commodities has a purely social reality' (Marx, 1974: 54). As pointed out above, value is always relative but in exchange there must be a universal source of equivalent value. There is no intrinsic value in exchange – nothing can be valued in itself: 'when a commodity acts as equivalent, no quantitative determination of its value is expressed' (Marx, 1974: 62). Marx points out that this is true of all measures. The weight of a pound of jam is equivalent to a pound of lead – but not to another pound of jam. Marx notes that there is at least some substance to weight equivalence: with weight there is a real physical phenomenon, heaviness, whereas for commodity value there is no inherent value, it is entirely socially constructed:

> the enigmatical character of the equivalent form ... escapes the notice of the bourgeois political economists, until this form, completely developed confronts him in the shape of money. (Marx 1974: 63)

Both the commodity and the money equivalent are social constructs:

> since the existence of commodities as values is purely social ... the form of their value must be a socially recognised form ... the equivalent form [as] thus social identified ... becomes the money commodity or serves as money. (Marx, 1974: 71, 74)

A key to Marx's analysis of commodification in the market is the way in which exchange value destroys use value. For Marx use values 'constitute the substance of all wealth' (Marx, 1974: 44). Unlike exchange value, use values can vary qualitatively in terms of use and labour input. Use value has a 'plain, homely, bodily form' (Marx, 1974: 54). In a very green-sounding phrase, Marx quotes William Petty who sees for use value 'labour as its father and the earth its mother' (Marx, 1974: 50). On the other hand 'exchange values ... do not contain an atom of use-value' (Marx, 1974: 45). This does not mean that commodities' exchange values have no meaning, but that their valuation in markets (e.g. their price) is not based on use value. Two things can be valued the same in a market, such as a car and some life-saving equipment, but their use is very different. This is ironic when we know that under a market system a car is seen as a wealth creator and the life-saving equipment as a drain on wealth creation, unless the latter is used within a privatised health service.

However, Marx goes further than to say that exchange value replaces use value. He shows how the 'form of the value' destroys the intrinsic value of things (Marx, 1974: 54). Commodity value is always relative to the equivalent, which has no value in itself. The equivalent only becomes money when it is a universal equivalent (and anything can become money) – but the ideal form of money is something that has no equivalent, i.e. that is value-less in commodity terms. Everything then becomes valued in terms of something that has no value other than its social existence (a dollar is worth a dollar) – so that anything valued as a commodity ceases to have value as itself or as anything else other than the value-less money – therefore we destroy use value by pouring resources and labour as products into the bottomless chasm of money value. One of the authors has described elsewhere this problem in relation to money security (Dordoy and Mellor, 2000).

It is also important to note that exchange makes no sense if property is held in common. People can only exchange what is their private property and therefore is alienable. Common ownership, control and use of resources is central to Marx's vision with a community of free individuals holding the means of production (we would say provisioning) in common. The total product of the community is a social product – some consumed as subsistence, the rest 'remains social' and is distributed according to prevailing social arrangements. Human labour would be allocated according to a social plan which would maintain 'proper proportion' between the different kinds of work to be done and the needs and wants of the community (Marx, 1974: 83). Common ownership of the means of production, distribution and exchange is central for Marx, where the idea of commodities would make no sense. For Marx 'the life-process of society, which is based on the process of material production does not strip off its mystical veil until it is treated as production by freely associated men and is consciously regulated by them in accordance with a settled plan' (Marx, 1974: 84). Under Marx's version of socialism the 'freely associated' producers would regulate their own work free from the duress of wage slavery. Division of labour, the use of money and production for exchange would continue, but profiteering would end. This theme, developed in the form of the 'national guilds' of guild socialism and its implications for the management of money as outlined in social credit thought, is explored in later chapters.

The political construction of the capitalist market

Free markets are, in the words of John Gray, Professor of European Thought at the London School of Economics, 'a product of artifice, design and political coercion'. Far from being the natural product of social evolution, *laissez-faire* is centrally planned. The free market is 'an end product of social engineering and unyielding political will' (Gray, 1998).

In neo-classical economics the market is rarely defined beyond the simple notion of an area in which buyers and sellers negotiate the exchange of a well-defined commodity. In mainstream theory individuals do not organise themselves: the market is seen as a natural or normal order consisting of the aggregation of individual bargains. Individual traders interact in this natural medium, independent of social institutions. The labour seller is just another trader. In fact, the notion of a network of independent individuals motivated by unadulterated self-interest entering into an unrelated series of contracts is unacceptable both in logic and practice. The fascinating question for economists is *how* individuals *do* organise themselves, and whose interests are served by such organisation (Hodgson, 1988).

Although subject to change and adaptation over time, routines and norms are essential in all forms of human relations. When interacting with others, no individual can plan intelligently unless others can be expected to act predictably, and the actor is able to predict with a fair degree of accuracy. Economic theory operates on the basic assumption that demand and supply are mediated through the price system in a process of *'tatonnement'*. The term, used by Leon Walras, the founder of mathematically based, general-equilibrium economics, describes the bids put forward by buyers and sellers, and adjustments made by both *before* trading takes place, in order to reach an equilibrium price at which demand and supply are in balance. The process of *tatonnement* is likened to a village auction, where the prices offered for cattle or furniture are mediated by an auctioneer before the sale is agreed. In theory, individual preferences mysteriously appear and collide in a mechanical process so that buyers are price takers. In real life, however, no sale ever takes place outside the social framework. The village auction market, like any market, is a social institution where the process of selling involves specific methods, customs or routines to reach price agreements. Publicity, transport, clerical work and storage are required to be in place before trading can begin. The marketing process itself can affect outcomes. Furthermore, even the small local market is supported by a legal framework defining ownership and appropriate forms of transfer of ownership of property, backed by the ultimate sanction of force.

The 'free market' extolled by capitalism is anything but 'free'. It is hedged around by a maze of centrally organised statutory controls, regulations and interventions designed for the benefit of national and transnational corporations (TNCs). Not the least of these is limited liability. As capitalism grew, the volume of interventions escalated to ensure the 'free' working of the system. The capitalist 'free market' economy has been centrally planned and controlled from its origins in the interests of the ruling elite. In a mixed economy democratic procedures may secure some concessions for the working class, but only in so far as they continue to serve the interests of the elite class (Hodgson, 1988: 152–3; Polanyi, 1944: 140–50).

The 'development' of the United States provides a clear example of the nature of statutory controls over the 'free market'. Corporate political involvement preceded the creation of the US. Private enterprise, in the form of the Virginia Company, the Plymouth Company and other joint-stock companies, was central to the settlement of the original colonies in the seventeenth century. The companies set up the settlements and held political power from the outset. The American Revolution can therefore be viewed as a revolt by colonial business interests against the mercantile (strong national economy, based on gold) policies of Britain. It has been argued that the Constitution of the US 'was an economic document drawn up with superb skill by men whose property interests were immediately at stake; and as such it appealed directly and unerringly to identical interests in the country at large' (Beard, quoted in Epstein, 1969: 21). The late nineteenth century saw the rapid growth of large national corporations or 'trusts', concentrating power in the production of railroads, steel and oil. These 'trusts' hand-picked political candidates and financed their election. Vast sums of money were involved: 'In 1896, the Standard Oil Company alone gave $250,000 to support the successful Presidential candidacy of William McKinley' (Epstein, 1969: 27).

How did the 'trusts' emerge? E.K. Hunt and Howard Sherman (1990) describe the fair means and foul whereby John D. Rockefeller established his oil empire through extinguishing most of the many small, independent operators and replacing them with a single cor- poration. Methods included forcing railroads to give rebates on the Standard Oil's *competitor's* shipments, in the process acquiring infor- mation on its competitor's 'shipper, buyer, product, price and terms of payment'. The information, with the rebates, allowed it to smash competitors. Between 1870 and 1879 Standard Oil came to own between 80 and 90 per cent of the nation's output of refined petroleum. The result was a wide gulf between the practice and the elegant classical economic theory of a free market in which a large number of small firms operate, none having the ability to substan- tially influence the market as a whole. Similarly, railroad companies manipulated and blackmailed politicians, governments and whole communities to gain control of transport systems, in opposition to, rather than in, the public interest. Communities were forced to offer hefty subsidies to railroad firms under the threat that the railway would run miles away from the town or settlement if payment was not forthcoming. The identical process continues to the present day as communities offer subsidies to incoming capital investment (Rowbotham, 1998: 153).

By 1880 co-operative collusion between the remaining firms became common practice. In place of the many small firms of the neo-classical dream, massive corporations co-operated to maximise their joint profits. When public pressure forced apparent concessions in the 1889 Sherman Anti-Trust Act, collusion between politicians and the corporations they sought to control resulted in legislation which was weak, vague and ineffective. Ironically, legislation of this type was used by the corporations to weaken trade unions, on the rationalisation that strikes constituted a 'restraint of trade' (Hunt and Sherman, 1990). In general, as Hunt and Sherman observe, anti-trust laws did nothing to maintain a large number of small firms. When government regulation did occur, it was designed to maintain monopolistic co-operation, enabling large corporations to continue to make extraordinary profits at the expense of the public. Meanwhile, corporate use of the mass media deliberately fostered the conceptualisation of an identity between corporate and national interests. In times of war and peace corporations were in pursuit of the common good. Conflicting interests were therefore by definition opposed to the national interest (Epstein, 1969: 32–3, 115–8. See also Korten in *Resurgence*, March/April 1999).

The growth of massive corporations takes control of institutions away from SMEs, farmers and local communities, and into centralised offices in distant capital cities (see Douglas' 1919 'Pyramid of Power' predictions, as described in Hutchinson, 1995: 43 and Hutchinson and Burkitt, 1997: 61–2). Under corporate capitalism the supply chain of finance and materials is controlled through the corporations: farmers and small producers are dependent upon the buying policy of large corporations, and must adapt their production technology accordingly. Even where production is 'contracted out', the corporations control the prices of inputs and dictate the market price. Corporate control of the production process is virtually complete. Prices, production, marketing and information flows are designed to meet the perceived interests of the large firm. This is the system that now operates as global capitalism.

Given the political reality of how the 'free' economy operates, neo-classical theory would appear to be what William Dugger has called an 'enabling myth'. He observes that 'enabling myths' 'justify racial supremacy, gender supremacy, class supremacy, jingoism, homophobia, and anti-Semitism' (Dugger, 2000: 66). Through enabling myths, 'top dogs' create the illusion of justification for their retention of power over the 'underdogs'. In the illusion of justification, three 'brute facts' are 'deeply institutionalized into the social fabric of the modern world':

> The first brute fact is that the top dogs have the capacity to field armies and police forces and to use them against foreign and domestic underdogs. They have the power of legalized violence. The second brute fact is that the top dogs have the capacity to buy the most educated and the most talented members of society and the capacity to form them into highly effective support groups of politicians, voters, theologians, lawyers, judges, writers, reporters,

editors, educators, managers and so on, as needed. They command legions of people and mountains of resources. They have the power of big money. Under capitalism they also can hire and fire workers. This is the third brute fact about today's top dogs. They have the power of ownership. They own the means of production. The underdogs must go to the top dogs for a job. (Dugger, 2000: 78)

Additionally, top dogs have the power to eradicate the history of how they came to acquire their power.

Enforcing the free market on a global scale

The international institutions that have supported the globalisation of the western capitalist market system are well known, the International Monetary Fund (IMF), the World Bank, the World Trade Organisation (WTO). A more local example is the European Round Table of Industrialists (ERT). The ERT, composed of chairs and Chief Executive Officers of 40 major European companies, consults with European officials on a regular basis. Arguably they have more power than elected governments (Hutchinson, 1998: 155–6). The power of these organisations, in some cases legal, overrides the sovereignty of national governments. Particularly notorious are the structural adjustment programmes (SAPs) imposed by the IMF and World Bank on countries who fall foul of the international market. It is, however, the WTO which has attracted most opposition in recent years.

Based in Geneva, the WTO was set up in 1995 by, and in the interests of, the international financial institutions (IFIs) and powerful transnational corporations. Its mandate is to regulate world trade to the benefit of its sponsors, by implementing the General Agreement on Tariffs and Trade (GATT) and 'supervising' the enforcement of national trade policies. According to critics, the GATT agreement 'violates fundamental peoples' rights, particularly in the area of foreign investment, bio-diversity and intellectual property rights' (Chossudovsky, 1997: 35; see also *New Internationalist*, issue 334, May 2001). Clauses concerning trade liberalisation and foreign investment are permanently entrenched in the articles of agreement of the WTO. These articles facilitate the policing of countries, including the imposition of conditionalities, according to international law. Powerful actors seeking to establish a global free market must ensure that the legal framework which defines and entrenches it must be beyond the powers of national legislatures to control. The notion of the all-powerful nation state, with its statutory authority over the political economy is belied by the fact that of the 100 largest economies in the world, nearly half are represented by transnational corporations while 500 companies control 70 per cent of world trade (Hines, 2000).

Transnational organisations like the WTO are seeking to project the 'free market' into the economic life of every society by compelling adherence to rules which release 'free trade' from 'encumbered or embedded markets that exist in every society' (Gray, 1998). Under threat of removal of trade and employment from their lands, sovereign states are persuaded to sign up to membership of the WTO. However, 'it is the WTO, and not the national legislature of any sovereign state, which determines what is to count as free trade, and that which is a restraint of it. The rules of the game of the market must be elevated beyond any possible revision through democratic choice' (Gray, 1998). Although the WTO appeared to be able to impose its free-market rules, it faltered on the most fundamental for global finance capital, the Multilateral Agreement on Investment. This would forbid any country from opposing inward investment. Effectively it would outlaw locally controlled economies. This was defeated in 1998 through a combination of NGO protest and opposition from national governments.

The social and environmental costs of the so-called 'free market' are such that it is incompatible with economic democracy or environmental sustainability. For example, corporate farming and biotechnology force farmers to abandon small-scale, eco-friendly agricultural methods in the name of market freedom, based on the notion of 'perfect competition' in which costs can be compared on a 'level playing field'. As a result, the full costs of production between different producers are difficult to determine with any degree of meaningful accuracy. Take two not-so-hypothetical farmers:

Cereals from farmer Smith are cheaper than farmer Jones'. And on this narrow comparison of market prices farmer Smith wins market share and is able to put his rival out of business. But what happens if it were known that farmer Smith's apparently cheaper prices result in part from intensive use of chemicals which, apart from boosting yields, also [degrade the soil], run off into rivers, kill wildlife and contaminate food?

Now if the full costs for contaminating and degrading the environment were incorporated into production, then the price of produce from the intensive farmer would dramatically increase and become uncompetitive. (*Farm Trader*, 6 Nov. 1997)

As a result of the historical evolution of markets under western capitalism, maximisation of short-term profit dominates policy formation, while the real costs of environmental impacts are not taken into account. Where farmers are in the same neighbourhood, some attempt may be made to compare the environmental costs of the two systems. Where competing farms are in different hemispheres, social and environmental cost accounting becomes even more problematic. 'Cheap' beef from Brazil or Botswana, where malnutrition is rife, only appears cheap because the full costs from destructive environmental and social impacts are not accounted in prices (*Farm Trader*, 1997; Chossudovsky, 1997; Lang and Hines, 1993; Harvey, 1998).

Challenging the market

The logic of market capitalism is not satisfaction of human needs, but meeting of 'effective demand', that is, demand backed by money. The institutions of capitalism have evolved as a means to create and consolidate elite power over the resources of the natural world and society such that the majority of people are forced to participate in its structures of accumulation. The strength of the dominance of market society is that it does not seem at all odd that most of humanity is now almost exclusively preoccupied with getting and selling for money whether by choice or compulsion. Within the richer societies such as Britain those in employment are working ever longer hours despite its being the fourth richest economy. Paid work is now a major source of social relationships and consumption is the primary leisure activity. Within market societies the celebration of individualism as consumerism has come to be identified as freedom, even if everyone wears the same logo. Unfortunately, that freedom has not been accompanied by equality, so that individuality as consumption is only available to a minority of the world's population. Capitalist institutions penetrate work, family and social life so that daily life ceases to be the site of production of goods and satisfactions through the design and creation of foods, clothes, furnishings and the arts. The wage slave culture of capitalism creates instead the twin dichotomies of the disutility of labour and its antidote, emulative consumerism, which we will discuss more fully in the next chapter.

If economic democracy is to be achieved, that is, the control by human beings collectively of the conditions of their existence, it is necessary to show that there is another way. It is necessary to go back to the fundamentals as Marx did, and Veblen and Douglas after him. All three authors rejected the thesis that working for money is a necessary fact of economic life. Economic democracy will not be achieved if the issue of money and value is sidelined by a class debate that only operates within the framework of bourgeois political economy. We have argued that the capitalist-defined means of production must not be confused with the means of provisioning human societies.

Basically, the mainstream economic assumption has been that 'the economy' as defined by capital produces wealth. *Then* the political process has been seen as sharing out that wealth. However, as Marx demonstrated, money is social and value is ephemeral (see Marx, 1974: Ch. 1). As we have argued, what that system produces is money. This money is issued into society on the basis of 'commercial' decisions. Investment is channelled to 'commercial' choices. This makes socially necessary expenditure 'uneconomic'.

Against this model we follow Marx, and later Veblen and Douglas, who saw *people* as undertaking a range of different tasks within a holistic society. In the following chapters we review movements seeking a more holistic and co-operative society underpinned by a practically based, theoretical analysis.

5 Marx, Veblen and the Critique of the Money/Market System

In the last chapter we pointed to three aspects of the capitalist market economy that are central to this book. The first is the exclusion of people from the means of their own provisioning. People are excluded from their means of subsistence – that is, they can no longer grow, catch or find their own livelihood. The second point follows from the first. If people do not have access to, or control over, their means of provisioning, then in money/market systems they have no choice but to earn money to survive. The third aspect is the nature of money/market systems, where money is capitalised and not just a useful medium of exchange. In capitalised money systems, money/credit issue is a means by which those who have control over, or access to, the money-creation process can establish ownership and control over the means of provisioning and production. In a commodified market system money is the means by which property and value is accumulated leading to further capitalisation. In short, money is capital.

A key distinction we have made is between the means of production and the means of provisioning. The former is defined by the money/market economy, the second represents the resources and processes that meet human needs. The market economy may meet some human needs, but that is neither its defining feature nor its primary function. What the capitalist economy prioritises as 'production' cannot be automatically deemed the most necessary for human well-being. It is merely the most profitable. This in turn means that the means of production represents at best a response to effective demand – that is, demand backed by money or the ability to pay. This in turn rolls back to the problem of who has access to money and how.

Economic democracy, therefore, must be about control over, or access to, the means of provisioning. The right to livelihood must be the basis of any democratic system. This is very different from the right to earn money through paid work. Since money is not a natural phenomenon, but a social construct, the economy it represents is also socially constructed. Economies are not universal systems or forces, they are social structures made up of real people trying to live meaningful lives. Inequality, unmet needs, impoverished lives are not the result of natural laws. They represent particular patterns of social relations. Any meaningful democracy must be based on economic democracy. Inequality in provisioning and therefore livelihood is a political question. What we mean by a right to livelihood/provisioning is that people should have at least democratic control, if not direct control, over the resources for, and conditions of, their own existence. We are not therefore advocating a wholesale return to subsistence in the sense of people growing their own food, although that may be very important for many people. The problem with an individualised approach to control over subsistence is that it is a privatised solution and our concern is with a more collective vision of economic democracy.

One of the confusions that arises in money/market systems is between needs and wants. Do people 'naturally' want to consume beyond what is immediately necessary or is consumerism an enforced 'pleasure'? We can never know the answer to this question unless people are free to make their wishes known in a democratic context. The so-called 'free' choice upon which the capitalist market bases its claims for legitimacy is rigged by the lack of choice about participation. A second confusion is between money-making and provisioning exemplified in the confusing use of the notion of 'wealth creation'. Capitalist market systems conflate money-making with creating 'wealth' for a society. The implication is that wealth as money-making is the same as wealth as well-being. Within conventional economics it makes perfect sense to define the arms trade as beneficial (i.e. money-making, 'creating' jobs), while the health service is a burden to 'the economy'. In fact, its theoretical framework is so closed that within conventional/capitalist economic thought there is no basis upon which to make the opposing case.

A further confusion that arises in money/market systems is between the utility and disutility of labour. Conventional economics assumes that labour is carried out in a money/market system primarily to get money for consumption. Labour itself is assumed to be a disutility. Ironically this notion is in direct contradiction to the claims for free choice within neo-classical economics. In a provisioning system the assumption of the disutility of labour would not be made. Central to many of the ideas we will be discussing in this book is the view that human labour can be pleasurable; it is the context that creates disutility. The ability of contemporary 'bottom-line' accounting systems to destroy utility in human activity is evidenced by the destruction of job satisfaction. Increased stress levels are evident in many professions such as teaching or nursing that were once a source of high status and pride for many people.

Many of these issues have been raised in the work of Veblen. Like Marx, Veblen saw economic systems as embedded in social systems, the institutional context. In this book we are arguing that there is a direct heritage between Marx, Veblen and social economic theorists such as the guild socialists and social creditors. Veblen's distinction between industry (creative activity) and business (exploitative activity) paves the way for a more holistic study of human economic activity. The sphere of industry, in Veblen's usage, includes all activities that transform materials for human use. He sees the special human capability to consciously act in a transformative way as generating a range of human capabilities, most of which require social co-operation and not merely individual effort. Because of the need for social co-operation, Veblen also sees individual creativity as being the product of the collective abilities of society over time, the common cultural heritage. The range of human capabilities is therefore changing continuously whilst providing satisfaction and pleasure through the processes of work as well as through corresponding acts of consumption. Veblen's approach challenges the orthodox assumptions that (a) consumption is how people get satisfaction and (b) labouring must be done under duress, as wage labour. Within Veblen's framework it is clear that unremunerated work such as domestic labour, whilst occurring within complex webs of social relations at one remove from wage labour, counts as part of what Veblen refers to as industry: it is effective; it is active; it is part of what makes us human; it is social. We see Veblen's work therefore as providing a bridge between the work of Marx and the later theorists we discuss.

Marx's legacy

As with Veblen, Marx's theories on political economy did not materialise out of thin air. As Marx's full and frequent footnotes indicate, his economics derived directly from extant scholarly works on the subject. Mark Lutz argues that he drew many of his key concepts such as the proletariat and class struggle from Sismondi (1999: 45). Marx's ideas have become part of the heritage of what Lutz has called 'humanist economics'. The works of Thorstein Veblen, together with that of the UK guild socialists and social credit movement, widely circulated and debated internationally throughout the century, drew heavily upon Marx's original works. In many cases they drew on themes in his work which had been largely forgotten or misinterpreted.

In keeping with the spirit of the times in which he wrote, Marx sought a 'scientific' explanation for the ability of capitalists to exploit the labour of the working class. He found it in the mechanisms governing production for profitable, finance-mediated exchange. However, discussions of the notion of the falling rate of profit, the inevitability of the demise of capitalism, the so-called 'transformation problem', and other such debates have tended to obscure Marx's fundamental observation that the creation of waged labour within a framework of (financial) capital is what capitalism *is*. A socialist society would be one in which labour ceases to be a commodity to be bought and sold on the market. From this perspective much so-called 'socialist' theorising about the economic capacity for improvements in the pay and conditions of labour becomes a mere apology for capitalism. Equally a concern with ownership and control of the means of production limits socialism to the capitalist agenda (Mellor, 2000b). It is not entirely unexpected that a focus on the conditions of labour and production should be emphasised when Marx's class analysis was so much based on industrial production. Recently Marx's categories have been substantially revised to include different class fractions as well as unpaid labour. Some examples of Marxian class analysis from Indian contexts are set out below to illustrate the variety, strengths and weaknesses of contemporary Marxian approaches.

Concentration on the exploitation (and alienation) of the working class by the capitalist class *within capitalism* gave rise to the assumption that Marx's political economy did not oppose the existence of wage labour but only its conditions. This is not the case. Marx was scathing about would-be reformers who suggested a 'fairer' redistribution of the product of capitalism while failing to work for its demise. One object of his ire was the US economist Henry George, who advocated a land tax. Claiming that a 'cloven hoof, together with the donkey's ears, peep unmistakably out of the declamations of Henry George' Marx railed against:

All these 'socialists', ... that ... allow wage labor, i.e. the capitalist system of production to continue, and by juggling with words fool themselves into the notion that by the conversion of the ground rent into a state tax all the ills of the capitalist system of production would vanish of their own accord. In other words, the whole thing is simply an attempt, douched with Socialism, to rescue the rule of capitalism, in fact, to rear it anew upon a firmer basis than its present one.

He went on to ask of Henry George whose work was acceptable to and drawn upon by the emerging neo-classicals (Blaug, 2000):

How did it happen that in the United States, where (relatively speaking, i.e., in comparison with civilized Europe) the land was, and to a certain degree (again relatively) is still accessible to the masses, the capitalist system and its correlative enslavement of the working class have developed more rapidly and shamelessly than in any other country? (Karl Marx (1892), 'Karl Marx on Henry George', *People*, 5 June. Reprint of letter dated London, 20 June 1881)

In the same letter Marx berates would-be 'socialists' who go along with the 'radical English bourgeois economists' for joining forces with industrial capitalists in their attack on landowners and quest to appropriate *rent* on behalf of the state – while continuing the system of wage labour which *is* capitalism. Fabian (UK 'socialist') economics based on the appropriation of rent would have been equally abhorrent to Marx, who refers to his own *Communist Manifesto* suggestion of appropriation of rents as a 'transitional' measure, and 'full of contradiction' (ibid.).

In his *Wages, Price and Profit* Marx takes issue with one 'Citizen Weston' who was predicting a rise in real wages as capitalism expands. Convinced that the workers would combine to overthrow capitalism, Marx urges the working class to continue with their 'every-day struggles' but

not to forget that they are fighting with effects, but not with the causes of those effects: that they are retarding the downward movement, but not changing its direction; that they are applying palliatives, not curing the malady. They ought, therefore, not to be exclusively absorbed in these unavoidable guerilla fights incessantly springing up from the never-ceasing encroachments of capital or changes of the market. They ought to understand that with all the miseries it imposes upon them, the present system simultaneously engenders the *material conditions* and the *social forms* necessary for an economical reconstruction of society. Instead of the *conservative* motto, '*A fair day's wage for a fair day's work!*' they ought to inscribe on their banner the *revolutionary* watchword, '*Abolition of the wages system!*'. (Marx, 1975: 78. Emphasis original)

Marx's *Wages, Price and Profit* is the text of an address to the General Council of the First International in June 1865 and was first published as a pamphlet in London in 1898 by Eleanor Marx with a preface by Edward Aveling. Marx concluded the address:

> Trades Unions work well as centres of resistance against the encroachment of capital. They fail partially from an injudicious use of their power. They fail generally from limiting themselves to a guerilla war against the effects of the existing system, instead of simultaneously trying to change it, instead of using their organised forces as a lever for the final emancipation of the working class, that is to say, the ultimate abolition of the wages system.

Writing on Marx in 1906, Veblen is more than likely to have read this publication, and his works suggest that he had.

Marx's original challenge was taken up in the UK by the branch of trade unionism known as 'guild socialism'. Unlike other 'socialists' such as the Webbs, who moved the debate in favour of labourism, guild socialists, and later the social credit theorists remained implacably opposed to 'wage slavery'. They undertook the tremendous revolution *in theorising* that was necessary to envisage the end of the wages system. From his anti-wage labour perspective, Marx would not have classed reformism, as seen for instance in the UK's Labour Party, or state communism, as socialism. For the guild socialists a socialist solution to the wages system would be based on local *producer* not waged-worker control of the production of goods and services. However, the revolutionary ideas of guild socialists were hampered initially by a failure to take account of the controlling influence of finance capital upon the economy. The guild socialist Orage at once recognised the potential of the contribution of social creditors such as Douglas as discussed in the next chapter, but this split the guild socialist movement because bourgeois 'socialists' like G.D.H. Cole could not or would not make the revolutionary leap in consciousness. They sought political democracy for *workers*, not an end to capitalism. It is true that Marx also rejected as utopian the producer-based co-operative experiments of the nineteenth century because they did not seek to confront the capitalist system directly but rather to undermine it by forming a parallel economy. In this book we are seeking to find a way to refound economic theory and practice so that a co-operative commonwealth such as Robert Owen envisaged could become a reality.

Thorstein Veblen's institutional perspective

Thorstein Veblen (1857–1929) has been described as 'probably the most significant, original, and profound social theorist in American history' (Hunt and Sherman, 1990: 122). His many books and articles are intellectually stimulating and continue to provide enjoyable reading, remaining highly relevant despite the passage of time. Veblen explored capitalism in the United States at the end of the nineteenth century and in the early decades of the twentieth century. His study of Marx informed his conceptualisation of the nature of capital (Veblen, 1990: 324–51, 409–76, first published in 1906) and his explanation of the unscientific nature of emerging neo-classical economic theory. It was, in fact, Veblen who coined the term 'neo-classical' (Hodgson, 2001). However, Veblen considered that it was an unlikely scenario to envisage a workers' revolution overthrowing capitalism based on workers' enlightened self-interest (utilitarianism). He foresaw the subversion of waged workers to capitalism through the twin attractions of patriotism and emulative consumerism (Veblen, 1990: 409–76). The workers would follow their masters in both war and the market.

The important link between Marx and Veblen is easily overlooked by commentators. For example, Philip O'Hara has argued that Veblen's 1906 paper on Marx demonstrated a 'rather partial' perspective on the works of Marx, as Veblen did not have access to the 'lost' manuscripts and relied heavily on secondary sources 'inconsistent with many of Marx's views' (O'Hara, 2000: 47). Furthermore, Veblen 'thought that Marxism was too teleological in its formulation of change', was 'misguided in his belief that Marx accepted the right of labour to the full product', and 'ignored teleological elements in his own theories' (O'Hara, 2000: 294). This is not our reading of Veblen's 1906 two-part essay on 'The Economics of Karl Marx and his Followers' in which Veblen discusses the mangling and misinterpretation of Marx by Marxists. Central to Veblen's argument is the need to take Marx's theory as a whole:

> Except as a whole, and except in the light of its postulates and aims, the Marxian system is not only not tenable, but it is not even intelligible. A discussion of an isolated feature of the system (such as the theory of value) from the point of view of classical economics (such as that offered by Böhm-Bawerk) is as futile as discussions of solids in terms of two dimensions. (Veblen, 1990: 410)

The depth and appreciation of Veblen's study of Marx is shown by his statement that 'there is no system of economic theory more logical than that of Marx' (Veblen 1990: 410). Veblen does not attempt to rephrase or restate Marx's teaching but makes the basic assumption that his readers can read Marx intelligently for themselves, noting towards the end of the first half of the essay, that:

> In all that has been said so far no recourse is had to the second and third volumes of *Capital*. Nor is it necessary to resort to these two volumes for the general theory of socialism. They add nothing essential, although many of the details of the processes concerned in the working out of the capitalist scheme are treated with greater fullness, and the analysis is carried out with great consistency and with admirable results. (Veblen, 1990: 428)

Veblen's perspective on Marx is far from 'rather partial'. In a footnote a page or two later, Veblen refers to 'a remarkable consistency, amounting substantially to an invariability of position, in Marx's writing, from the *Communist Manifesto* to the last volume of the *Capital*. ...'

> The main position, and the more important articles of theory – the materialistic conception, the doctrine of class struggle, the theory of value and surplus value, of increasing distress, of the reserve army, of the capitalistic collapse – are to be found in the *Critique of Political Economy* (1859), and much of them in the *Misery of Philosophy* (1847), together with the masterful method of analysis and construction which he employed throughout his theoretical work. (Veblen, 1990: 434)

In other words, Veblen is not relying on secondary sources. In his essay Veblen's purpose is to contrast the original 'Marxism of Marx' with the 'scope and method of modern science' (Veblen, 1990: 437). Marxism emerges as 'the image of the struggling ambitious human spirit', while modern science, which for Veblen was centrally organised around Darwinian evolution, is of the nature of a mechanical process:

> The neo-Hegelian, romantic, Marxian standpoint was wholly personal, whereas the evolutionistic – it may be called Darwinian – standpoint is wholly impersonal. The continuity sought in the facts of observation and imputed to them by the earlier school of theory was a continuity of a personal kind, – a continuity of reason and consequently of logic. The facts were construed to take such a course as could be established by an appeal to reason between intelligent and fair-minded men. They were supposed to fall into a sequence of logical consistency. The romantic (Marxian) sequence of theory is essentially an intellectual sequence, and it is therefore of a teleological character. The logical trend of it can be argued out. That is to say, it tends to a goal. On the other hand, in the Darwinian scheme of thought, the continuity sought in and imputed to the facts is a continuity of cause and effect. It is a scheme of blindly cumulative causation, in which there is no trend, no final term, no consummation. The sequence is controlled by nothing but the *vis a tergo* of brute causation, and is essentially mechanical. (Veblen, 1990: 436)

Note the use of the past tense in the first sentence, contrasting Marx's own study and teaching with that of his followers including, in the later years, Engels (Veblen, 1990: 437). Veblen was monitoring the evolution of scientific positivism, anticipating the later near-total demise of reason in the study of political economy. The word 'teleological' is used here in an entirely different sense from that implied by O'Hara (2000: 294), applying rather to the reasoning process itself than to material outcomes. A further footnote in the same essay by Veblen is equally helpful in placing our present work, alongside that of Marx, Veblen and Douglas, in the broader context of economic and social theory:

> The fact that the theoretical structures of Marx collapse when their elements are converted into the terms of modern science should

of itself be sufficient proof that those structures were not built by their maker out of such elements as modern science habitually makes use of. Marx was neither ignorant, imbecile, nor disingenuous, and his work must be construed from such a point of view and in terms of such elements as will enable his results to stand substantially sound and convincing. (Veblen, 1990: 437)

Veblen warned that interpreting Marx from a positivistic standpoint distorts his system, casting doubt on his conclusions. Veblen is in no doubt that Marx believed human beings capable of rational thought about the material circumstances in which they found themselves, that they could study their history and adapt their institutions from a rational perspective. From a 'Darwinian' perspective, however, instinct replaces rational thought and humans are reduced to rational calculators deprived of intellect (Veblen, 1990: 435–6).

For Marx and Veblen, studies of political economy must challenge capitalism on all its premises. If they do not do so, they remain 'safe', to be tolerated by capitalism, or subsumed by it. In the first decades of the twentieth century Veblen was concerned at capitalism's ability to subvert the institutions of 'higher learning' to its own ends, as in his prophetic text 'The Higher Learning in America' (1918). However, it is ironic that most post-Veblenian institutionalism remains within the capitalist paradigm, unable to fight free of the assumption that the institutions of capitalism have been designed with the common good in mind, and have somehow become corrupted. Political democracy is thought to be the underlying philosophy of capitalism. Under this paradigm democratic socialism could be introduced through force of reasoned argument without any need to question production and distribution assumptions, still less the wages system itself. Minorities have only to voice their discontent through the appropriate channels and all will be well. Political democracy in this sense cannot embrace economic democracy in the sense we are using it here.

Veblen's *The Theory of the Leisure Class*, published in 1899, was dismissed by economists as an amusing lampoon of the American way of life. However, Veblen sought to enlighten the majority of people motivated by the 'instinct of workmanship' as to the true nature of capitalism. In his view the business class of absentee owners were subverting industry, controlling production according to their greed for profit, degrading the work process and sabotaging the potential for industry to provide for the needs of all. If the working people realised that, far from contributing to the production process, the capitalist 'pecuniary' interests were at the root of economic and social malfunctions, the workers would break free of the laws, institutions and governments of the 'pecuniary business culture' and transform industry to meet the needs of the people as a whole.

For Veblen, capitalism relies on two basic mechanisms of cultural conditioning. First, is the condition of 'chronic dissatisfaction' associated with 'emulative consumption' (consumerism). Poverty, in this case, is not so much associated with the abject poverty of total material deprivation, rather it is the 'spiritual' poverty associated with the social degradation of labouring for a money wage. The 'leisure class' is distinguished from the labouring classes through a taboo on productive labour, and through its conspicuous and wasteful consumption of expensive, ornate and useless objects as well as its pursuit of sport and the arts. Once a subsistence minimum has been reached, workers seek to acquire and consume more objects offering the illusion of leisure and status, going into debt and seeking career advancement as a means to transcend their chronic dissatisfaction. Once on this treadmill workers identify with their employers, seeking their favours and rejecting calls for industrial action. Focused upon obtaining more in order to rise up the social ranking, workers blame themselves rather than the system for their feelings of disillusion.

Second, capitalism relies on patriotism and military discipline to maintain its aggressive imperialist expansion. For Veblen, the pursuit of profits by the absentee owners of business knew no national boundaries. The domination of foreign lands, or control of their domestic governments, could bring rich profits to capitalist countries. Patriotism and nationalist sentiments could ensure that waged workers identified with corporate interests in continuous military and economic expansion. Military-style discipline was also useful in securing obedience and co-operation in the workplace. Veblen saw the ethos of workmanship as being founded on co-operation, individual equality, interdependence and pride in workmanship (intrinsic satisfaction in work). Since these traits are subversive to the divisive production-for-profit system, it is necessary to instil relations of competition and subordination based on military discipline, not only in the armed forces but also in the workplace.

The direct cultural value of a warlike business policy is unequivo-
cal. It makes for a conservative animus on the part of the
populace. ... Military training is a training in ceremonial, arbitrary
command and unquestioning obedience. A military organisation
is essentially a servile organisation. Insubordination is the deadly
sin. The more consistent and the more comprehensive this
military training, the more effectually will the members of the
community be trained into habits of subordination and away
from that growing propensity to make light of personal authority
that is the chief infirmity of democracy. This applies first and most
decidedly, of course, to the soldiery, but it applies only in a less
degree to the rest of the population. They learn to think in warlike
terms of rank, authority, and subordination, and so grow progressively more patient of encroachments upon their civil rights.
(Veblen, 1904: 185–6)

The institutional framework of society, inculcated through the
educational system, enables the 'captains' of industry to sabotage
the 'progress in the industrial arts' which would otherwise lead to
an equitable economic system. The continued ability of absentee
owners to exploit their workers depended upon the learned habits of
the culture of subordination, coupled with that of emulative consumption and the subversion of knowledge in favour of myth and
the ceremonial.

For Veblen (1899, 1990, 1998) the 'instinct of workmanship' was
in contrast to the 'predatory instinct'. Although he labelled these
traits 'instincts', they are more accurately described as learned
patterns of behaviour. The instinct of workmanship included all
socially useful, co-operative activities associated with provisioning,
craft, arts, 'industry', caring, nurturing and educating (the 'parental
instinct'), and invention (the 'instinct of idle curiosity', 'idle' in the
sense that knowledge is not sought for gain). These traits are responsible for growth and progress in the human economy. They also fulfil
the basic human need for affection, sharing and social concern, and
are expressed through the more creative and co-operative activities
normally undertaken by women and the 'common man'. In his
essay on 'The Instinct of Workmanship and the Irksomeness of
Labour' published in the *American Journal of Sociology* in 1898, Veblen
drew attention to the distinction between working as a wage
labourer, performing irksome labour for a money reward, and undertaking wholesome work to meet human needs. For Veblen,

economic theory sets common sense on its head with its emphasis on the disutility of labour:

> Many a discussion proceeds on this axiom that, so far as regards economic matters, men desire above all things to get the goods produced by labor and to avoid the labor by which the goods are produced. ... According to the common-sense ideal, the economic beatitude lies in an unrestrained consumption of goods, without work; whereas the perfect economic affliction is unremunerated labor. Man instinctively revolts at effort that goes to supply the means of life. (Veblen, 1998: 78)

The assumption of an 'aversion to useful effort' for Veblen goes against the evidence of nature where no other species exhibits 'a consistent aversion to whatever activity goes to maintain the life of the species' (1998: 78). He goes on to note that within orthodoxy the aversion to effort extends only to *useful* labour. Strenuous mental and physical effort may be put into war, politics, sports and other leisure activities. 'Ceremonialism' and 'sportsmanship' were characteristics of the non-creative 'leisure class'. It is only where pecuniary gain is involved that 'Economic Man' emerges as 'a lay figure upon which to fit the garment of economic doctrines', emancipated from the laws of natural selection, uniquely fitted for economic survival (Veblen, 1998: 79). On this basis agriculture, arts and domestic labour receive little or no 'pecuniary' (financial) reward, work is degraded to wage labour and self interest rather than workmanship is the prime motivating factor. Technological progress is 'sabotaged' to serve the financial interests of the capitalist class (Veblen, 1948: 431). Capitalists with their 'vested interests', the 'absentee owners', the 'leisure class' and the 'captains of industry' were opposed to the interests and aspirations of the 'engineers' and workers.

For Veblen the 'predatory instinct' in human societies is associated with the notion of 'private' property: 'Ownership began and grew into a human institution on grounds unrelated to the subsistence minimum. ... Property set out with being booty held as trophies of the successful raid' (Veblen, 1899: 36–7). In contrast, Veblen regarded the provisioning of society as true *economic* activity, and criticised neo-classical economists for failing to recognise that their analysis was flawed in so far as they confused 'pecuniary' wealth with real wealth.

Whenever the institution of private property is found, even in a slightly developed form, the economic process bears the character of a struggle between men for the possession of goods. It has been customary in economic theory, and especially among those economists who adhere with least faltering to the body of modernised classical doctrines, to construe this struggle for wealth as being substantially a struggle for subsistence. ... It has not been unusual for economic theory to speak of the further struggle for wealth on this new industrial basis as a competition for an increase in the comforts of life – primarily for an increase of the physical comforts which the consumption of goods affords. (Veblen, 1899: 34–5)

For Veblen it is the *possession* of material wealth, and the honour which its *'conspicuous* consumption' confers, which is the desired end of accumulation. The style of house, clothes and foodstuffs confers status rather than intrinsic satisfactions. The seizure and retention of private property through violence received institutional legitimisation, giving rise to class-divided societies. In such societies the majority of the population are engaged in 'industrial' pursuits, providing the necessities of life from commodities supplied by the natural world. The common cultural inheritance is employed in the farm, household, workshop and factory, in the management of the real economy; 'oikonomia' to use the Aristotolean term (see Daly and Cobb, 1990: 138). However, a substantial minority are engaged in 'chrematistics', the manipulation of property and wealth. Non-industrial employments such as war, arts, government and sports signify the leisure class. What is seen as socially useful becomes distorted. We can see in current society that entertainers and sports people are highly 'valued' whereas people meeting the basic needs of the human community such as the garbage worker or working farmer are accorded little status.

The pursuit of chrematistics exposes the fundamental division within economic systems. Veblen drew a distinction between industrial (real) and financial capital. Industrial capital is the material means of industry which can be physically employed in production. Financial capital, on the other hand, refers to financial wealth which can be employed for purely financial ends (Veblen, 1990: 308). Capital of the latter type can consist in pieces of paper and blips on computer screens indicating credits issued and debts incurred. Finance capital is the controlling force in global capitalism, operating under the shadowy illusion of the existence of a theoretically 'free' market. As many people have observed, international capital operates as a global casino, exercising rights without responsibilities. In it is vested the power to govern the institutional framework of markets and property rights under which global economic activity takes place.

For Veblen the division between real capital and financial capital is complex. It cannot be argued that real capital has a physical existence whereas financial capital does not, as supra-physical aspects of real capital, such as the knowledge of how to use equipment, exist too. While there is scope for overlap between real capital and finance capital, Veblen draws the two categories apart in order to expose the false claim that production can be rooted purely in the finance-capital sphere: it cannot. Similarly, financial capital has both physical traces and social/subjective aspects. The main distinction between real and financial capital is their relation to human activity and outcome. Real capital requires the participation of knowledgeable humans to work. Farms, factories, kitchens, gardens: they are meaningless without people. However, finance capital is unproductive even with its associated staff. Wall Street, the brokering houses in the City of London, the stock exchanges: they all produce nothing. The capabilities of humans can only be exposed in the context of 'real' capital. Finance capital is a tangential phenomenon. Finance capital in capitalism has real effects, but only in conjunction with what Veblen called 'real capital' in the human economy.

For instance, Veblen provides a neat example of the 'doublethink' employed in neo-classical economics when the factors of production are described in purely material terms. John Bates Clark, an early American marginalist, dismisses the notion of capital as financial (money) value. In his view, it would be more accurate to regard capital as 'a fund of productive goods', having a purely physical existence. However, as Veblen notes, Clark goes on to use the term 'capital' to describe the mobility of capital from one industry to another. In his view, when capital goods are transferred, it is done in this way: when a piece of machinery wears out in one industry, it is replaced by investment in a different type of machine suitable to a different industry. Veblen refers to Clark's own example of the transfer of capital from a whaling ship to a cotton mill. Plainly, this is 'not a matter of the mechanical shifting of physical bodies from one industry to the other'. Capital *goods* are not transferred. The continuity in ownership of the 'capital' rests in the 'legal rights of contract, of purchase and of sale' (Veblen, 1990: 196). Finance capital intervenes to change the nature of exchange relations, like money as in the example of the sweet and the biscuit.

In practice, 'capital' is a financial fact, not a matter of physical machinery. The significance of this observation in clarifying the mechanisms determining the processes of production, distribution and exchange cannot be overstated. The value of capital depends upon the intention or 'state of mind' of the valuers: it is no longer a material fact to be observed 'objectively'. Capitalism upsets all concepts of 'natural' returns to the factors of production according to their productivity. However, as we argue, it is not even possible to talk of 'real' factors of production. These are distorted by capital. Hence our distinction between the means of production and the means of provisioning. It is only within a framework of economic democracy that human activities can be turned to both use and utility.

The dilemma of the current economy is that the activities of giant corporations undermine general welfare and utility while providing the money conduits for commodified provisioning. As Paul Dale Bush has argued 'the economic waste that is inherent in ceremonial encapsulation of resources and technology by the military–industrial complex is also the source of secure income for millions of Americans' (quoted in Hunt, 1994: 56). Free from 'outdated' checks and balances, giant enterprises promote military, pharmaceutical and agribusiness ventures in the pursuit of profit, regardless of the destructive effects on social and ecological life-support systems. In order to create and maintain the hierarchy of power, privilege and distinction, the large firm has to dominate all other institutions in the social life of western civilisation. Free inquiry and the expansion of intellectual horizons give way to ideology, training and research designed to meet the needs of large corporations, while dissenting voices are skilfully discredited or violently attacked (see Hynes, 1989; Korten, 1995; Rowell, 1996; Hutchinson and Burkitt, 1997; Ho, 1999; Steingraber, 1998; Halsey, 1992; Monbiot, 2000).

For Veblen, the true wealth of any society is created by the co-operative activities associated with the 'instinct of workmanship', although today we would not use such a gendered concept. Material products whether useful tools or ceremonial artefacts do not constitute the real wealth of society. Rather, wealth is embedded in the abundance of skills and knowledge of techniques and processes whereby a society provisions itself. Take away the spears, containers and digging sticks of a pre-agricultural social group, and they will make more and survive. Take away their knowledge of local flora, fauna, foods, medicines and designs of containers and other tools, and they will be unable to provision themselves through the use of the 'instinct of workmanship'. The 'common cultural inheritance' remains the source of wealth in all forms of human society, including capitalism. It owes its existence to social, rather than 'private' or individual efforts. As will be discussed later, the cultural inheritance can be seen as the basis of 'social credit' in society. Marx makes a similar observation about the 'capital' of pre-industrial society being knowledge rather than tools (Burkitt, 1984: 44) The isolated, solitary male hunter is a myth; to be human is to be part of a social group. Throughout history work traditionally associated with women has been central to the accumulation and development of social wealth (Veblen, 1899: 21–4; 1990: 324–6). Veblen showed that he was aware of this particular problem when he argued that the invisibilisation and trivialisation of domestic work was part of the process of taking control and demanding tribute that emerged among status-mongering, militarised, controlling, dominant, male elites.

Class, work and waged labour

Although social stratification has existed throughout human history, Marx and Veblen document a new phenomenon emerging with the industrialisation of agriculture, manufacturing and mining, that of class. More than Marx Veblen distinguishes between hereditary castes and lineages capable of oppressing some of the people some of the time and capitalism's ability to eradicate non-capitalist values and satisfactions. Veblen's 'leisure class' did not merely exploit the working class economically. More significantly, it destroyed traditional notions of obligation to all members of society, replacing them with a right to an income through employment. The 'working class' right to work for a money wage set capitalism apart from previous forms of social organisation by divorcing rights from obligations. Furthermore it has universalised slavery to the machine, as illustrated in the Chaplin film *Modern Times*. It has created a class of workers obliged to leave their souls at the factory gate in order to subject themselves to the will of the employing class. The consolation is the illusion of liberty through consumption so that even the poor in a monetised economy could aim through purchases of 'cheap' food, clothes and entertainment to achieve the promised world of the advertisement. Even those who feel themselves to be emulating the 'leisure class' of white, western, middle-class males remain enslaved to the monetised economy. The irony is that, however hard they try, however many designer clothes, meals, houses, cars, furnishings and holidays they consume, waged and salaried workers remain enslaved to the system. They are not free.

It is very important to distinguish between work and employment (labour for wages). Work does not occur only in places conventionally regarded as places of paid employment. It may take place in homes, factories, warehouses, farms, schools, hospitals, rivers, lakes, at sea or among the trees of a forest. Work may be a transformative, sensuous activity in any of those places. What the capitalist money system has done is break up the many activities that comprise human work. Here capitalism has been most skilful, rewarding highly certain activities useful to its purposes, minimising rewards to certain forms of essential work and failing to reward other forms at all. Most marked has been the gender division between high- and low-valued work. We concur with Veblen in questioning Marx's faith in a (male) working-class revolution to overthrow capitalism (Veblen, 1990: 452–4). Potentially, a united, waged, labour force could have provided the power base to end capitalism. What was lacking was motivation. Far from uniting in the solidarity of enlightened self-interest, members of the 'working class' have sought waged or salaried employment as a means of personal empowerment (and in this economists are no exception). The general idea has been to move as an individual out of the labouring classes, setting up small businesses and/or sending children for a better education to remove them from physically, emotionally and spiritually degrading work in mills, mines and farms, placing them in positions as administrators, educators, politicians and the like. The same is true for third world elites as for individuals and their families in the so-called developed world.

In many ways the concept of class has served capitalism well. Division into classes with inherently competing interests diverts attention from the quest for liberation from capitalism and its replacement with a holistic economic system designed to function for the welfare of all in co-operation rather than competition. The emphasis on dualisms, on difference, on opposing interests is the very substance of capitalism. Opposing interests compete for a 'fair' share of the 'limited' cake. Higher financial and other rewards are secured by key sections of capitalism's workforce, leaving much essential work unpaid and depressing financial and other rewards to casual and unorganised labour. As individuals and families move up the socio-economic ladder they leave behind categories of individuals increasingly trapped in a widening poverty and empowerment gap. Access to resources in terms of access to land, materials, knowledge and time are increasingly rationed by the money economy.

The complexities of class within capitalised money/market systems has been somewhat obscured by Marxist thinking that narrows the emphasis to capital–labour relations. This not only ignores the problems of unpaid work but also cannot make connection with the position of debt-based, small-scale property ownership such as the peasant landholder. Veblen questioned Marx's prediction that agribusiness would absorb the small proprietor, converting them to landless labour. On the contrary, as early as 1906 Veblen suggested that socialists and small peasant farmers should have common cause in resisting finance capitalism (Veblen, 1990: 451–2). However, Veblen was a voice crying in the wilderness. Describing farming in Canada during the years immediately prior to 1914, Street (1933: 109) notes that 'the whole country was run on credit'. It was the practice for a young bachelor to work for a year or two until he had enough money to buy a plot of virgin land on credit. He would purchase a 'chunk of prairie' for from ten to fifteen dollars an acre, 'paying one dollar per acre down, and leaving the remainder of the purchase price over a period of ten years at six per cent'. Horses and equipment were similarly purchased on credit, making it essential to 'mine' the soil to remain financially solvent. The simplistic and dualistic class analysis failed to unite the interests of peasant farmers with those of the industrial/urban working class. This split opponents of capitalism along meaningless ideological divisions. Henceforth the small farmer, classed as 'bourgeois' by 'socialists', sought to oppose the hated financial capitalism by adopting an ideology on the far right. Recently the problem of landholding has been given a much more favourable hearing on the left in relation to claims for land rights on behalf of indigenous peoples.

The dualistic version of class relations developed in the older industrialised countries is even more problematic when applied to countries across the world facing capitalisation and globalisation. The labour/money relationship is particularly complex in societies that retain traditional economic and social forms. Ashok Mitra has shown how the rural bourgeoisie in India are politically linked with the urban industrial bourgeoisie (Mitra, 1977). Both, he found, had differing relations with international capital and therefore needed to be considered in their empirical context and not merely according to prior theory. The Marxist Amit Bhaduri has distinguished the production-oriented landlord class from a merchant class involved mainly in trade and moneylending (Bhaduri, 1973, 1977, 1983, 1986). Both Mitra's and Bhaduri's class relations schemas have their foundations partly in the actual Hindu caste system with its inter-marriage rules and occupational orientation for particular caste groups. They thus represent particular class categories operating within twentieth-century Hindu, or Hindicised, culture (Bujra, 2000). Bhaduri's class analysis suggested that the techniques of production would be held back by the production-oriented landlord class if they thought they could make more money through lending to tied peasants than through revamping capital-intensive agricul-tural techniques. Bhaduri's model is an interesting exploration of the reasons for (and functions of) usury, but says little about the ethics of moneylending or the mutual subjectivity that develops when peasants engage in dependent relations with a landlord. Moreover, Bhaduri's modelling exercise was falsified by events: the Green Revolution occurred in the very parts of northern India on which Bhaduri's models were based, further disrupting traditional farming practices.

Although admirably empirically-grounded, these highly theoret-ical class analyses share with conventional economics a lack of awareness of unpaid labour. The domestic work of women and dependants in the landlord, bourgeois and merchant capital classes is totally ignored. Women, implicitly, are assumed to wear the class clothing of their husband or father and to share his class alliances. Meanwhile the class structure among poor people is also ungendered and the authors appear to be unaware of non-capitalist social relations, except in so far as the 'peasants' are, household by household, separate from capitalist labour relations and therefore not included in the class of proletarians. Some authors have improved the situation regarding options for class analysis in the Indian context. Utsa Patnaik created a methodology for measuring the amount of exposure to surplus-value exploitation of different rural worker households, the index of exploitation (Patnaik, 1987, 1988). One measures the number of days a household is employed by others and compares it with the number of days a household employs labour on its own land. Patnaik's Index is useful if the class structure is strongly polarised, but soon generates multiple rural social classes if one allows for non-wage-based social relations to be taken into account. Outside India, in African, Latin American, other south Asian, and East Asian countries a whole plethora of Marxist class analyses could be listed. Many empirical analyses in the Marxist tradition use labels like 'landless worker', 'marginal peasant', 'subsistence peasant', 'middle farmer', and 'large farmer' in order to allow *households* to rest at different points along a spectrum from employee (presumed to be landless) to employer (assumed to have a lot of land).

Empirical research nowadays belies this continuum-based approach to class relations in two ways. Firstly, among 'workers', individuals do not conform to the expectation that the Index would generate at household level. One researcher, Lucia Da Corta, has measured the class location of individuals, facilitating a gender-aware analysis of changes in the class structure in south India (Da Corta and Venkateswarlu, 1999 and 2001). Secondly, among 'employers' we find a similar deviation, with individuals taking salaried jobs, thus becoming *employees*, whilst their rural asset base places them in the relation of *employer* with respect to workers in their place of birth. Further empirical research has shown that women and some men actively avoid engaging in wage labour. One reason for this is that wage labour implies a capitalist relation and a price of labour which may be exploitative. Instead, many workers and people from small farms choose to share their work through 'exchange labour' (Olsen and Da Corta, 1990). In this institution no money changes hands. A verbal agreement that someone will do three days of this in exchange for other people doing three days of that is sufficient. Therefore, the notion that economists can go out into the field for research while ignoring exchange labour is problematic for political economy. A holistic approach to work in all its forms must be the starting point. The study of class relations has traditionally centred on the employment relation, whereas work is done under diverse household, village, patriarchal, family, and employment relations. In a sense, then, workers work while 'labour' undertakes wage labour.

Even moneylending is complex in the Indian context. Harriss-White argues that the group of people who engage in trade and moneylending is actually much more differentiated than Marxist theory or Indian Marxist writings might suggest. Observations from both southern and northern India show substantial differentiation among traders and moneylenders (Harriss, 1989; Crow and Murshid, 1994). The different categories of traders and their interactional patterns have been explored through an examination of their assets and the scale of their trading activities (Harriss-White, 1999). These findings must then be considered in the context of the power relations existing between buyers and sellers at each stage in the goods market in which the traders are engaged (ibid.; and White, 1993). A trader might act monopolistically *vis-à-vis* indebted farmers who sell to him/her, but in turn act as a competitive, powerless seller in wider grain markets. In the latter case the absence of loans may preclude large-scale trading, forcing them into dependency relationships as clients. This approach is confirmed by detailed empirical work in Bangladesh (Crow, 1999). It now becomes possible to move away from a crude *a priori* class analysis and closer to an empirically grounded, complex, carefully specified set of social relations. Social class is now just part of the set of resource factors and interrelated subjectivities such as gender and ethnicity that go into shaping social relations. Social relations cannot be merely based upon the ownership of private property but are also grounded in how people participate in various markets. The class 'location' of a person cannot be read off simply from their assets at birth. A new, reinvigorated empirical Marxism is required. A gender-relations angle and an awareness of self-subsistence and shared subsistence activities become essential. A range of research is progressing in this area at present.

To date, much Marxism, like classical political economy, has often been non-, pre-, or anti-feminist in that it ignores the common property and private property which is an integral part of the tools of domestic or subsistence work. In this context people use houses, trees, cooking equipment, land, water, and animals to create a decent living environment for families or household members 'when they come home'. However, the means of provisioning are not necessarily privatised. The classical Marxist meaning of 'private property' does not apply to some of the means of provisioning used in domestic and subsistence contexts, since these are often not individually owned at all. Take cooking stoves and firewood. Firewood may be collected as a common good, or bought; the stove and the wood are then used by domestic workers without quibbling over whether they, their son or husband or mother-in-law 'owns' them. Thus, households and subsistence farming are realms/times/spheres where the terminology of capital–labour do not apply. Also, as we have pointed out earlier, the notion of means of production is not sufficiently broad to account for work done outside explicitly capitalist social relations. This is why we prefer the concept of means of provisioning.

The same principles apply to forms of work/activity that do not at first instance appear to be in the 'subsistence' sector. Students making videos or acting as disc jockeys on pirate radio stations; kids playing in the street and making up games to improve the quality of leisure through co-operative activity (building a den, making a tree swing, creating complex fantasy-scenario games), musicians playing music for free together – all are 'working' in the 'subsistence' or self-provisioning sector. The quality of life is immensely enriched by what people do, often collaboratively and usually socially, in their supposedly free time. Unfortunately, these collaborative activities are chased out and closed down by the progressive domination of people's time with labour-market activity. As capitalism continues its avalanche into people's lives, it overtakes, alienates and encloses time. Even leisure activities become connected to the employment/market relation. Payment is made in order to see a video, to play a fantasy game, or to have a shoulder to cry on (therapist).

By ignoring voluntary work and neglecting its role in social reproduction, Marxists using the traditional concept of socially necessary labour linked to production/waged labour have an overly limited conception of what counts as important human activity. The concept of socially necessary labour is unnecessarily restricting our vision to the capitalism-based activities of employers as they extract surplus value. A worker is not necessarily an employee. In this book by workers we mean not only those engaged in public institutions that produce goods, as in factories, but also to those who produce at home for use among family and friends. We elide the employee/inactive distinction commonly found in labour-market economics. As is well established among feminists we make visible the subsistence and productive work done on farms, gardens, in homes, in living rooms, in huts, in bedrooms and bathrooms and kitchens, and by watertaps all over the world. At the same time we must be careful about romanticising the subsistence sector. It may be that as found in 1990s south India, rural women *wish to* move into formal employment relations in ever greater numbers, but are actually stuck in a marginal subsistence status (Olsen, 2001). Women also have little chance to enjoy small-scale property ownership as in many regions of the world property deeds lie mainly in men's effective control. It is often men who have moved out of the subsistence economy and into waged work as rapidly as they possibly could under the urge to modernise, urbanise, and get jobs with proper contracts.

To say that the capitalised money/market system is exploitative is not to say, as Veblen acknowledged, that people do not willingly participate. By seeking emulative status waged workers may collude in working in the waged economy all day and then working in the non-cash economy to create a 'good' family, local school or neighbourhood. Women's voluntary time (and men's) is known to underpin many good works. These activities are not fully capitalistic and not fully privatised, e.g. local clubs; Girl Scout/Boy Scout Troop equipment; Oxfam shops; sewing machines in the home. The expectations for behaviour are more rooted in traditions about family life, farm work or how clubs should be run. These aspects of capitalist society have been ignored and made invisible during the times when (a) conventional economics ignored them since they are non-market and (b) Marxist economics ignored them since they are non-market. In the twenty-first century economics may be ready to acknowledge these activities, but only to incorporate them into conventional economic categories by attaching a monetary value to them. As Sen has argued, if developing human 'capabilities' is to be the aim of economics in the twenty-first century (Sen, 2000), then let these capabilities be seen as social and let them be appreciated as ripe fruits in their historical light rather than as personal 'capital' in a commercial light.

Work as transformation

If we take a transformative approach to social action we can see people as agents of their own progress rather than having to wait for the capital–labour conflict to erupt in an employees' revolution (Bhaskar, 1993). This notion of people acting from where they stand, in diverse economic situations, is held in common with the feminist approaches in the micro-finance literature (Chapter 9). In our view, reclaiming possession of creative capacities, transformative skills, sensuous abilities to make things convey joy to/with others involves a mental transformation. However, this cannot be seen at just an individual level. The pleasures of productive work are not attained alone but rather in conjunction with the generations that came before and the people with whom one co-operates today. People also work in consideration of those who are to come. Whether we are referring to household and family life, to farming, to wider market transactions in food and other products, or even to money transactions, one can appreciate the social human achievement of well-being. Capitalism tends to make us forget this basic well-being, basic social-ness of existence. Capitalism tends to make us reckon things up in money terms. This fetishisation was heavily critiqued by Marx and many later Marxists. In this book we explore the possibilities already available for empowerment in the specific sense of increasing power held *with* others rather than merely the overturning of power held *over* others. We find that grass-roots movements are providing examples of alternative practices, but that what is needed is an economic theory within which their practice can be expressed. We begin this process with the work of the guild socialists and social creditors in the next chapter.

6 Guild Socialism and Social Credit

During the final decades of the twentieth century the vast body of writings on so-called 'alternative' political economy has been studied, if at all, for its curiosity value rather than for its intrinsic content. Academics aligned on the left or right of the political spectrum have studiously avoided engaging in reasoned argument with Morrisonian, guild socialist, social credit, distributist and other writers save to attach labels of fascism, communism or utopianist idealism to the work of guild socialists, social creditors and other questioners of the nature, purpose and direction of economic 'progress'. We feel it necessary, therefore, to trace the history of the guild socialist and social credit movements in order to place the writings of Douglas in particular within their political and historical context.

In this chapter we explore the legacy of the guild socialist and social credit movements. We introduce the idea of producers' and consumers' credits in a democratised banking system within a radically revamped production and distribution scenario in which the interests of producers and consumers cease to be in conflict. We see these arguments as reinforcing our case for re-evaluating the properties of money as the basis of an ecologically sustainable socialist political economy. As we have argued, capitalist economics survives by seeking to consign 'alternative' bodies of economic thought to the non-recyclable bin. By reviving consciousness of a vast literature, logical and coherent in its opposition to capitalism, we open up the possibility of achieving an egalitarian and sustainable economic democracy. Consciously or unconsciously, the future is built upon the past. For too long the conscious appraisal of past theory and practice has been sacrificed on the altar of post-modern cynicism or mindless progress to an increasingly unpleasant and uncertain future. In this chapter we explore the history of UK-based movements drawn from literature written and widely circulated far beyond the borders of the UK, in the US, Canada (French and English-speaking), Australia and New Zealand. We make no apology for analysing UK literature. It is a matter of history that guild socialism and social credit originated in the UK.

From labourism to social credit

Marx's conceptualisation of a mass working-class movement united in its opposition to the evils of capitalism and determined to overcome them was echoed by the UK Fabians, the intellectual wing of the Labour movement. However the Fabians took up little else from Marxist thought in their quest to protect the interests of organised labour under capitalism. Meanwhile, state communism in the Soviet Union sought to eliminate self-motivation by directing a blanket uniform 'working class' of labour through a centralised bureaucracy. The error of diverging from socialism as a goal can in part be attributed to Marx's own 'transitional' proposals in the Communist Manifesto. Labour as disutility to be rewarded according to its productivity became a basic tenet of a 'socialism' designed to protect the rights of workers under capitalism. By contrast to both labourism and communism, syndicalism and guild socialism sought to overthrow capitalism by reclaiming the communality and utility of production. In Spain, France and the United States syndicalism based upon individual 'craft' unions or 'industries', e.g. miners, transport/railway workers, sought to co-operate with each other, using strikes to gain *political* power and hence *economic* control over their industries (Burkitt, 1984: 116–31). Similarly the guild socialist movement in the UK sought control, not only over the *means* of production but also over the *processes*, the skills, crafts and 'intellectual property' of the different industries. Rejecting the notion of individual private profit, they developed the theme of service to the community so that producer and consumer could work in partnership for the common good (see, e.g. G.D.H. Cole, 1919).

The labourist approaches to socialism also stemmed from the misrepresentation of Marx's labour theory of value which led not only to the imagined 'transformation problem' but also to the notion that the physical labour of waged workers was the sole source of social wealth. By implication engineers, artists, scientists, farmers (as distinct from farm labourers), domestic workers (paid or unpaid) and above all intellectuals did not contribute to the creation of wealth in society. State and other 'socialisms' could therefore classify such 'non-workers' as bourgeoisie, to be converted into workers or eliminated (except, of course, for the ruling elite). We follow Veblen

(1990: 445) in noting that Marx's labour theory of value can be replaced with a more general theory of social value without damaging his thesis. The more general notion of the *social* theory of value is encapsulated in the social credit theory that we describe below. From this perspective money has value because of its ability to represent the value of *all* commodities and services produced and exchanged by society. However, the *necessity* to work for money, i.e. the continued commodification of labour, would need to be eliminated under socialism, if it is to be socialism as economic democracy rather than a paternalistic (state) capitalism.

Social credit represented the case for economic democracy on the grounds that wealth is produced by and through society in co-operation rather than competition: hence individuals and firms were not entitled to appropriate private fortunes at public expense. Money should be a servant available to society, not the master of society. The question of who has the rights to issue money into a society becomes, therefore, a critical one. The idea of money as representing social credit necessitates an understanding of the relationship between individuals and society as represented by money. From such an understanding flows the awareness that the creation of a meaningful political democracy awaits economic democracy. However, recognition of such a grounded approach to socialism depends upon a rejection by the majority of people of the socially destructive and environmentally devastating drive to produce and consume (and to produce producers and consumers) under the present system of debt-created money and banking. It also requires a realisation that the labourist aim of the 'right to work' is not a radical political aim. The demand should be a right to livelihood.

Until 1922 socialism in the UK was a rich intellectual landscape capable of embracing the medievalism of Arthur Penty, William Morris and Ruskin, Marx's philosophy and economics, syndicalism and some elements of Fabianism without logical inconsistency. After 1922 doctrinaire labourism swept the broad school of guild socialism into the margins in its will-to-power *within* capitalism, eliminating alternative routes to socialism. In doing so it narrowed the base of socialism and its history in much the same way as mainstream economics denied the pluralism of its history. Labourism was strongly identified with the trades unions, but organised 'labour' never represented the whole of the working class. Women, the unemployed, agricultural labourers, the non-unionised workers in sweat shops and outworkers of all kinds were largely excluded from the unions. Managerial and white-collar workers also formed separate organisations, fragmenting the ability of organised labour to determine economic outcomes. Recognising this, the guild socialists sought to enlarge and strengthen the movement in order to abolish wage labour altogether and with it the notion that labour is merely a commodity with a price determined like those of other commodities. The uniting of the interests of producers and consumers formed a secondary plank in the guild socialist platform.

The guild socialists envisioned all trade unions and professional organisations being vertically integrated into 'guilds' on an 'industry'-wide basis, with all workers, no matter how skilled, being united in a common purpose. Each trade and profession would create its own guild. Within the nation as a whole all economic life would be covered by guilds, chartered by the state but run on a decentralist basis with input from local consumers and the local community as a whole. With an effective monopoly of labour, the guilds could demand its full price, distributing it as incomes, but not as wages for work. The socialism which gave rise to social credit had its origins in the decentralist trade union movement associated with guild socialism and bore very little relationship to the Old Labour notions of centralised state control over labour from the cradle to the grave. Equally, New Labour bears no relation to the radical potential of this rich tapestry of socialist thought despite its 'Third Way' claims. With the guild socialists we contend that only a socialism offering *economic* democracy can provide true political freedom, equality and comradeship.

The origins of social credit

The link between guild socialism and social credit was based on a collaboration between the guild socialist Alfred Richard Orage (1873–1934) and the originator of social credit theory Clifford Hugh Douglas (1879–1952). Guild socialism aimed to break the artificial bond between employment and payment of a personal money income. However, until the arrival of Douglas on the scene, Orage and the other guild socialists were at a loss to explain the role of money under guild socialism, or under capitalism for that matter. This was despite considerable exploration of the newly emerging science of economics (Hutchinson and Burkitt, 1997: 9, 18–22). Orage was originally a member of the Fabian Arts Group, a wing of the Fabian Society which he formed with Holbrook Jackson in 1907.

They purchased a bankrupt magazine, the *New Age*, which provided a platform for guild socialists, including Arthur Penty and S.G. Hobson, distributists such as Hilaire Belloc and G.K. Chesterton and a range of leading intellectuals covering the arts, politics and economics. Virtually from its inception, the *New Age* criticised statistical 'gas and water' socialism dependent upon a capitalist economy, exploring instead workable alternatives to capitalism. The *New Age* was widely read throughout the trade union movement.

The meeting of Orage with Douglas at the end of World War I gave rise to an association which continued until the death of the former in 1934. Writing in 1926, Orage described his relationship with Douglas. From the very first he was impressed by Douglas' understanding of the relationship between finance and industry, and with his grasp of economic affairs. 'In the scores of interviews we had with bankers, professors of economics, politicians, and businessmen, I never saw him so much as at a moment's loss of complete mastery of his subject' (Orage, 1926). Between 1918 and 1924 the 'Douglas/*New Age*' texts appeared in hardback versions, including *Economic Democracy* (1919), *Credit-Power and Democracy* (1920), *The Control and Distribution of Production* (1922) and *Social Credit* (1924). These texts first appeared in serial form in the *New Age*, together with numerous speeches and articles, all of which went through many reprints, remaining available throughout the twentieth century. The close collaboration between Orage and Douglas, which established the guild socialist economics subsequently known as 'social credit', ended in 1922 when Orage went to Fontainebleau to study with G.I. Gurdjieff. Although Douglas continued to promote social credit until his death in 1952, giving rise to a worldwide movement and innumerable books, pamphlets and periodicals on the subject, powerful interests became more concerned to discredit social credit than to enter into a reasoned debate with its proponents. Early appreciation of this trend drove Orage to abandon the editorship of the *New Age* in 1922. However, he continued to promote social credit in the US and on his return to the UK at the end of his life and even died while broadcasting a talk on the subject (Hutchinson and Burkitt, 1997).

Douglas and social credit

Douglas' ideas were first published as articles in the *English Review* of 1918–19 where he argued that the capitalist system was designed to lead to waste and warfare rather than peace, co-operation and (self-) sufficiency. The four *English Review* articles formed the basis of Douglas' first, most comprehensive book, *Economic Democracy*. According to Douglas, political democracy without economic democracy was an empty sham. The four *English Review* papers were entitled 'The Delusion of Super-production', 'The Pyramid of Power', 'What is Capitalism?' and 'Exchange and Exports'. In these articles, and *Economic Democracy*, Douglas explored the nature of finance-driven economic change.

As Douglas' social credit ideas outlined in this chapter were published in the UK in the years immediately following World War I, they predate and anticipate the miners' strike, the General Strike, the great depression of the inter-war years, Keynes' *General Theory* and national income accounting (GDP/GNP). With minimal acknowledgement it was drawn upon by economists working within the framework of orthodoxy, including Keynes, G.D.H. Cole and James Meade (Hutchinson and Burkitt, 1997). Taken as a whole, Douglas' work provides the basis for development of a non-equilibrium economics in which sufficiency can take precedence over economic growth, competition and the quest for profit. Production would cease to be dependent upon wage labour, while a realistic balance between production and distribution could be maintained. The Douglas/ *New Age* texts as a whole, formulated around the guild concept, outline a socialist system of finance tailored to serve socialist rather than capitalist ends, providing a coherent economics for socialism.

The main themes of social credit are a critique of the circular flow model of the economy (the A+B theorem described below), the utility of work as opposed to the disutility of labour, a view of society's wealth as the common cultural inheritance as distinct from intellectual and other private property, and the concept of the national dividend, that is, the distribution of the wealth of society as a social right. The ideas were brought together in a 'Draft Mining Scheme' described below. The dominant theme in social credit is the role of money in determining production, distribution and value under capitalism. As social credit ideas are incompatible with capitalist economics, each social credit theme if examined in isolation can be rejected as implausible or unworkable. However this is only the case if they are examined within a conventional economic framework, i.e. *under capitalism*. If these ideas are explored as a whole we argue that they demonstrate that there *is* an alternative to capitalism, and one worthy of debate.

As we have already noted, Douglas' work, rooted in the political economy of guild socialism, was recognised as *politically* incompatible with mainstream economic theorising (see Hutchinson and Burkitt, 1997: 83–128). Like Marx and Veblen, Douglas presented the case for reform of capitalist political economy. His basic thesis was that financial institutions determine how society allocates real resources when they create credit for specific forms of industrial development without taking account of social or environmental responsibilities. Finance is no neutral facilitator of exchange, but is central to political economy. Recognition of this crucial point paves the way for consideration of alternative ways forward as, for example, in the Draft Mining Scheme.

Although the Douglas texts abound with notions of sufficiency, social equity, sustainability, international peace, co-operation and responsibility, they do not incorporate a mechanical blueprint for a 'social credit' economy. Rather than focusing on specific schemes and proposals, Douglas sought initially to raise consciousness of the possibility of, and scope for, change. Recognising the evolutionary nature of institutions, he stressed the need to evaluate the resources, productive flows and institutions of a country at the point of considering legislation to adapt the financial system. It was also important to consider whether local or national financial reform of any kind would require a national legislative framework if it were not to be corrupted to the service of capitalism.

The basic theme of 'social credit' is that new money should not be created as debt by private interests. Rather, it should be created as 'credit' on behalf of the community as a whole. How could this be done? This is the tricky question. The conventional socialist answer would be to nationalise the banks (see Hutchinson and Burkitt, 1997: 98). However, this would merely result in an Orwellian creation of another elite set as under state communism. Douglas' ideas centred on two basic forms of money-creation.

1 *Consumers' credit*: money could be allocated directly to consumers in the form of a 'national dividend' on the strength of the universal claim to a share in the common cultural inheritance. With the use of sophisticated computer systems, 'consumers' credit' of this type could be calculated according to stocks and flows of wealth creation and consumption. The calculation of non-financial definitions of wealth creation and depreciation would form an essential feature of the new economic system. The

notion of a national dividend or basic income is explored in a later section.

2 *Producers' credits*: a slightly less familiar notion, but closer to existing practice, is that of 'producers' credits' linked to the just price and based on the 'A+B' theorem as explained below. Instead of attempting to recoup the full costs of *past* production of the product, producers would sell at the 'just price' (free of the profit and interest payments of debt-finance) of their present costs. They would be compensated for certain additional 'B' costs through a central clearing house. Although complex, it was argued that the existing system is no less complicated in its actual operations. The effect of financing production in this way would be to replace debt financing with a system of credit finance.

Both producers' and consumers' credits relied on the notion of the 'just price' to be calculated on the basis of costs of production, together with calculation of the relationship between production and consumption coupled with depreciation.

The Draft Mining Scheme

In 1920 Douglas had extensive discussions with the leaders and rank and file of the Miners' Federation of Great Britain (MFGB) which was affiliated to the UK Labour Party. Published amid mounting concern at the effects of capitalist financing upon prices, wages and employment in the mining industry, the Draft Mining Scheme was designed to bring production and employment under local community control through decentralisation of management and finance within the statutory framework of the nation state. The original document was accompanied by a commentary by Orage. Referring to contemporary debate on the subject, especially the Draft Bill for the Nationalisation of the mines drawn up by the MFGB, Orage presented the case for decentralisation of the finance and administration of the mining industry in the UK (Douglas, 1920: 149–212). The Draft Mining Scheme highlighted the economic benefits of subsidiarity, that is, devolution of decision-making to the lowest practicable unit. In the 1920s, railways were being grouped into six well-defined districts, each administratively autonomous, to the benefit of personnel and their working conditions. Uniform conditions imposed upon industrial areas differing widely in natural and social resources would create all the evils and waste of regimented bureaucracy. The division of mining areas by their natural or geological areas would ensure a general local administration in harmony with the local conditions. The corresponding devolution of administrative control would facilitate creation of an identity of interests between workers, their management structures, consumers and the local communities in which they live. These ideas mesh very clearly with contemporary ideas of the localisation of production and bio-regionalism in green thinking.

The 'Draft Mining Scheme' can most accurately be described as a consciousness-raising exercise. As the use of the adjective 'draft' indicates, the proposal was intended as a basis for discussion, rather than a dogmatic blueprint. The scheme envisaged a national network of statutorily endorsed 'producers' banks', linked to the decentralised regional management structures of individual industries. It contained scope for recognition of the mutual interdependence of producers and consumers, and the dependence of both upon the local community and its natural bio-region. The scheme was directed towards mining for historical reasons as coal represented the major source of the nation's fuel supplies (see Hutchinson and Burkitt, 1997: 72, 95). Although the mining industry was used as a contemporary example, the concept of 'producers' could be extended to include other productive manufactures, agriculture, retail, services and professions. Furthermore, local banks would evolve to serve local communities, covering the full spectrum of production. A strikingly similar conceptualisation lay behind José Maria Arizmediarrieta's founding of Mondragon's Working People's Bank.

We argue that the 'steady-state' economy envisaged by Daly (1973) and others as discussed in Chapter 8, could be created on the basis of the ideas set out in the Draft Mining Scheme. Such an economy would be dependent neither on a continuation of the destructive and alienating forces of capitalism nor on the draconian elimination of capitalism through state control. On the grounds that 'it is not Capital that is evil, but capitalism' the original scheme contained provision for the gradual elimination of 'absentee ownership' (Douglas, 1920: 175–6). A clause allowing for capital already invested in the industry to continue to receive a fixed return (though without the ability to fix prices) was designed to avoid the political and economic impracticalities of confiscation without compensation. Under social credit all would be entitled to their share of the product of the common cultural inheritance. What was produced and consumed would no longer be determined by *financial* profitability, but by the free play of the forces of supply and demand determined by a truly free and equal market.

Under the Draft Mining Scheme, existing separate colliery companies in each of the defined geographical areas would be required to amalgamate into statutory companies or, alternatively, to set up working agreements that would answer the same end. Such working agreements are a common feature of capitalist operations. Their explicit recognition under a statutory framework would eliminate financial competition and bring the industry under the control of the local community. In this way money can be used as the textbooks suggest, to facilitate economic choice. In each area a Producers' Bank would be established and recognised by the Government as an integral part of the mining industry. Douglas and Orage assumed that following the Draft Mining Scheme as a pilot in one 'industry', other 'industries', including services and professions, would be affiliated to the Producers' Bank.

The Producers' Bank, set up by a vertically integrated trade union on behalf of all workers in the industry would become an integral part of the (mining) industry. As the producer of wealth, affiliated with the national clearing house, the Producers' Bank measures and represents the real wealth created by the industry. Four crucial points need to be spelled out: (a) The nature of credit; (b) the workforce as a whole, in the form of the trade union, represents the Credit or positive wealth of the industry; (c) the function of the Producers' Bank; and (d) the affiliation of such a Bank to the Clearing House.

(a) The nature of credit

Social credit thinking sees two kinds of credit – real credit and financial credit. A nation's real credit is the correct estimate of its ability to produce and deliver goods as, when and where required by the potential consumer (i.e. the potential, not the actual supply of goods). Real credit depends upon two factors: the ability to produce and the needs to be satisfied. Either is useless without the other. The producer of goods that nobody wants is of no more value than a potential consumer of what is not produced. The consumer, in other words, is quite as necessary to the production of real credit as the producer, the real credit being their joint and common creation. Not only is the consumer a necessary factor in the production of real credit, but the community at large is even more indispensable. Economically regarded, a nation is an association of people engaged in the production of real credit. In this sense the state, as the custodian of the real credit of the community, may be said to represent the interests of producer and consumer equally, since both are equally necessary to the creation of real credit. Since, however, producers and consumers between them make up the whole community, we may conclude that real credit is social or communal in origin; that it belongs neither to the producer nor to the consumer, but to their *common* element, the community of which they each form a part.

Financial credit, on the other hand, is the correct estimate of the ability to deliver *money* as and when required. Real credit is based upon goods (and services), whereas financial credit is based upon money, and money, as we know, does not necessarily stand in a valid relation to goods. Financial credit is one remove from real credit, since money itself is only of value in so far as it is based upon goods. What is the function of financial credit? It is to set in motion and to direct real credit; money 'makes the wheels go round'. Before a producer can begin producing boots, s/he must gain control of raw materials which are already in existence. How does s/he do it? Suppose s/he has no money or purchasing-power with which to go into the market, or to pay employees: s/he has only an ability to produce boots. Under these circumstances s/he is therefore compelled to 'borrow' purchasing-power or financial credit, as a means of obtaining control of the goods s/he needs in order to begin to produce. The usual organ for the issue or lending of such financial credit is a bank. A bank is, in addition to being a custodian of money and valuables, a dealer in financial credit.

(b) The workforce (labour) forms real credit

Labour is essential for all forms of production: therefore, the workforce is entitled, alongside the community, to be regarded as depositors in the venture. Financial credit rests on real credit, which in turn resides in the workforce and the community. The scheme envisaged the gradual elimination of absentee capitalist financial interests. Note that in using the concepts 'workforce' and 'labour' the authors of the Draft Mining Scheme were using familiar terminology in order to describe the transition stage towards socialism.

(c) The function of the Producers' Bank

A bank issues financial credit against real credit through the medium of money. Therefore, the producers' bank represents the real credit created by the industry, contributed by the workers who increasingly become its depositors as producers rather than as waged or salaried labour. The function of the Bank is to issue financial credit in line with the creation of real credit by the industry and the need of the public (consumers) for the products of the industry.

(d) The affiliation of the Producers' Bank to the Clearing House

Affiliation of local Producers' Banks to the national clearing house is an essential feature of the scheme. Through this mechanism, the currency of the new credit-creation mechanism is given statutory endorsement. The move also provides the facility for government access to funding for payment of a national dividend/basic income and other social provision. Though unfamiliar, the new accounting system would be no more complex than the present system, while maintaining the scope to be a great deal more rational in the allocation and conservation of social and ecological resources.

The case for socialisation of credit

The starting point for Douglas' work was his observation that while socially desirable schemes were not implemented for want of finance, socially destructive activities such as warfare and the production of armaments faced no such limitations. While working at the Farnborough Aircraft Factory in 1916–18 he had the opportunity to see a war economy in operation. In his *English Review* articles of 1918–19 Douglas predicted that economic instability would result if the economy was converted from wartime to peacetime productivity purely on the basis of financial profitability. In particular, he noted the contemporary misconception that 'profitable' production of consumer items of dubious practical value would have to be stimulated so that incomes could be paid out as wages, and taxed to 'pay' for the war, i.e. to repay the National Debt incurred during the war (Hutchinson and Burkitt, 1997: 54–7). Production for exchange on the basis of financial profitability would lead to wasteful competition in international markets, deliberately fostered by 'export credit schemes' in order to increase exploitation of wage labour and resulting in inherent political instability (Hutchinson and Burkitt, 1997: 69–70). In this, Douglas was merely voicing a common contemporary concern echoed by Keynes in his *The Economic Consequences of the Peace* (1919).

With many current resonances, Douglas noted that even in the period before World War I the drive for profit meant that the manufacture of consumer goods far outstripped requirements for everyday life. New products were being introduced to the market with the sole purpose of achieving financial profitability. New designs of cars and sewing machines were introduced through advertising to the extent that advertising costs exceeded the costs of manufacture. Meanwhile, the new model, 'not novel in any real essential' served merely to 'depreciate the value of the previous year's fashion' (Douglas, 1918: 429). Changing fashions in clothes, furnishings and food processing were diverting resources to the satisfaction of financial profitability, with perceived status (emulative consumption) predominating over the satisfaction of basic needs. Produced for short-term status rather than long-term use value, the 'wealth' so generated could more accurately be termed 'waste'. The labelling of 'basic' and 'subsistence' as a 'backward' sign of poverty by the advertising 'industry' created the illusion of material progress measurable in terms of the possession of things. In the process cultural, emotional and spiritual satisfactions were reduced to optional, unquantifiable ephemera. In Veblenian terms, emulative consumerism was essential to drive the capitalist economy. Additionally, large-scale production of armaments represented the supreme example of wasteful use of resources.

The 1914–18 World War had involved a vast expansion in the speed and volume of output in the main manufacturing countries across the world, including Britain, America, Japan, France, Italy, Germany and Austria. The capitalist nations now had the technological capacity to divert a vast potential of productive resources to repair war damage and provide for peace. However, the decision to introduce new technologies would depend upon the availability of finance for its production and use. The potential existed to eliminate routine and repetitive tasks, while dramatically reducing hours of work and at the same time producing a *sufficiency* of basic needs for all. If private financial profitability dominated decision-making, people would end up working longer hours producing a stream of superfluous items, reducing their real quality of life and destroying the natural environment through pollution and waste. Furthermore, the extra production could not *profitably* be absorbed in the home market. It therefore becomes necessary to produce more, and consume less, so as to increase exports in order to restore and maintain the value of the £ sterling. Each national currency has a 'price' in terms of other national currencies, determined by relative demand and supply. Hence:

> this clamour for super-exports as a means of 'stabilising' exchange is based on the desire to raise the price of the English pound in the international money market for exactly the same reason that the fruit merchant wants to raise the price of plums in the fruit market – because there is more profit for him. It is not based on a desire to increase the purchasing power of the consumer expressed in terms of American goods, because the demand that American goods shall not be allowed to enter this country [i.e. for protective tariffs] comes from the same quarter. (Douglas, 1919a: 370)

The financially motivated search for new markets would be acceptable if the majority of the people benefited from improved quality of life, in terms of shorter hours of work and a sufficiency of material needs. However, the production for export policy sought to restrict the import of cheap consumer goods, to maintain the price in the home market. Cheap raw materials were therefore imported so that workers could be forced to expend long hours in the production of manufactured exports for financial profitability. As Douglas predicted, the post-war UK government introduced an export credit scheme, financed from public money, to facilitate manufacture of capital goods, machinery and transport, to stimulate trade and create a 'strong economy' (see Hutchinson and Burkitt, 1997: 69–72).

As we have seen, Douglas anticipated an incredible expansion of production and consumption, involving massive waste of productive resources through depletion of energy and raw materials, in order to maintain a volume of production of 'cheap' items for which markets would have to be found. Under the existing financial system, the alternative to a massive increase in production would be unemployment, i.e. a failure in income distribution. In short, 'the present system of unregulated currency and credit, administered in their own interests by international groups of financiers and super-industrialists' would inevitably lead to a *rise* in the cost of living 'measured in terms of intensity of effort' accompanied by a *fall* in the standard of life 'in terms of security, leisure and freedom' (Douglas, 1919a: 369). The unregulated financial system was unsustainable socially and ecologically. Eventually, economic instability and collapse would lead to the realisation that 'the chief crime of the capitalist was that he was such a very bad capitalist; in that he neither recognised his assets, nor met his liabilities' (Douglas, 1918: 432).

The solution, Douglas argued, was to reduce money to a medium of exchange so that supply and demand could operate according to textbook theory. New products and new technology would be introduced by producers (workers) in an industry, rather than for the financial profit of absentee landlords. Douglas questioned 'whether the accepted principles of price making are so sacred that a world must be brought to ashes rather than that they should be analysed and revised' (Douglas, 1919a: 169).

Douglas' social credit theory which emerged from the study of Marx by UK guild socialists was combined with the Veblenian institutional approach to the study of the economy through Orage's transatlantic connections. Certain specific proposals flowed from these writings, including the National Dividend (a guaranteed basic income) and the Draft Mining Scheme for the finance of industry on a decentralist (localised) basis as described above. As Douglas stressed throughout his writings, his proposals were suggestions rather than blueprints. Nevertheless, they had in common a vision of the end of 'profiteering' capitalist finance. The prime purpose of Douglas' work was to gain understanding of how the capitalist economy works. If finance is a man-made phenomenon, it is possible to study its role in the processes of production, distribution and exchange with a view to directing those processes to socially desirable and environmentally sustainable ends. Once the principles of the workings of capitalist finance were understood, it becomes a matter of mere accounting to adjust prices and money flows to desired purposes. Under the existing system complex adjustments are undertaken every day in order to drive the wheels of business and commerce towards profitable but not necessarily socially useful ends. No matter how complex these adjustments might be, they remain human calculations, not the workings of a clockwork universe designed by some great Economist in the Sky. If studied from an informed perspective, society's 'credit' could be used to end, or at least reduce, the tendency to economic warfare and military conflict. Social credit is not, however, a reformist measure; it cannot be grafted onto the capitalist economy in order to make it work better.

Douglas' A+B theorem and the flawed circular flow model

Social credit as a body of theory aims to explain the social/communal nature of money and credit. This is in marked contrast to the mainstream view of economic systems. As we argued in Chapter 2, to explore the role of money and credit in the economy we must first examine the limitations of current economic thinking. Central to our analysis and to Douglas' work was a critique of the model of the circular flow and its failure to account for finance capital. He presented his critique in his 'A+B theorem' and his analysis chimes in well with the work of Schumpeter on the same question. The 'static' analysis of the circular flow in conventional economics can account for slow but continuous change, as in the evolution of a small shop into a major retail chain. Furthermore, economists do not need to account for changes external to the economy. Change may occur in 'non-social data' as in climate change or other natural conditions. Equally, 'non-economic social data' including 'the effects of war, changes in commercial, social or economic policy, or in consumers' tastes' may give rise to change in the socio-economic system (Schumpeter, 1934: 62). None of these external changes invalidate the static circular flow analysis.

However, if dramatic, discontinuous change can be attributed to an *economic* cause, the circular flow analysis is inadequate to predict or explain the change. It is limited to investigating the new equilibrium position *after* change has occurred. Under mainstream theory change due to *economic* causes appears to 'magic' a new equilibrium position out of thin air. Schumpeter used the term 'new combinations' to describe discontinuities arising from *economic* causes. The formation of new combinations involves transfer to different uses of existing factors of production already in the economic system. This is not done by reserving funds from existing development within the circular flow. New combinations require fresh funds in the form of credit. Even the 'greatest combine' possessed of great wealth cannot finance a new combination by returns from previous production (Schumpeter, 1934: 69). Schumpeter distinguishes between entrepreneurs and capitalists, although he argues that over their careers most 'captains of industry' act in both roles. As he sees it, those who carry out new combinations (enterprise) are entrepreneurs, even if employed as managers or financiers and not heading firms as owner managers. The entrepreneur's function is 'to combine the productive forces, to bring them together ... *for the first time*' (Schumpeter, 1934: 76. Emphasis added).

Douglas' observations on the working of the capitalist economy led him to fundamentally challenge the circular flow equilibrium model that lies at the heart of mainstream economics and justifies a *laissez-faire* policy. He argued that even in its own terms there could never be an equilibrium within capitalised market systems. This was encapsulated in his A+B theorem. Douglas called his analysis the 'A+B' theorem in order to suggest that decomposing the notional price of a good would reveal some anomalies in capitalist pricing. If we cannot assume a single production-and-consumption period, in which markets clear as Say's law and the circular flow appear to indicate, it becomes necessary to clarify the relationship between finance on the one hand and production and distribution (consumption) on the other. The A+B theorem offers one way to approach this problem.

In an exchange economy production takes place *over time*, as a good passes from raw material to finished product at the retail outlet. At each stage of production finance is required so that labour can be hired and raw materials or semi-manufactured goods bought. The tanner buys hide from the farmer, the shoemaker buys leather from the tanner, the shopkeeper buys shoes from the shoemaker and sells them to the consumer. Although all costs must be recouped in the selling price, goods available for purchase in the present period must be paid for with wages earned in the present period. Wages paid out in the past, as the product passed through earlier stages, are no longer available to spend on present goods. Meanwhile, present production is not yet available for purchase. Savings and investment, i.e. mediation of money through the capital markets, are the compensating factor that adjusts actual prices in practice. In this way Douglas stressed a direct relationship between capital investments and exchange prices. This viewpoint overlaps with orthodox economics but decomposes the sub-elements rather differently.

It is necessary to bear in mind that Douglas was not trying to save the economic system from boom, bust and eventual collapse by feeding new money ('funny money') in to compensate for a real or imagined shortfall. Rather, he questioned the fundamental necessity for a continued expansion of production which locked the mass of workers (including professionals, educationalists and academics) into wage/salary-slavery, emulative consumerism and perpetual economic insecurity. The 'A+B theorem' was nothing more than a description of the relationship between production, and the distribution of money incomes *over time*. Having calculated the flow of costs and wages in a number of industries during the 1914–18 war (Hutchinson and Burkitt, 1997: 11–12) Douglas came to the following conclusion:

> A factory or other productive organisation has, besides its economic function as a producer of goods, a financial aspect – it may be regarded, on the one hand as a device for the distribution of purchasing power to individuals through the media of wages, salaries and dividends; and on the other hand as a manufactory of prices – financial values. From this standpoint its payments may be divided into two groups:
>
> Group A – All payments made to individuals (wages, salaries and dividends).
> Group B – All payments made to other organisations (raw materials, bank charges, and other external costs).
>
> As the rate of flow of purchasing-power to individuals is represented by A, but since all payments go into prices, the rate of flow of prices cannot be less than A+B. Therefore a proportion of the value of the product at least equivalent to B must enter the economy to compensate for the shortfall in A in relation to prices. The additional finance is advanced in the form of loan credits or export credits. (Douglas, 1920: 21–2)

It is possible to quibble with some of the detail of the Douglas analysis. Despite certain inconsistencies, however, Douglas' basic observation holds: present distribution of incomes buys past production, but is only partly financed by present sales (Group A payments representing all finance of the circular flow) and must be supported by the advance of loans in respect of future productive output, which are also paid out in present wages. The purposes for which loans are made, i.e. what will be produced in the future, is determined by financiers in collaboration with absentee owners on grounds of financial profitability. The circular flow becomes a continuous flow, sustained by a perpetual increase in the volume (value) of output deemed financially profitable. This analysis renders meaningless the orthodox economics assumption that labour is rewarded as a factor of production for its contribution to productive outcomes. The more central role is that played by financial capital in the productive process.

The continuous flow nature of production and distribution over time is central to Douglas' theory. Like Schumpeter, he recognised that commodities exist in two time periods, the one in which they are produced, followed by the one in which they are consumed. Goods are not distributed in the same economic period as that in which they are produced. It follows that there is no *necessity* for the total amount of money available in the consumption period to be identical with the total sum of prices attached to goods during the past production period and available for present consumption. When the circular flow is established it may, as Schumpeter noted, lead people to work within established networks of production and consumption. There is, however, no natural tendency to equilibrium. On the contrary, in 'normal' periods of economic growth, new investment, generated as debt by the financial system, will be paid out in wages in the present period, alongside wages and other payments to consumers as reward for their contribution to the productive process in the present. The result will be an increase in prices, since the consumer goods available for purchase in the present period cannot be increased *in that same period*. When the (increased amount of) goods produced in the present period appear on the market in the future period, an increased element of past costs will be incorporated in their price.

In Douglas' view, economic change cannot be accounted for within the circular flow, where time and prices stand still, money is a mere medium of exchange, technology is fixed, markets clear, capital is not accumulated and history does not exist. Attempts to explain economic change within the framework of mainstream theory become difficult, if not impossible, to sustain. The appearance of new goods, new technologies, new markets, new resources and new monopoly positions cannot be resolved by or through the circular flow concept, no matter how sophisticated attempts to do so may appear. Change occurs in the real-life economic system when new finance capital is introduced. All new capital, however, forces change in the use of existing resources, drawing some to new forms of profitable production, rendering other resources redundant, and establishing new routines of economic interaction.

7 Institutional Critiques of Capitalist Finance

The credit basis of capitalism

Money as credit forms the basis of the capitalist economy, distinguishing it from non-exchange or simple market economies. While non-capitalist economies use money for non-commercial purposes or limited exchange, capitalism is defined by production for exchange financed by credit. As new combinations enter the circular flow, old firms are forced out. In their turn, the old combinations were founded on credit in a previous period. However, credit, as financial capital in the form of 'money or money substitutes' (as in bills of exchange) does not produce. That is done by real factors of production: labour, raw materials and tools. Credit provides the new capitalist (the entrepreneur) with the essential *access* to the means of production without which new forms of production cannot take place (Schumpeter, 1934: 71–80). In creating a new enterprise, the capitalist swims *against* the circular flow. Without this analysis periodic crises in capitalism are difficult to explain in conventional terms of savings and investment.

Finance already existing within the circular flow can be regarded as 'a kind of certificate for completed production' which has increased the social product. Equally, it can be seen as 'an order upon, or claim to, part of this product' (Schumpeter, 1934: 73–4). Hence access to 'the national dividend is usually to be had only on condition of some productive service *previously* rendered or of some product *previously* sold' (Schumpeter, 1934: 73–4, emphasis added). Where new credit is created to finance new combinations, that credit will affect the price level. The issue of new bank notes not fully covered by equivalent withdrawals, together with other credit payments advanced for the financing of new combinations, enters the circular flow as it is paid out to wage earners or owners of already-produced means of production. It therefore competes for a share of the existing consumer goods in the circular flow of that economic period (Schumpeter, 1934: 73), raising price levels. The money so created is indistinguishable from that already in the circular flow. Its effects are, however, very different.

The banker is in a position to produce new money out of nothing. He also acts as a middleman, allocating reserve funds and savings deposited with him, so that the total demand for free purchasing power rests with the financier:

> He stands between those who wish to form new combinations and the possessors of productive means. He is essentially a phenomenon of development ... He makes possible the carrying out of new combinations, authorises people, in the name of society, as it were, to form them. He is the ephor [overseer wielding effective power] of the exchange economy. (Schumpeter, 1934: 74)

As a result, the private or state banker holds sole rights to issue what is, in fact, social credit to people or institutions of their choosing. Although banking practice differs from country to country, it has certain universal features. Money enters the economy through a financial institution which determines the purposes for which it will be used. The price of money (interest rate) will govern aggregate demand for money but will not determine supply. That is determined by the banking system because there is no market-clearing equilibrium price for money. Moreover, virtually all credit is allocated by administrative decisions. As Hugh Stretton explains:

> there is no market alternative to administrative allocation of loans. The practical alternatives, and the policy questions, are about *who* should allocate credit, and *who* should decide the guidelines under which they do it. (Stretton, 1999: 629. Emphasis original)

Financial institutions decide which individuals and firms should receive advances of credit, and which should not. Equally, they decide which industries are to be developed, and where. Throughout the history of industrialisation, major social policy decisions have been made at the stroke of a banker's pen. Moreover, although banks do look after people's money, it is an illusion to imagine that they only lend out 'other people's money' when making a loan for investment purposes. As we have already observed, if banks did no more than lend out *already existing money*, no new investment could take place.

The headquarters of the capitalist system

The issuers of credit are therefore, and always have been, central to the political economy of capitalism. Meanwhile, across the board, economists have asserted 'with rare unanimity, even with impatience and moral and intellectual indignation' that money has no essential function to play in the economy (Schumpeter, 1934: 95). Dissociating himself from popular 'error' through a painstaking step-by-step argument, Schumpeter is led to accept two 'heresies':

> first ... the heresy that money, and then ... the second heresy that also other means of payment, perform an essential function, hence that processes in terms of means of payment are not merely reflexes of processes in terms of goods. (Schumpeter, 1934: 95)

Money, and other means of payment (credit instruments, including bills of exchange), comes into existence as debt (as credit is advanced). The purposes for which it is advanced quite definitely affects economic outcomes (Schumpeter, 1934: 96ff). Economic 'progress', or 'development' as Schumpeter calls it, depends upon the advance of finance capital. The existence of finance capital cannot be accounted for in the circular flow.

Schumpeter defines finance capital as *'that sum of means of payment which is available at any moment for transference to entrepreneurs'* (Schumpeter, 1934: 122. Emphasis original). With some reservation, Schumpeter identifies the capital market with the money market, noting that without 'development' there would be no money market, merely a highly organised 'central settlement bureau, a kind of clearing house or bookkeeping centre for the economic system' through which transactions were settled through 'credit means of payment' (Schumpeter, 1934: 124). Under the dynamics of capitalism, however, finance capital is private, not social.

> The money market is always, as it were, the headquarters of the capitalist system, from which orders go out to individuals, and that which is debated and decided there is always in essence the settlement of plans for further development. ... Thus the main function of the money or capital market is trading in credit for the purpose of financing development. Development creates and nourishes this market. In the course of development it is assigned still another, that is a third function: it becomes the market for sources of incomes themselves. (Schumpeter, 1934: 127)

Under capitalism, finance capital determines the type and quantity of production for exchange. Hence the productive system determines distribution of incomes within the community and mediates social relationships through the medium of money. Having reduced money to a mere *numéraire*, mainstream theorising appears to argue that individuals and firms 'save' money which they invest in the various ways shown. How they acquire *any* money, whether to spend or to save, is left as an unexplained mystery. Here we are dealing with the principles underlying the money economy, and they are quite simple: banks create finance for specific purposes. That finance flows through the economy in highly complex circuits, the detailed study of which lies beyond the scope of this work, save to indicate that its very complexity has been allowed to obscure the role of money in determining production, exchange and distribution.

The cyclical problems besetting the international economy since the industrial revolution have given rise to all manner of discussions as to the relationship between credit (money loaned into being) and prices. Debate has mainly centred on the causes of periodic booms and slumps, with a view to creating continuous economic growth. In an essay entitled 'Credit and Prices', first published in *The Journal of Political Economy* in 1905, Veblen makes the commonplace observation that, in prosperous times, credit expands and there is a general rise in the level of prices, while crises and depressions see a shrinking of credit and a decline in the general level of prices (Veblen, 1998: 115). Which is cause and which effect is not immediately obvious, but that the two phenomena are linked forms a reasonable assumption. Veblen goes on to explore the phenomenon of credit extension, noting that banking is profitable because the banker lends more money than he has or more than he has borrowed. Banks provide two basic services: they (a) discount commercial paper and (b) make loans on collateral other than bills of sale. In performing task (a) banks authenticate the issue of credit, increasing the demand for goods, since the volume of credit and hence the volume of money values available for purchase has been increased. Equally, in making a loan on collateral representing property not intended for sale the banker creates a new volume of credit:

Such a transaction creates credit and so adds to the borrower's funds available for purchase, and therefore increases the effective demand for goods, and in doing so helps to enhance prices. In such a transaction the banker lends funds which he does not possess. ... Hence borrowers are enabled to borrow more in the aggregate than all the funds that the ultimate lenders have to dispose of – more than the whole of the funds seeking investment as loans plus that collateral which represents property sold or seeking sale. The purchasing power placed at the disposal of debtors is larger because of the banker's mediation than it would be without it. (Veblen, 1998: 127–30)

The discount received by the banker on repayment of the loan enables him to lend more, causing a continuous rise in the volume of credit and in prices. Meanwhile economists fail to question the 'motives and aims' of the businessmen who seek credit and of the traffickers in credit, the bankers and brokers, presuming beneficial results to society as a whole as credit and prices expand (Veblen, 1998: 127). Hence society's credit (money) is created and distributed for reasons of personal gain and motives unconnected with the common good, while economists assume that this is not the case. In these circumstances the suggestion that money should come into existence as producers' or consumers' credits appears a reasonable proposition. The question, 'But where is the money to come from?' can be turned around by examining where existing money comes from.

National dividend

At the heart of social credit is the claim that the issue of money/credit is a social question. This rests on a fundamental commitment to economic democracy. Social creditors argue that all members of society are entitled to a share of the social product by right. This is particularly important for those in the 'developed' world who are denied access to traditional means of subsistence by the evolution of capitalist property rights. This social credit case is based on the argument that the wealth of a society is based on the common inheritance of the body of cultural knowledge and natural resources handed on from generation to generation. This leads to the social credit proposal that at least a proportion of personal incomes be paid in the form of a basic income or 'national dividend' available to all citizens regardless of employment status. Payment of a national dividend is not dependent upon taxation of incomes earned by firms or individuals 'earning' money from production. It is a direct payment paid through, and calculated by, a 'National

Credit Office' and modelled on reversal of the national debt, taking the form of 'consumers' credits' issued directly as money incomes.

If money – credit – is created as loans by bankers out of nothing, it may equally well be created by a National Credit Office, replacing the National Debt Office of the country concerned. However, it is not suggested that money should be created on a whim. That is certainly not the case under the capitalist system of debt-money creation. Careful calculations are made by all concerned, and a state seeking to control its own money-creation processes would require the banking system to account for the relationship between real wealth and money prices. The flow of buying power to individuals and the total prices of goods for sale need to be compatible. Accordingly, social credit theory argues for 'Just Price' or 'price adjustment' proposals to bring prices and quantities of goods for sale into balance. According to this notion, price is determined by the cost of consumption (using up of materials and energy) during the period of production. During production money flows to consumers. However, at the point of sale the flow of goods onto the market may not be matched by the flow of money. Eliminating the boom and slump of the bankers' debt system, price adjustment regulates the flow of buying power in relation to production, ensuring that the total spendable incomes equal total retail prices.

Although the proposal to convert National Debt into National Credit, along with other social credit concepts were explored by economists still wedded to the capitalist system such as G.D.H. Cole and James Meade, a great deal of further research on alternatives to capitalist financing remains to be undertaken. The current financial system is introducing constant change on a massive scale, impacting on the everyday lives of people across the globe, affecting work practices, built environments and the wild and domesticated flora and fauna upon which all human life depends. In this climate, regulating the regulator of economic activity – money – through a just-price mechanism appears more rational than continuing with capitalism-as-we-know-it.

Reclaiming the common cultural inheritance

Veblen, Douglas and other theorists in the early decades of the twentieth century were aware that the common cultural inheritance of skills, knowledge and technology, produced communally through past generations, was capable of providing a sufficiency for all. The resources and techniques necessary to enable the community as a whole to provide the good life for all, without waste of effort or resources, already existed, as demonstrated by the vast quantities of production destroyed in the conduct of World War I. Subsequently, during the Depression years, the dumping of food and other consumer goods in order to maintain price levels was documented in social credit literature (see Hutchinson and Burkitt, 1997: 151–5). The Depression years saw newspaper headlines declaring 'Herring glut threatens starvation', 'France welcomes mildew', 'Hurricane helps sugar position' and 'International plan for destruction of cocoa' (see Hargrave, 1945 for details). As early environmentalists, the guild socialists argued that resources could be mobilised to less wasteful ends, given the political will unhampered by capitalist economic theorising.

Veblen noted the fundamental flaw in emerging economic theory, that the 'natural-rights' of ownership was the product of past labour of the owner.

> This natural-rights theory of property makes the creative effort of an isolated, self-sufficing individual the basis of the ownership vested in him. In doing so it overlooks the fact that there is no isolated, self-sufficing individual. All production is, in fact, a production in and by the help of the community, and all wealth is such only in society. ... Production takes place only in society – only through the co-operation of an industrial community. This industrial community may be large or small ... but it always comprises a group large enough to contain and transmit the traditions, tools, technical knowledge, and usages without which there can be no industrial organisation and no economic relation of individuals to one another or to their environment. ... There can be no production without technical knowledge; hence no accumulation and no wealth to be owned, in severalty or otherwise. And there is no technical knowledge apart from an industrial community. Since there is no individual production and no individual productivity, the natural-rights preconception ... reduces itself to absurdity, even under the logic of its own assumptions. (Veblen, 1998: 33–4)

In short, wealth is produced communally. Any economic theory allocating economic rights on grounds of individual productivity is patent nonsense. Fundamentally opposed to private exploitation of labour and the other means of production, social credit theory echoed Veblen's observations. Douglas had great faith in the ability of modern technology to provide sufficiency while removing the necessity for onerous routine tasks. In a social credit economy exploitation of the many by the few would become a thing of the past. In Douglas' view, technological development was created by the community as a whole, and arose out of the common cultural inheritance. Like Veblen, Douglas held that there were virtually no rights to be assigned to individuals on the basis of their *individual* contribution to the productive process. Furthermore, the introduction of labour-saving machines reduced the demand for labour, rendering wage labour redundant. The answer was not to create further productive work for those displaced, churning out a mass of unnecessary fashion objects and armaments. The aim should be to create an income for all from a system of production designed to provide profit for profiteers claiming individual rights over the common cultural inheritance of designs, processes and intellectual property. The way forward was to provide all citizens with the inalienable right to an income, a national dividend, independent of work status, on the basis of advances in technology based on the cultural heritage held in common.

The utility of work versus the disutility of labour

Following Marx, the guild socialists observed that under capitalism workers had no control over the management and conditions of production and were denied ownership of the product of their industry. Furthermore, they lived under perpetual economic insecurity, dependent upon an employer for wages. The availability of wages was determined by changing profitability of production for their employers in terms of changing technology and demand. They viewed trade unions, operating within the national legislative framework but with autonomy at local level, as the basis of the post-capitalist productive unit. The locally controlled productive unit of an industry would offer workers at all levels control over the product of their labour, an income regardless of employment status, and control over production.

In his introduction to William Morris' selected works, Cole drew attention to Morris' belief that:

the ordinary things men made ought to be so made as to be a 'joy to the maker as to the user,' and that where most men spent their working days joylessly making ugly things, the death of civilisation was at hand. (Morris, 1944: xvii)

The socialism of Morris like that of Marx was very different from the labourism which sought to keep the workers in waged labour while assuming that labour would be unpleasant and unwanted under employment relations. Employment as disutility versus leisure as utility perhaps overstates the position. If engaging in work were a truly voluntary choice (which would be possible if the circumstances of life were generally secure and did not lead to threats about the implications of *not* engaging in work), then work could assume aspects which were perceived as unpleasant in an immediate sense yet acceptable given that the work of transformation is a valued activity leading to highly desired outcomes. Work which contained a combination of unpleasant and pleasant aspects could be chosen and freely engaged in. Thus, a stress on the utility of work does not deny the disutility of work but insists on the person involved agreeing on the basic purposes and the acceptability of *work as a means* to achieve them. Such a view is holistic and does not separate a person's time as a happy consumer from their time as an unhappy employee. Work, in this holistic sense of meaningful transformative activity, is usually done with other people and one can engage in a discussion about improving the conditions of work. This is so regardless of whether we refer to paid or unpaid work. This view of the acceptable conditions of work has much in common with the ideal of Habermas and the Frankfurt School who said that under conditions of social and economic inequality persons can hardly even recognise, much less easily enunciate, their own true interests.

A society in which members are equally regarded, fundamentally economically secure, and well represented politically is a society in which opinions about how work should be done (and should be changing) can be democratically exchanged in a constructive atmosphere. Economic democracy is a *pre-condition* for people engaging in truly productive work. Otherwise their 'productive' work remains a means to their own oppression and the suppression of their desires. Furthermore, the guild socialist definition of an 'industry' extended far beyond that of manufacturing, to include health, education, farming and many other necessary elements of the social or 'real-wealth' economy, the value and significance (and even existence) of which are ignored by capitalist economic agents in their search for financial profitability (Hutchinson and Burkitt, 1997: 18–22). For guild socialists such as Penty this would include the arts, the professions and agriculture in the realm of 'work' (Penty, 1921). A holistic approach to the nature of work would break down the association of the arts, politics and other activities with the 'Leisure Class' as identified by Veblen.

Personal income and the utility of labour

Veblen's dismissal of the inherent disutility of labour was echoed throughout social credit literature. Douglas, for example, highlighted the absurdity of the notion that the provision of full employment would end starvation and poverty. The poor and dispossessed need an *income*, or access to the means of subsistence, not waged labour in the capitalist production system. As far back as 1919 Douglas noted that demands for a minimum wage and the right to full employment were based on the notion that labour was a commodity to be bought and sold (Hutchinson and Burkitt, 1997: 65). However, proposals for a national dividend payable to all citizens regardless of other income sources, and not funded by taxation, remained incomprehensible within mainstream economic orthodoxy.

Proponents of economic liberalism cite Smith (1776), who demonstrated in *The Wealth of Nations* that state intervention tended to distort the self-corrective mechanisms of a competitive market that comprised small buyers and sellers each too small to influence individually the market price of commodities exchanged. Significantly, although labour was theorised as a factor of production, i.e. as a commodity, lifelong total dependence upon a money wage from industrial/commercial employment was most uncommon in Smith's time. Labouring families continued to emerge from the countryside, retaining some links with the land and its subsistence economy. Therefore, economic theorists could presuppose the existence of a reservoir of labour which may be 'called onto the market' according to the demands of capital. Despite Keynes' influence, neo-classical theory has yet to address comprehensively the phenomenon of involuntary unemployment, i.e. the failure of income distribution due to the denial of access to land-based subsistence and its effects in depressing wage rates. Economic liberals continue to ignore the powerlessness of landless labour and the necessity for welfare provision to compensate for the appropriation of land from village communities. Esping-Anderson (1996) demonstrated that post-1945 attempts in Sweden to decommodify labour in order to establish a genuinely 'free' supply of labour met resistance from both domestic and global capital. 'Workfare' and 'welfare to work' programmes reflect the power of international capitalism to demand labour in return for an income. In practice, income as reward for 'disutility' remains an empty concept under conditions of enforced employment indistinguishable from wage slavery.

Pure disutility of labour belongs to a slave state. Where the master/employer owns the means of production, and the labourers are being denied access to land, tools, skills and time, a simple reward and punishment system may apply. Neo-classical theory operates on an extension to this system, regarding 'labour' as the factor/wage-slave to be bought and sold as a commodity. In the 'instrumental' view of work, labour 'necessarily painful, is a means to an end, considered to be desirable or pleasurable, such as earning money, which in turn is a means to other desirable ends, like buying goods or gaining leisure' (Lee, 1989: 231). Within this system labour is rewarded by a basket of commodities which, beyond a basic subsistence minimum, are 'wants' artificially stimulated by the system (Hodgson, 1988: 20). Above a certain minimum income higher wage rates may draw forth an increased supply of labour resulting in a rising supply schedule, as the textbook model suggests. However, at an increased wage rate the worker enjoys a greater income for any given number of hours expended. If this income exceeds the substitution effect (of more highly remunerated labour for leisure), a backward-sloping supply function for labour will occur. In these circumstances workers would logically exercise their freedom to acquire leisure by reducing the number of hours worked. The possibility of reverse labour supply schedules should, in theory, preclude the existence of a determinate equilibrium wage. This indeterminacy destroys the apparent precision of the neo-classical income distribution theory. Furthermore, as Juliet Schor (1991) reminded us, under capitalism the ability of labour to vary its effort in response to fluctuations in its price, on the model implied by orthodox economic theory, is limited by the institutional restraints imposed by 'free market' capital. The effective choice for workers is usually between undertaking longer hours or leaving the labour market completely to face unemployment and total income loss.

In reality financial reward is one factor among many drawing 'labour' onto the market. Price is not the sole, or even the dominant, factor. Consequently, the supply schedule for labour may well run horizontally or even in reverse. There is no evidence that it *must* slope upwards and so intersect with the demand curve in line with mainstream general equilibrium theory. Once labour is conceptualised as utility, the notion of a unique, determinate, labour-market equilibrium ceases to retain its theoretical credibility. Furthermore, as Wright and Smye (1997) demonstrate, individualism and competition may create an abusive environment in the workplace. Competition between colleagues, the 'blaming culture', long hours, irregular hours and stress all stifle initiative. Such conditions are counterproductive, both for the firm and the employee. Furthermore, as Wright and Smye observe, higher salaries fail to compensate for such abuse. In terms of job security and satisfaction it is in an employee's interests to seek out a co-operative working environment, if necessary accepting a lower salary.

Once the theoretical bond between money income and work, crucial to mainstream economic theory, is broken, orthodoxy must be rejected as implausible and impractical. It then becomes necessary to examine credible alternatives, such as those encapsulated in the social credit literature, to unite coherent theory with sound practice, facilitating an economy capable of developing useful, effective and good work. Social credit can encompass the vision of an end to wage-slave labour with a view to creating a sufficiency of the means of subsistence. Social credit offers an enhanced dignity of labour and the possibility of abolishing the drive to wasteful and ecologically destructive economic growth. It distinguishes between production of wealth and production of waste. However financially profitable the latter might be, however much employment it might create, its disutility to the community can be analysed under so-called 'alternative' socialist theorising (Hutchinson and Burkitt, 1997: 65–9).

Sufficiency and economic democracy

The concept of 'sufficiency' is particularly difficult to understand when coming from a capitalist perspective. Capitalism operates on the ingrained assumption that value can be measured in terms of 'more' or 'less', coupled with the belief that money provides a measure of value free from subjective personal opinions. Douglas argued that to accept money as the measure of value was in itself a matter of subjective personal opinion, demonstrating that wasteful use of human time, depreciation of machinery and the degradation of material resources are invariably accounted as *additions* in terms of national accounting under capitalism (Hutchinson and Burkitt, 1997: 49, 62–5). Car accidents, oil spills and other disasters are accounted as *additions* to GDP (a form of accounting introduced around the time of World War II; the concept of GDP/GNP accounting may, ironically, have been derived from Douglas' work) since the use of emergency services, insurance claims, replacement of damaged property and clean-up operations all register as positives in terms of money accounting.

At the start of the twenty-first century, a bushel of corn sells in Canada for less than $4, while a bushel of cornflakes sells for $133. In capitalist accounting terms, the cornflakes have been processed, packaged, transported, stored and retailed, adding money value along the way. It is dubious, to say the least, whether the nutritional value added, even accounting for convenience, is anywhere near that measured in money terms. The degradation of the environment and disutilities of labour involved in the total sum of processes taking the product from cradle to table and disposal may well result in an overall negative rise in value *even in money terms*. This capitalism does not do. We take a further example, that of apples and processed apple sauce. Apples grow well throughout the UK. It takes a few seconds to core an apple and pop it next to the roast in the oven. Within minutes the skin can be peeled away (and composted, no waste packaging to dispose of) leaving a delicious, flavoursome apple sauce to go straight onto the table. Yet, at the height of the apple harvest and during the following months during which apples are easily stored fresh, supermarket shelves display apple sauce in jars and packets of powder to be reconstituted. Not only have these apples been stored and transported, often across the world, but the processes involved reduce flavour, convenience and nutritional value at the point of consumption. Yet by 'a process of arithmetical leg-erdemain known as cost accounting the value of the original matter ... is increased' by these operations by a sum equal to their total financial costs (Douglas quoted in Hutchinson, 1998: 133).

The core argument of the guild socialist/social credit perspective is that the goods, services and all the real wealth of society is created in common by individuals acting as co-operative members of society. Money – society's credit – regulates access to the wealth society produces. Guild socialists argued that 'absentee landlords', to use Veblenian terminology, were unnecessary to the production of the wealth and welfare required by society. A critique of the notion that

under capitalism finance drives the productive process, simultaneously determining incomes and production, was the central theme
of Douglas' social credit theory. He argued that there can be no pre-
sumption that change in pursuit of private financial profit will
necessarily result in an increase in general welfare; social wealth will
only be created by socially created and directed credit. While
Douglas had much in common with guild socialism, he had some
differences, particularly his faith in machines. His proposals for an
unearned income alienated him from the Fabians and the trade
union movement. His suggestion that bankers conspire against
society as a whole made him an easy target for ridicule or for the use
of his ideas in ways that betrayed their guild socialist origins. Nevertheless, his penetrating analysis of capitalist economics continues
to provide the basis for a non-equilibrium economics of sufficiency
and sustainability.

Social credit addresses the relationship between the individual and
society as represented by money/credit. From the social credit
analysis flows an awareness that the creation of a meaningful
political democracy awaits economic democracy. Common
ownership is a human right. It is one which must be exercised in
conjunction with the wider community to which people are
accountable. One of the problems in comprehending the social
credit conceptualisation of the economy is the difficulty of eradi-
cating the deep-seated notion that productive work is inextricably
linked to the acquisition of a money income. Social credit provides
a possible route towards the replacement of global capitalist
oppression with a socially and ecologically sustainable socialism.
However, no technical 'reform' can replace the need to study and
research the political economy in all its aspects in order for it to be
governed and regulated by an informed citizenry.

The right to an unearned income for all is modelled on the notion
of payments to owners of capital. It represents a universal right to a
share in the proceeds of the common cultural inheritance. A
national dividend payable to all would introduce a truly free market
in labour. With a secure income, albeit a modest one, workers can
negotiate the terms on which their labour is sold. Furthermore, if
the model of the Draft Mining Scheme is followed, work in industry
and agriculture ceases to be undertaken on the orders of an absentee
owner interested only in financial profitability. It is the *producers*
who determine the terms of their own participation in the
productive process.

In the last decades of the twentieth century ecological and feminist economics have raised issues about the negative impact and unfair allocation of waged work. Feminist economics has been concerned with the inequalities of income, power and status of socio-economic minorities including women, the sick, elderly and disabled and those discriminated against on grounds of race or creed. Within the theoretical framework of mainstream economics there is no basis for arguing for discrimination in favour of so-called 'minorities' and those with *de facto* low income, status and power. Equally, there is no economic basis for arguing that people should not have to do dangerous and unnecessary work in order to earn an income. However, payment of a secure income coupled with the changed work environment implied in the Draft Mining Scheme offers the capacity to overcome many of the problems highlighted by contemporary feminist and ecological economists. This was recognised by social credit writers in the first decades of the twentieth century. They wrote of a 'birthright income' based upon the productive capacity of the community and offering 'economic independence and freedom' to all. Women would no longer face the stark choice of dependence upon a male breadwinner or accepting wage slavery in competition with men. With a secure income all members of the community could determine the terms upon which they participate in 'economic' activities (Hutchinson, 1995: 38).

8 New Critiques: Green Economics and Feminist Economics

It seemed by the late twentieth century that the critique of the capitalist market system, and particularly the role of money at its heart, had been silenced for good. The long period of post-war reconstruction, the political eclipse of the labour movement, the global reach of the capitalist market and the long stock market boom seemed to show that liberal capitalism signalled the 'end of history' (Fukuyama, 1992). Capitalism was as good as it was going to get. Problems such as the financial crises in Mexico, Russia or Asia were dismissed as inevitable hiccups, nothing the IMF could not solve. Even when the Japanese economy lay down and went to sleep and the new technology bubble burst, economic theory and policy ploughed on regardless. Although the global market economy seemed to be sweeping all before it there were glaring problems that it could not meet or control. The first was the impact of industrial and commercial expansion on the environment. The second was the marginal socio-economic position of many families, communities and countries particularly in terms of health and poverty. The third was the destruction of local provisioning systems without any alternative market mechanisms taking their place. The old critiques may have been scorned and silenced but new critiques and new versions of old critiques were emerging. In particular, arguments from greens and feminists pointed to the inadequacy of money/market systems in embracing the damage to the environment and the lives and work of women.

Ecology and economics

One of the earliest links between ecology and economics was made by the Scottish scientist Frederick Soddy (Alier, 1987; Merricks, 1996). He argued that all life depended upon energy, and human activities were no exception. Soddy was concerned that the exploitation of fossil fuel would result in future impoverishment when supplies ran out. Soddy also condemned the commercial use of science, arguing that it should be seen as 'communistic in its inheritance and communistic in the spirit of its application' (quoted in Merricks, 1996: 69). In effect, he argued for a steady-state economy and for monetary reform as a solution to the destructiveness of the money-based market system. Soddy claimed that his economic thinking derived entirely from his scientific analysis of physical systems, but he had read Silvio Gesell, Arthur Kitson, Keynes, Douglas and Orage (Merricks, 1996: 62). For Soddy, people were so besotted with 'token-money' and the 'virtual wealth' of paper money that they did not pay attention to the real damage and poverty that surrounded them. Like Douglas, Soddy's ideas were rejected by the Labour Party. As Merricks points out, Soddy's politics continually shifted and changed but he did not join any other political group as his main concerns were environmental. He did, however, forsee war as an outcome of the economic crises of the 1930s.

Despite the concerns of scientists such as Soddy, the dynamism of post-war reconstruction and the central role of the US seemed to offer a future of limitless progress. The expansion would be led by science, technology and business. In 1949 President Truman launched the campaign for development, or rather against underdevelopment. 'Development' (or 'maldevelopment' as Shiva has called it (1988)) was to bring the whole world into the commercial and industrial age on the US model. This process continued relatively unchallenged, particularly on environmental grounds, until the 1960s when the possible consequences of the introduction of noxious chemicals into the environment was raised by Rachel Carson (1962), the issue of population and carrying capacity by Ehrlich (1968) and Hardin (1968), the disjunction between environmental and economic systems by Georgescu-Roegen (1971) and Daly (1973) and the capacity of the environment to meet human needs by an industry-sponsored MIT study (Meadows *et al.*, 1972).

The concerns raised by Rachel Carson have continued apace as people have become increasingly disturbed by the contamination of the environment and food sources. A market response has been a growth in organic food markets and 'natural' products generally. However, green consumerism, although sometimes powerful as in the case of the use of CFCs or GM foods in the UK, is only a choice for those who already have sufficient economic resources to affect the market or those who have the time and knowledge to search out appropriate products. The problem of toxicity is one of political ecology, that is, the social distribution of ecological goods and bads. Poorer people have less choice about the food they eat or the conditions in which they live. A particular example is the disposal of toxic waste in the US in poor, Black areas (Bullard, 1990; Hofrichter, 1993). This has led to a general concern about environmental justice and environmental racism, where poor and non-white communities not only suffer more from environmental problems but are targeted by environmental policies that adopt a Malthusian approach. Exclusionist policies are central to Hardin's idea of a 'lifeboat' ethic where each country/community would calculate the population-carrying capacity of their region and prevent people from climbing on board. It is not hard to imagine who would be in the boat and who in the water.

Apart from the racist implications, while the lifeboat analogy might have made sense for a resource-rich country like the US with a low population density, it had little to offer the crowded countries of Europe who draw their resources from around the world. The rather simplistic notion of 'too many people' directed at the youthful and dynamic populations of the 'Third World' has been tempered by an increased awareness of the problem of global inequalities and the need to address consumption in the rich, population-stable states with their massive global ecological footprints (Wackernagel and Rees, 1996). There is little sign, however, of a willingness on the part of governments in the richer countries to address seriously the problem of consumption. In the case of the US Bush administration there has been a refusal to accept any limits on consumption of carbon.

Despite the failures of subsequent governments to address adequately the issues it raised, the Limits to Growth study (Meadows *et al.*, 1972) was a landmark challenge to the optimistic assumptions of post-war industrialism. The study carried out a computer projection of human population, agricultural production, natural resources, industrial production and pollution. It concluded that given 'growth trends in world population, industrialisation, pollution, food production and resource depletion the limits to growth on this planet will be reached within the next 100 years' (1972: 24). These conclusions have led to considerable technical debate from those who see such assumptions as far too pessimistic, such as Julian Simon (Simon and Kahn, 1984) to those such as Tom Athanasiou who see evidence of the Limits to Growth being realistic and perhaps even underestimating the levels of soil erosion (1997: 63). Athanasiou also points out that a growth rate of 3 per cent doubles production in 25 years, while David Booth argues that 'the forces driving economic growth are also driving environmental change' (1998: 170). Despite increasing concern about pressure on the environment, finance-driven economic growth is still seen as a solution to the main policy issues of the age. Poverty is to be solved by expanding the cake rather than confronting the political problem of the redistribution of wealth. Unemployment is to be solved by more jobs rather than questioning the need to make guns to eat bread. Population growth is not to be resolved by directly empowering women to give them control over their own bodies, but by the 'economic empowerment' of women as a by-product of growth and development.

Herman Daly and Nicholas Georgescu-Roegen both challenged the growth model at the heart of economic theorising and particularly aimed their critiques at the circular flow model. They argue that the circular flow model assumes a closed system and ignores the fact that environmental resources, particularly energy, operate on entropic principles. Drawing on the laws of thermodynamics they argue that the first law points to the absolute scarcity of matter in that it can neither be created nor destroyed, while the second law shows that energy moves in an entropic direction. So, while the sum total of matter remains fixed and can be reassembled into new forms, the energy used in the process loses a proportion to entropy, that is to an unusable state. While the circular flow model assumes perpetual motion, energy is moving in a linear direction. Neither growth nor perpetual motion are sustainable in the long run. Even maximal environmental efficiency in production will not overcome the problem of entropy. Daly also questions the optimistic assumption that human technology can replace or repair, or even take over from natural capital, by replacing it with 'man-made capital' (2001a: 19). For Daly, the aim must be a steady-state economy which has as far as possible a circular metabolism – that is, it aims to re-use and re-circulate resources. However this will only minimise, not overcome, entropy. The question then remains whether a debt-based capitalist market economy can operate on steady-state principles. Can capitalised and debt-based money systems exist without growth?

Environmental or ecological economics?

A starting point for all green economics is that existing industrial economic systems (capitalist or state socialist) have not taken account of ecological resources or ecological damage. Natural resources are treated as a free good which only gain a price when they are owned and/or used by humans. The assumption behind this approach is that the natural world is unlimited or that natural resource shortages will be overcome if necessary by human ingenuity. Even where the damage that human activities do to the environment is acknowledged, the inability of the environment to absorb the outcomes of human activity is not costed into production. Any loss of, or damage to, the environment is externalised by the money economy, that is, it is not taken into account in calculating the price of goods or the costs of production.

A broad distinction can be made between environmental and ecological economics, although nomenclature is often very loosely used. Environmental economics in general addresses the ecological issue from within a framework of conventional economics, whereas ecological economists take a more critical position. However, Herman Daly, a founding editor of the journal *Ecological Economics*, who criticises mainstream economic theories of circular flow and growth still uses terms such as 'natural capital' drawn from mainstream economic rhetoric. Natural capital is widely used to describe the regenerative and assimilative capacities of the ecosystem over time as well as the body of existing resources. The most reformist of environmental economists argue that economic systems can be adjusted to take account of environmental costs and values in the depletion of 'natural capital'. The capitalist economy, it is argued, can internalise environmental externalities, the market can become environmentally wise. A variety of solutions are offered from environmental accounting, assessments and audits to various proposals for green taxes or pollution permits. These ideas have been put forward most recently in Kyoto, but earlier attempts to adopt environmental accounting systems at the international level fizzled out because of the pressures of globalisation (Daly, 2001b: 31). Even if implemented, the Kyoto proposals would only cut emissions by 2 per cent at best over ten years as opposed to the 60–80 per cent that is needed.

Daly points to the way that international trade does not even follow the correct rules of accountancy. For primary producers the exploitation of their stores of resources is treated entirely as income rather than as depreciation of capital. For most countries of the world, insolvency beckons on this basis, because natural resources are being rapidly diminished. The powerlessness of primary producers was illustrated in mid 2001 when Indonesia, in an attempt to boost its national income, expanded export of tropical timber. This caused a collapse in world prices such that Indonesia was forced to increase output even further to keep up income. Most of this precious wood ended up pulped into paper. Daly does, however, follow conventional environmental economics in arguing for resource taxation. Like many green economists he criticises taxes on people as encouraging the move to mechanisation and therefore resource inefficiency. He argues that energy or throughput taxes would encourage more efficient use and the benefit would go to the community as a whole. However, this model still leaves the market supreme. Efficiency, therefore, is only in market terms, not based in use values. For example, development rights in resources would go to the highest bidder rather than to the local community without assets. Also, taxation would not stop resource use. Daly himself points to the problem of globalisation where the disembedding of the global economy means that the main regulatory level, the state, is disempowered. In the face of the 'race to the bottom' any tax or regulatory law would be met with a withdrawal of capital to an easier target.

James Robertson, while advocating eco-taxes, is aware of their regressiveness (2001). Eco-taxes work their way through to the whole population and therefore are paid equally by the poor and the rich. To overcome this problem Robertson advocates a resource-tax-funded basic income that would compensate those with lower incomes. He acknowledges the irony that, if the eco-taxes are successful in reducing pollution, the payment of a basic income may be undermined. However, he assumes by this stage that there will be a 'people-centred society' which is 'less employment centred and state-centred' (2001: 82). It is unclear if this is still to be a basically capitalist market economy. Certainly the taxation base means a re-circulation of earned income and not an income based on social credit. Like many green economists and new economics theorists he sees the globalised market as somehow fading into the background and becoming irrelevant as small-scale local economies develop. Equally Daly, despite his criticism of conventional economic thought, still sees (regulated) market mechanisms as having a role and has no solution at all to the issue of wage labour: 'as for unemployment, I'm not sure I know the answer to that one, maybe a public sector employer of last resort, ecological tax reform raising resource prices, job sharing, various things' (2001a: 26).

For Canadian ecologist William Rees the looming crises in the ecosystem present

> an opportunity for humanity to correct an historical error and develop a gentler, more balanced and stable relationship with the natural world. This view also raises moral considerations such as the need in a limited world for more equitable sharing of the world's resources. (quoted in Carley and Christie, 2000: 27)

Given the dynamics of global capitalism, it is highly unlikely that it will either fade away or take on its moral responsibilities. As Michael Jacobs has argued, the problem with market economies is both power and money. He sees the ecological degradation of the environment in market economies as resulting from the invisible elbow (1991: 25) rather than the invisible hand. Elbows can inadvertently knock things over, but they can also be used to knock people and environments out of the way. If the economic externalisation of environmental damage is a sin of omission, then it may be possible to incorporate it; if it is a sin of commission, the problems become more intractable. As Booth has argued, in the framework of a capitalist economy where the aim is economic gain, there is every incentive to externalise costs as 'gain-seeking promotes cost externalisation' (1998: 17). Following Schumpeter's notion of creative destruction, he argues that each new generation of industry produces new environmental problems. Although some ageing industries will respond to regulative efforts, the urge to dynamic growth and the recirculation of capital in new ventures continually produces new externalised social and environmental consequences.

Paul Ekins, an early advocate of green economics, hovers between a radical and a reformist perspective on whether the market could be reformed. Certainly, for Ekins sustainability will not be achieved as a (by-)product of economic optimality and cannot be left to the wisdom of commercial enterprises or the logic of the market. The market system can only continue if

> a combination of technical change and efficient public policy begins to deliver both economic growth and improvements in environmental performance such that ... disturbing environmental trends ... become less threatening ... If not, then those who continue to insist that the environmental will impose its own,

perhaps catastrophic limits to growth ... may well be proved right. (2000: 326)

Jacobs argues that a distinction must be drawn between financial growth and growth in the real economy. For him it should be possible to get more money out of less production, through efficiency and better-directed production to meet need (1991: 61). A similar approach is taken by those who argue for 'factor four', to do twice as much with half the resources (Weisacker *et al.*, 1997). This may be possible, but it would not be a capitalist economy following the logic of money-capital accumulation.

Both ecological and environmental economics have shown that the money-valuing process within the market is inadequate in environmental terms. The problem for any solution that does not challenge the money/market system is that it leaves the role of money as a measure of value in place. Since all decision-making involves some assessment of costs and benefits, however intuitive, it has proved tempting to accept the 'contingent valuation' notion that a money value can be placed upon non-traded facilities such as silence, clean air, water, beauty and so on. Although, in theory, placing a notional money value on factors outside the money economy may seem to aid decision-making, these tools are used by advocates of projects likely to be opposed on non-economic grounds as a means to overcome opposition (Hutchinson and Hutchinson, 1997: 228–30). Economic solutions such as cost–benefit analysis, contingent evaluation or eco-taxes assume that assessment can be made in money terms or at least claims that there can be a commensurate measure of value (Jacobs, 1991). The problem is that there may be no way of achieving a common measure of value between monetary or consumption benefit in the current time period and the consequences of resource loss for the future. For Booth pollution permits or other resource-exploitative rights would seem to make the assumption that payment in economic (read money) terms allows the moral right of destructive behaviour (1998: 18). This leads to the problem of incommensurability that has been identified by ecological economists (Alier, 1987). As Jacobs argues:

The incommensurable nature of environmental and other non-marketed values (such as human life, community, culture and so on) makes the whole process futile – if not actually dangerous. (1991: 202)

For Teresa Brennan a market system can never incorporate sustainability, as its whole functioning requires the exploitation of surplus value from the environment. She argues that profitability depends on the range and speed of circulation and therefore 'the essential contradiction in production is between the reproduction time of natural energy and the time or speed of exchange for profit' (1997: 177).

Brennan sees the role of the environment in much the same way that Marx traced surplus value to labour but with worse consequences, arguing that in terms of their creation of surplus value, 'there are no real grounds for separating labour-power from other natural substances' (1997: 179). While capitalism does pay the minimum for the reproduction of labour through the wages paid to the worker for her/his labour-power, it does not, and cannot, pay for the environment, because the reproduction of the environment is beyond price. What, for example, is the cost of the replacement of non-renewable fossil fuels laid down millions of years ago? What is the replacement cost of pure groundwater when the aquifers are contaminated? For Brennan, 'nature is the source of all value, and ultimately of all energy, but the inherent dynamic of capital is to diminish this value and this energy in favour of time and technology' (1997: 179).

Funtowicz and Ravetz see ecology as the analysis of complex emergent systems and therefore beyond costing or explanation (1994). Mellor argues that the embeddedness of humanity in an interactive environment means that the outcomes of human activities are always uncertain, even though the environment may be knowable and malleable in parts (Mellor, 1997a). Uncertainty and incommensurability do not mean that choices are not made (do we preserve the forest or build the highway?), but these cannot be made on a money-value basis. This is why Ellie Perkins has argued for a discourse-based evaluation, where people can discuss and debate decisions drawing on a range of criteria (2001). For Jacobs 'achieving the Green Economy will not ultimately prove a question of economics' (1991: 253). It will be a social, aesthetic or moral question, a politics of consumption (Jacobs, 1991) or a politics of nature (Mellor, 1997a).

The capitalist dynamic lies at the base of the push for post-war 'development' and more recently for globalisation (Hines, 2000). As Adams has argued, 'the green alternative ... issues a challenge to the very structures and assumptions of development' (Adams, 1993: 200). In a debt-based money economy where wealth is defined primarily in privatised production terms, there is little hope that governments can ever be in a position to challenge the dominance of corporations (Monbiot, 2000). As O'Connor (1973) pointed out, a state that requires capitalist economic growth to maintain the resources it needs to manage capitalism, particularly when the latter is in crisis, is doomed to failure. O'Connor argues that capitalism in face of the environmental consequences of its actions faces a 'second contradiction'. It is destroying the material (social and environmental) conditions of its own existence (1988). However, unlike the workers of the first contradiction who are predicted to take over control of the means of production, distribution and exchange, by the time capitalism has been destroyed by the second contradiction, the conditions for human existence may be destroyed beyond repair. Whole areas of material renewal and social co-operation that underpin the economy are ignored as 'non-economic' factors until they have a commercial impact. This is not wise use of resources since, by the time a problem affects the formal economy, it is too late. Global warming, loss of species diversity, soil erosion, death of coral reefs, holes in the ozone layer, melting of ice caps, resource wars over water and land, rising asthma and pollution levels, multiple increases in childhood diabetes and other environment-related diseases, and a host of other interlinked causes for concern, have each been repeatedly dismissed. They are seen as (a) not really happening, (b) normal, (c) beyond human control or (d) nothing to do with economic activity. Despite decades of documentation of causes for concern, economics-as-we-know-it provides few clues as to likely causes, and even fewer routes to sustainable solutions.

Ecology and food provisioning: from soil cultivation to soil mining

Debates around the modern economy have tended to focus on the manufacture of goods, services and consumption. Food provisioning through agriculture and the sustainability of the land has been marginalised. This ignores the fact that, however sophisticated a society might appear, produce from the land remains essential to maintain human existence. Traditional farming methods in all non-industrialised economies take account of the necessity to maintain the fertility of their land, albeit in very different ways. In Africa, for example, slash-and-burn agriculture was generally derided by European expatriates, although it was an effective means to rekindle fertility on thin soils. Agribusiness farming invariably disrupts natural cycles, leading in the long term to degradation of the resources essential to human life. Failing to replenish the earth, it removes matter from the land to supply raw materials, creating wastes in distant places. As Harriett Friedmann explains, commercial farming

> turns natural substances (from anywhere) into 'resources,' and divides multiple products into commodities (to be sold anywhere) and 'wastes' (with no good place to go). Resources, or inputs, are external to the linear material process of industry, and the market that connects raw material regions with industrial regions cannot link either one to living cycles. Resources must be depleted; wastes cannot be absorbed. (Friedmann, 2000: 488)

Sustainable agriculture is based on the principle of 'returns' to land, sea and air. It contrasts starkly with globalised agribusiness that is based on commercial cycles capable merely of diminishing returns – staved off, in the short term, by petrochemical additives leading in turn to pesticide, fertiliser and herbicide poisoning of ecosystems, with loss of species diversity. Friedmann (2000) explores the relationship between commercial exploitation of the soils and cultivation of natural resources. 'Post-animal humans appear to eat commodities rather than other living beings. Our need appears to be less food than money' (Friedmann, 2000: 481).

The temptation to convert the human relationship with the land and its peoples into a money relationship is not new, dating from at least biblical times (see, for example, Amos 8: 4–7). However, capitalism has successfully overcome dissent to its extermination of all but money values by devaluing local and home production of the basic necessities of all aspects of life. Opposition to agribusiness has often been portrayed as mistaken nostalgia for a non-existent golden age or a perverse refusal to acknowledge the reality of 'progress'. Meanwhile excellent works on the disadvantages of commercialisation of agriculture have been systematically silenced (Hutchinson, 1998).

Friedmann provides a refreshing view of the heritage of good farming and sustainable use of the land, particularly in Europe (2000: 486–8). She observes that peasant farming systems evolved according to local climate and local configurations of soils and water. In general they involve interdependence of cultivated plant and animal species so as to preserve a self-renewing agronomy based on holistic indigenous knowledge systems. It is noteworthy that, while within the English-speaking world the term 'peasant' connotes poverty and ignorance, elsewhere it normally denotes independence from wage labour. Friedmann points to the English High Farming practice of using the four-crop rotation of wheat, turnip, barley and clover which enabled soil fertility to be maintained and improved without recourse to petrochemical fertilisers or pest controls. Evolving from peasant agriculture of the medieval three-field system, the High Farmer sought to compensate for wheat output through animal manure derived from winter forage crops, the growth of which added nutrients to the soil. Nightly enclosure of sheep in moveable folds (fences) brought nutrients grazed from uncultivated land to the cultivated fields. Farmers achieved biological pest control through experience of different rotations (Friedmann, 2000: 490). High Farming was an early form of capitalised agriculture which combined ecological sustainability with social inequity. It was superseded by the rise of full-scale commercial farming in the New Worlds.

Unlike the European countries from which its colonisers originated, the North American continental farming tradition did not emerge from peasant agriculture. From the outset, plantation cropping was designed to maximise financial returns so that agricultural supplies and everyday necessities could be bought in wherever possible. The fertile soils of the prairies were stripped of the herds of buffalo, then of the tough prairie grasses which together created a rich soil environment. As 'exotic' grains were imported for bread-making, and European cattle displaced the buffalo, the soils continued to yield crops for export to urban centres and for overseas trade until the folly of abstracting without return resulted in the dustbowls of the 1930s. Production of sugar, cotton and other mono-cultured plantation crops continues to result in similar breakdowns in soil composition, and hence fertility. As a result of the introduction of agribusiness farming, the replacement of human and animal labour by tractors, harvesters and other fossil-fuel-driven machinery and the separation of grain cultivation from livestock farming, soil fertility and the ecological systems dependent upon it, created over millennia, were destroyed within two centuries, in some places within decades (Friedmann, 2000: 491–2). However, the destruction went virtually unnoticed within a social and economic system based upon the accounting values of money. In the process of the development of agribusiness farming, money for the purchase of inputs and sale of outputs replaced traditional considerations of social obligation and the maintenance of soil fertility. Prairie farming is also mining non-renewable sources of groundwater.

Unsustainable agriculture now exists on a global scale. It cuts across the cycles of the seasons, breaking the ties between the food producer and consumer while removing nutrients from one location and depositing them as wastes in another. As cycles and societies are disrupted, the all-providing global economy draws a mask over reality, creating the illusion that all will be well so long as the money economy remains strong. The Finnish eco feminist Hilkka Pietila (personal communication) has warned that global technological enhancement of agriculture to produce new varieties and multiple harvests in warmer climates for export to the north will undermine the possibility of self-sufficiency in harsher climates such as Finland. This is already leading to a worrying decline in stocks of species and varieties able to survive in northern lands. If the global system breaks down, it may well be too late to revert to local indigenous agriculture. Already, the knowledge of local wild foods and the preparation and preservation of local fresh seasonal food is disappearing.

Non-local agriculture is not only ecologically unsustainable but also chronically unhealthy. Motivated purely and simply by the profit motive, the commercialisation of farming and food production has purported to be supplying cheap food for all while in fact producing the most expensive food on earth. In money terms, agribusiness has been subsidised on a massive scale, with vast sums being spent on pharmaceuticals, environmental clean-ups and medical care to compensate for the effects of unhealthy diets of 'cheap' junk food. The production of 'cheap' chicken, turkey, pork and dairy products involves revolting cruelty, while a cocktail of chemicals is added to fruits, vegetables and grains as they progress towards the final junk-food product. Processing, packaging and transportation of food and drink over vast distances leads to further resource use and pollution.

A preference for the seemingly cheap, mass-produced foods on the supermarket shelves needs to be set against such costs as fossil fuels for farm machinery, transportation, refrigeration and wastage. Marian Van Eyk McCain calls for people's attention to be drawn to the hidden costs of the globalisation of food:

Remind them to include the environmental and health costs related to pollution, global warming, soil quality and waste

Garden Economics
(Frances Hutchinson)

Our garden in the North of England, has a plentiful summer harvest of strawberries, raspberries, black currants, red currants, gooseberries and loganberries, while autumn finds plums, pears and apples in abundance, not to mention peas, beans and other vegetables. Each planted variety has been selected as suitable to the local climate while offering excellent flavour. Together with blackberries and other wild fruits and fungi, surplus fruits and vegetables can be stored in various ways to see us through the winter. However, fresh is always best in terms of flavour and nutrition. Although there is no comparison between our produce and the anaemic apologies for fruit and vegetables sold in supermarkets (even under the label of 'organic', since the time lag from farm gate to table results in loss of flavour and nutrients) it is 'uneconomic' to sell fresh produce.

In money terms our produce is uneconomic. To pick and transport produce to a retail outlet would at those prices bring in a reward of about a penny per hour, not accounting time spent pruning and caring for the plants during the year. Fresh produce is always problematic, since it deteriorates very quickly. Seduced by the artificially bright and standardised imports, busy shoppers ask few questions about the source of the foods they place on the family table. Ironically, many protestors at third world debt, famine and injustice still purchase foods grown as cash crops, exported from lands where people are starving because they were forced off their farm lands so that cash crops could be grown. Furthermore, it is 'uneconomic' for even small residential institutions – retirement homes and retreat houses – to prepare local fresh foods. Because of adverse currency values and cheap wages, imported processed foods are cheaper than locally grown and prepared food. It is not unusual to see apples left to rot under the trees while oranges, bananas and pineapples are served on the table. As tropical fruits replace hardy northern fruits, knowledge of how to cultivate, prepare and store different varieties of apples and other produce for consumption throughout the year is fast disappearing. Total dependence upon a long chain from farm to table appears at best very unwise, not least in view of the potential for breakdown of the system. It only appears 'economic' to import food over vast distances because the farmer is paid so very little when forced to sell to huge combines.

disposal, charged back to them as taxpayers. Let them work out what those imported products (not just avocados, but milk and potatoes!) have cost in terms of the loss of local sector employment in our own countries or exploited labour in someone else's. Have them figure out the true cost, to them, of government subsidies to agribusiness or the loss of fertile land to highways and parking lots. (2001: 53)

Through this process locally grown foods are revealed as the 'true bargains'. Furthermore, money paid for them remains in the locality, 'rather than swelling the profits of some transnational corporation with rich shareholders' (ibid.).

As Jules Pretty explains in the same issue of *Resurgence* the real costs of modern farming means that 'we actually pay three times for our food – once over the counter; twice through our taxes which are used largely to support one type of farming; and thrice, to clean up the mess caused by this method' (2001: 8). Drawing on research from the University of Essex, Pretty calculates that the total externalised costs of UK agriculture (damage to air, water, soil, biodiversity and landscape; and to human health through the effects of pesticides, nitrates, micro-organisms and other disease agents including BSE) were, at a conservative estimate, £2,343 million in the UK in 1996.

One idea to support locally produced food and local employment is community supported agriculture (CSA). In the UK the 1990s saw the emergence of community support for agricultural production based upon financial and practical forms of co-operation between producers and consumers. An early introduction to CSA provided by Trauger T. Groh and Steven S.H. McFadden detailed the development of 'community supported farms and farm supported communities' (Groh and McFadden, 1990). Through these schemes local consumers take it upon themselves to support a local farm by undertaking to cover the financial risk and providing labour and other resources as members buy shares in the farm or commit themselves to purchase the entire crop in advance of harvest. Schemes take a variety of forms, creating workable economic alternatives while reconnecting local communities around the basic issue of food, helping to heal the earth and restore the environment. The subsequent history of CSA and similar projects has been well documented (Brandt, 1995; Meeker-Lowry, 1995; Norberg-Hodge *et al.*, 2000). Connection to local banking on the Douglas model would greatly strengthen the CSA concept.

A Farmers' Markets movement is also gathering pace in the UK: information on alternatives to reliance on environmentally and socially degrading food supplies is available from a variety of voluntary organisations, including the Soil Association <www.soilassociation.org> and the International Society for Ecology & Culture (ISEC) <www.isec.org.uk>. A recent publication of the latter organisation carries information on a variety of commonsense ways to reduce the human ecological footprint. A small town in Vermont, for example, has a project for transforming vegetable waste from local restaurants into eggs supplied back to the restaurants, saving the expense of landfill (Norberg-Hodge *et al.*, 2000).

Socially responsible finance

Another way in which people are seeking to ameliorate the adverse ecological (and social) effects of the capitalist market are mechanisms whereby people can direct surplus earnings towards social or environmental investment. However, ethical banks and building societies must operate according to the principles of 'sound finance'. They are subject to statutory legislation, which they must observe stringently or risk immediate closure. For example, Richard Douthwaite reports the case of a Danish community bank closed by the government following its refusal to charge interest on new loans (1996: 164–7). However, although returns on ethical investments are usually lower than conventional rates, they enable investors to support, and benefit from, increased social stability, equity, environmental sustainability and community empowerment through the investments their loans help to create. Social and ecologically responsible loans are made available in the UK through banks like Triodos which only finance businesses and enterprises that deliver social and environmental benefits, such as organic farming, renewable energy, social housing and fair trade (see ethical investment websites).

The Ecology Building Society and other similar ventures, facilitate community projects, ecologically sound building and sustainable farming projects. Further examples can be located through the Ethical Investment & Research Information Service (EIRIS). While such banks have very limited opportunity to make new money available, mainly recycling savings, they do show a large demand in society for social and ethical control over where investment is made.

Operating within the capitalist financial framework, these financial institutions are nevertheless facilitating ecologically and socially sound investment, while at the same time providing solid foundations for development of economic democracy. One problem is that the notion of social and ethical investment is being used by mainstream investment companies to describe quite limited aims. Instead of positively looking to invest in socially useful products they mainly refrain from investing in obviously harmful ones.

Women and economics: the marginalisation of women

In the same way that mainstream economics has failed to account for, and take account of, the natural environment, it has also marginalised and externalised much of the lives and work of women. It is no coincidence that the hero of neo-classical economics is 'economic man' (Ferber and Nelson, 1993; Feiner, 1995, 1999). Specific studies have shown that gender issues are repeatedly marginalised as a result of implicit male bias in both macro-economic and micro-economic theory (Bakker, 1994; Hewitson, 1999; Nelson, 1993). Women's domestic work is not valued; when in employment they are paid less than men; and they are proportionately less likely to achieve higher positions. Under capitalism the power to allocate resources and determine access to finance in order to exercise 'effective demand', becomes almost exclusively an elite male prerogative. For women whose work is often not paid or is low-paid establishing effective demand is difficult (Waring, 1989). Even where women have entered into 'malestream' professions, their pay and career opportunities are often more limited than those of men of equivalent status, whilst most still have to juggle paid and unpaid work.

One response of feminist economists has been to bring women back into economics, to bring them 'out of the margins' (Kuiper and Sap, 1995). Similarly to the complex relation between environmental and ecological economics, feminist economics hovers between a reformist and a radical approach. It lies between looking for a challenge to conventional economic thinking, and inclusion within it. Neo-liberal feminist economics is recognisable by its empiricism, its desire for Pareto-optimal ('value-neutral') policy recommendations, and its use of neo-classical economic models. This approach is compatible with orthodox neo-classical economics because it tends to address the immediate problem of gender inequality within the economic system rather than more profound gender-relations issues. It rests upon a conception of science which privileges facts and figures whilst ignoring the realm of social and human experience in so far as these activities are not commercialised. Those who have offered a more fundamental challenge have been described by Elson as feminist critical economists (Elson, in Bakker, ed., 1994: 38). However, if feminist economists want to keep working, they are faced with the problem of making compromises with neo-classical economics. Without the compromises, the critical economists feel, correctly, that they will be rejected by the profession.

One solution to the problem of exclusion of both nature and women has been to 'count them in', but this does nothing to question the system of valuing in the first place. Many women have been happy to be counted in as they demand equal opportunities within the mainstream economy, but that is different from challenging economics as a model.

Through the prism of 'economic man', women are deemed to be inherently non-economic. Their needs and contribution are externalised relative to the money economy. As Nelson argues, 'the association of women and nature ... as [both being] passive, exploitable resources is not just co-incidental or incidental to neo-classical analysis' (Nelson, 1997: 156). Malestream economics has adopted 'separative' thinking (1997: 158): 'Again and again, western philosophy identified women (and slaves or 'barbarians') with nature, matter, passivity, and the body and all of these with a lower order than (dominant) men, reason, thought and activity' (1997: 157). Radical feminist approaches to economics have questioned the way in which economic systems are constructed (Folbre, 1982, 1993, 2001) and drawn parallels between the treatment of women and the treatment of the natural world (Mellor, 1997a).

Ecofeminist political economy has explored the links between the embodiment and embeddedness of human individuals and institutions and the exploitation of women's labour and planetary resources (Mellor, 1992, 1997a). Embodiment signifies that humans exist within vulnerable and needy bodies that are subject to a life-cycle. Embeddedness means that all human activity is located within an extra-human natural environment that generates its own needs and dynamics. From an ecofeminist perspective the exclusion of the environment and women's work from the formal economy is not accidental: it represents a material relation in the construction of the boundaries defining the framework of economic value. The economic benefit to dominant individuals, groups and societies of the current boundaries of economic activity is the exclusion and exploitation of the environment, women and other subordinated peoples (Mellor, 1997b). From this perspective there cannot be a simple economic solution based on the incorporation of hitherto externalised costs. Ecofeminist political economists argue that women are treated in the same way as the environment in male-dominated economic systems, used and abused, externalised and ignored. Furthermore, the justification for this treatment is that women are somehow representative of nature, their lives are dominated by domestic non-economic imperatives.

The development of a money economy can be seen as a means of building boundaries between those who can join and those who cannot; between those things that are valued and those that are not (Mellor, 1997b). The mainstream economy represents the con-struction of a valuation system represented by money. In doing so it values most highly, and places most emphasis upon, those things that are important to men and to capitalism: luxuries, mechanical production, movement (railways, cars), toys, communications, armaments, sports. These activities are defined as wealth-creating/money-making, which is hardly surprising because they are by definition highly valued in money terms and therefore deemed as creditworthy within a debt-money creation system. The valuation system of the male/money economy is a tautology. What is valuable in money terms is valued by money. Those who have the power to determine value are those who have control over money systems. Outside are those activities deemed secondary, not valued, dependent: the Cinderella activities of basic needs, emotional and physical care. These are assigned to the public economy or to the non-money social economy which have no 'right' to debt-money. Public-sector expenditure in accounting terms is a liability not an asset/investment. There is no public or mutual 'capital' until it is privatised.

The concept of economic choice as understood within neo-classical economics reflects a social condition where it is assumed that vital needs for human survival and efficacy are already in place – that is, that the economic actor's physical materiality is secured. If this were not the case, it would not be possible to maintain the fiction that needs are indistinguishable from wants. Human beings necessarily have a material relation to their bodies (embodiment) and to the environment (embeddedness). Where these are ignored, the burdens and consequences fall onto less powerful groups – women, poor and marginalised communities – and onto the ecosystem. This is not to make an essentialist statement about the nature of women or the planet, but to point to the economic consequences of deep structural inequalities. In such a perspective, 'the economy' identified by neo-classical political economists, and taken on board largely uncritically by Marxism, is a social construction of privilege resting on a deep, yet largely unacknowledged, material base (Mellor, 2000a).

Although women are disadvantaged in money/market systems what is externalised is not women as such, but women's work. 'Women's work' is defined as human activities associated with the body, provisioning both physical and emotional needs (Nelson, 1993). Such work, associated with the body and the life-cycle, constitutes labour offering little choice unless people are to suffer through ill health or neglect. This work has been described as 'imposed altruism' (Mellor, 1992: 251). As it is largely imposed upon women, it is identified as 'women's work'. The distinctiveness of this work is its temporal and spatial location. The work must be done where the body is located (no virtual reality here) and within the framework of its temporality, the daily cycle (rest and replenishment), the life-cycle (childhood, old age) and the time-scale of disease. This work cannot be fitted into the schedules of paid work, as it has to conform to the needs of 'biological time' (Mellor, 2000b), the time it takes to grow old, grow up or get well.

It should not be assumed, however, that, because 'women's work' is devalued within present economic systems, it should be seen as necessarily alienating work. Arguably, the work of caring for others and meeting basic needs should be seen as the most valued and satisfying of human activities. Women's work can be performed by low-paid and low-status men (e.g. cleaners, janitors), by higher-status men if the social coding is changed (chefs) or by male choice in the home (New Man), but it is still seen socio-economically as women's work. Where women do this work wholly without pay their only link to effective demand is through the paid work of others, the family wage, or redistributed taxes. However, women's work, together with all the other non-market relations between and within households, in communal, social and political institutions, are crucial to the nurturance of actually existing economic structures. Any definition of economic rationality that excludes non-market relations and considers them irrelevant is not neutral and opens up the question of what is meant by 'rationality' in this context. A major challenge to economics from feminist economic theory lies in women's unpaid domestic and subsistence work, the work that sustains the basics of human welfare (Mies, 1986). Regardless of how this work is put on the political agenda (wages for housework, calculation of the value of women's work, radical critique of the family) the challenge to the male-dominated/capitalist economy is to explain why it is not recognised and why it has been left as an unacknowledged externality (Waring, 1989; Folbre, 1993). Nelson's answer is that 'women perform the bodily care and daily provisioning that must remain unacknowledged for the masculine self-image of active autonomy to be maintained' (1997: 158).

Environmental and gender issues have been brought together particularly sharply in parts of the world where the global market is having a negative impact without bringing any perceived benefits. Many studies have shown how important women are to rural and non-market economies (Sachs, 1996). There is also evidence that there is a profound shift from early approaches which sought to bring women into development (WID) toward rethinking gender relations in a fundamental way (Pearson and Jackson, 1998) and challenging the negative impact of development on women and the environment (Harcourt, 1994; Braidotti *et al.*, 1994). The debate has widened to bring together ecology, class issues and racism, as well as fundamental questions about capitalism, into the debate over gender.

Within the 'aid industry' there is a move towards research and practice aimed at attaining 'sustainable livelihoods' (Carney, 2000). Carney's work shows the problem with importing capitalist notions such as 'capital' into a wider social framework embracing complex livelihoods. Five capitals are identified: natural, physical, social, human and financial. The sustainable livelihoods framework offers an improvement over purely income-oriented, anti-poverty research because the former approach is more holistic. However, the study of sustainable livelihoods couched in 'capital' terms may neglect issues to do with social conflict, intra-household inequalities of distribution, gender, and the abuse of the natural environment. It may not recognise the contradictions that households face. For instance, if the aim is to enable a household to earn more money, then investing in a boy's education might be the best strategy since men earn more than women for a given level of education. On the other hand, if the aim is to improve the household's farming assets then educating a woman may be best where local circumstances mean that women tend to be the stewards and managers of farming activity. Such contradictions cannot be addressed by a framework that sees financial 'capital' and natural 'capital' as equally important because they are both measured by the 'universal' yardstick of money.

For example, for people to increase their 'personal social capital' they need to invest time in community activities. However, when waged labour enters a local system, time devoted to communal activity comes into conflict with time necessary for domestic work (unpaid) and with paid, and therefore valued, employment. No allowances are made in the framework for the costs of investing time in social capital, and (as pointed out by Fine in two publications, 1999 and 2001) a rational economic man approach to household decision-making is not appropriate when there are underlying conflicts of interest. Of course, these points have been made by many feminist economists, Naila Kabeer being a principal exponent of the notion that interests are not the same as subjectively identified needs (Kabeer, 1994). Tension, arguments, contradictory desires: these are the reality for vulnerable people in poor households. It is no good simply telling them that all kinds of capital are good. For development 'experts' to argue in such a way makes them appear simplistic. The sustainable development model summarised by Carney seems to confuse capital as a means to various ends with capital as an end in itself. An unintended effect of having the five-capital model is that all routes to human welfare are reduced to, and reinterpreted as, capital-related routes. Capital thus becomes both means and end, both a mode of relation and a desired outcome. Maureen Macintosh also warns against inappropriate importation of the northern concept of the household. From her research on sub-Saharan Africa she shows that income sharing, eating together and co-operative forms of work spread well beyond people who live together (2000: 127). It this context the notion of an individual economic 'actor' is an irrelevance.

Rethinking the economy

The idea of individual reward, so central to formal economic systems, is a meaningless notion in the context of human welfare. Most of human caring and welfare exists beyond the market. However, as market values invade they make non-market support systems less and less viable. Economic orthodoxy asserts that social claims are parasitic on the wealth-creating (money-making) sector. This is a nonsense. In fact, it is the so-called 'wealth-creating sector' that is parasitic on all the unpaid work, exploited labour, expropriated resources and degraded environments that sustain it. We could visualise a pyramid of creation, with domestic work and social reproduction at the base, public labour relations in the middle, and cash exchanges including wage payments at the top. Even if the top were creamed off, the foundations would still remain firm. However, it doesn't work the other way around: the cash economy would stop immediately if all the unremunerated work of billions of people were not done daily. Marxian socialism (rightly) identified the role of class exploitation in the creating of surplus value, but this needs widening to embrace all the other 'underlabourers' that give life to 'economy'.

As Julie Nelson has argued, modern preoccupations with choice-theoretic and individual choice models have hijacked the basic meaning of economics as embodied in the work of Adam Smith and Alfred Marshall. The basic meaning of economics, in her view, is 'the provisioning of the necessaries of life' where economics is 'centrally concerned with the study of how humans, in interaction with each other and the environment, provide for their own survival and health' (Ferber and Nelson, 1993: 34). We would go even further and argue that the 'provisioning' of a society is not an economic question, but a political one. The decision to hand over provisioning to 'the market' or 'the state' is a political one that in a market economy presents economics as 'politics in disguise' (Henderson, 1988). Henderson sees the money/market economy as merely the icing on a three-layered cake. The first layer is the public sector. The second is the social economy of unpaid community and household work. The third is the natural world. Figure 8.1 also aims to show the framing of the money/market economy within the natural and social worlds.

The notion of 'capital' arises during capitalism and has its roots in the system described by Marx, where finance capital begins to shape all bourgeois valuations of things, including people. This notion, 'capital', represents a dangerous ontology on which to base a 'sustainable development' paradigm. The word 'capital' implies too much. It implies a stock, a separation of capability from its social basis, a de-linking of nature from that which is 'man-made'. In reality these things are all related. We use a social-relations approach to re-vision the capabilities people have. No single diagram would do this approach justice, but Figure 8.1 tries to set things out in a

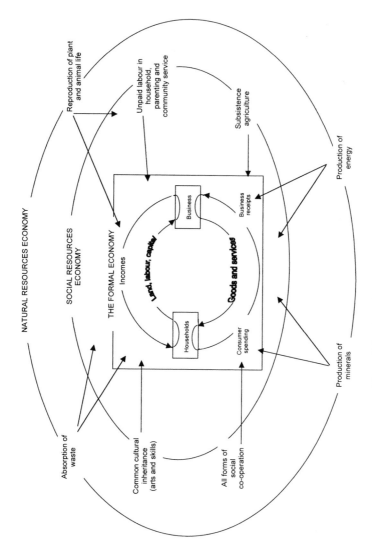

NATURAL RESOURCES ECONOMY

SOCIAL RESOURCES ECONOMY

THE FORMAL ECONOMY

Reproduction of plant and animal life

Unpaid labour in household, parenting and community service

Subsistence agriculture

Production of energy

Incomes

Land, labour, capital

Business

Business receipts

Goods and services

Households

Consumer spending

Production of minerals

Absorption of waste

Common cultural inheritance (arts and skills)

All forms of social co-operation

Figure 8.1 Foundations of the circular flow

180

way that differs from both neo-classical economics and from the sustainable development approach. For instance, in the figure we show technology not as 'capital' but as a common cultural inheritance rooted in the social realm. Social co-operation, too, is not a 'capital' but rather a set of social relations. Financially valued outcomes can only be a subset, an offshoot, or a set of epiphenomena relative to the basic realities of social co-operation. Thus, whilst co-operative organisations are often seen as failures in financial terms within capitalism, to their participants they are important as loci of supra-commercial ways of being. The commercial valuation is tangential to the reality of that being. Wage labour, unpaid labour, food production all now appear as primarily linking the natural world (power, senses, stomachs, arms and legs) with the social world. Granovetter (1985) argued that neo-classical economics sees the economy too much as disembedded from society, but we go further. We displace commerce as the perceived home of economic action, and replace it with the social (and hence politically rich) home of the public realm.

Clearly our perspective, like that of most feminists, questions the public–private divide, which in itself varies from culture to culture. In the public sphere, in schools, politics, the streets and shops, people are being reproduced, educated, socialised, incorporated. Therefore, as long argued by feminist Marxists (Hartmann, 1979; Himmelweit, 1995) the supposed divide between private reproduction and public production needs to be broken down. We have attempted to overcome this by using the word 'provisioning', which embraces activities that are now spread across the formal, informal and social economies. This involves rethinking many categories of modern social and economic thinking, with capital being first and foremost of these. In our view, one strategic form that resistance to capitalistic domination can take is re-visualising economic forms as social relations. This view is derived from Marx's critique of commodity fetishism. However the critique can be applied more widely: not only to the excessive focus on prices as values of goods, but also crucially to two other sub-realms of the economy. Firstly, an excessive focus on wages as the value of labour makes a serious mistake by fetishising the labour market as a locus where values are determined. Secondly, an excessive concern with interest rates as the supposed value of money, or as the relevant index of the cost of claiming future earnings now, reifies interest rates as the 'price' of money. Neo-classical models use the demand–supply interaction to suggest that interest rates are the 'price' of money, equilibrating the supply and demand in loans/savings markets. As we have indicated, however, that model masks a false representation.

As John Brohman (1995) has argued, neo-liberals ignore the state and have a simplistic and/or single-element approach to power relations. They thus ignore the complexity and richness of social conflict, while neglecting factors that differentiate markets as well as culture and history. Neo-liberals also tend to stress disciplinary divisions, fragmenting the social sciences and in the process suppressing serious debate. As positivists, they can relate effectively only to positivist science. Like Marx we would want to look at economic systems in terms of social relations. Contemporary social-relations theorists have a *praxis* orientation. For example, social-relations theorists treat labour relations quite differently compared with money-markets. Like feminists and Greens they see work as occurring outside markets as well as inside them. It can, therefore, be recognised that generalisations about markets, including equilibria, role of transactions costs, information or supervision issues, become impractical. A more meaningful analysis emerges through the unmasking of the social relationships underlying and surrounding money exchanges.

Re-visioning cash purchases as social relations

Consider buying a packet of apples in a supermarket. The packet is weighed and priced, giving the two items of information most central to the decision to purchase, the quantity being purchased and the price to be paid. The packet may also contain some information on the source of the apples, perhaps the country of origin, South Africa, France or New Zealand. The packet may show the name of the store selling the apples, but is unlikely to give much more information about the fruit.

Somewhere, a plot of land has produced an apple tree. The tree has been tended by people whose subsistence needs have been met from the environment. The apples have been harvested, sorted, crated, transported and documented through a complex administrative process, passing through a series of complex social relations which lie outside the weight/price axis.

Reference to Fig. 8.1 facilitates the imagining of the apples from different viewpoints:

- To the purchaser in the money economy, the apple is uniform in quality. From the cash economy view, the commodity has weight and price.
- To the purchaser the apple can also be viewed as part of the reward for waged labour. Under the social economy view, the commodity draws the purchaser into the social relations of exchange.
- To the person eating the apple it assumes use value. The natural world viewpoint links the social world with the body.
- It is also possible to trace the apple from hand to hand, from the original growers through the processes bringing it to the hand of the eater. The integrated view establishes a direct relationship between the lives of each person in the growing, processing, transport, wholesale and retail chain.

The process can be reversed, or started at any point in the chain linking producer to consumer. Once the process of purchase and sale is taken out of its purely monetised context, new theoretical vistas emerge. Notions of service and social responsibility can enter into consideration. For example, in the UK parents are advised never to allow a child to eat an apple without first removing the peel because of its toxicity. To what extent should the grower/producer ensure that poisonous pesticides should be avoided due to their ill effects on the health of consumers? To what extent should the consumer insist that the use of toxic substances in the production and processing not only of apples but of all food, fuel, fibres and so on, does not adversely affect the health of those supplying the labour along the chain of production, and those living under the shadow of the pollution left in its wake? To what extent can producer (as in paid labourer) or consumer materially affect outcomes? These questions cannot be keyed in artificially to mainstream economic theory while business continues as usual.

9 New Ways of Thinking About Money and Income

In recent years social and environmental critiques of the failures of the capitalised money economy have led to a number of proposed economic alternatives and monetary experiments. The impetus for new economics initiatives are varied, and include the instability of money systems, the collapse of local economies, a reaction against consumerism, damage to the environment and a desire for democratic control of economic systems. Some approaches seek to build out from personal lifestyle changes (voluntary simplicity, downshifting), others to reform income distribution (Basic/Citizen's Income), others to create local autonomy (LETS, local money and exchange systems) or to put money and credit into the hands of people who have been financially excluded (micro-finance, micro-credit). In this chapter we will explore a number of these initiatives, reviewing the extent to which they contribute to the demands of economic democracy in the terms we have outlined. In particular, we examine the potential they offer for placing money systems in the hands of the people using them in a way that will ensure democratic control over the means of provisioning, while facilitating the creation of a sustainable environment.

Local currency and exchange systems

The motivation for action at the local level is to create, or recreate, a dynamic local economy. Often this is accompanied by a desire to create a particular type of economy, more sustainable, more democratic. Broadly, local initiatives fall into two types: mutual credit systems which operate on a membership basis, and local currency systems which operate at community level. 'Local' in the latter context depends on the size of the community and could be a geographical area or a shared community of interest. Both types have a long lineage, certainly back to the capitalist market crisis of the 1930s. However, since both types operate within a framework of national and international currencies, it is important to see how far they are seeking to solve the symptoms created by the financial system rather than to bring about fundamental reform of the system itself. The 1930s in particular were a period of insecurity in national currency systems, and of currency shortages and many monetary experiments were temporary expedients. The classic example of a local currency is the Austrian Worgl stamp scrip and of a mutual credit system, the Swiss WIR. We analyse these together with a number of more contemporary initiatives.

Local money

Scrip is a form of money that does not qualify as legal tender. Historically it was issued by employers or by local landowners to control the expenditure patterns of their employees or tenants. Current examples are air miles or internet currencies such as beenz or i-points. Douthwaite and Wagman refer to such scrips as 'auxiliary currencies' since they operate alongside, and are even backed by, the national currency (1999). The Worgl experiment was influenced by the ideas of Silvio Gesell (1862–1930). Gesell argued that the issue of money should be seen as a public service and therefore a fee (demurrage) should be paid for holding it. Money would therefore always decline in value and there would be little incentive to hoard it and prevent its circulation. In 1932, Michael Unterguggenberger was the mayor of Worgl. The Austrian town of around 4,500 people had nearly one-third of the community out of work and an empty treasury. The mayor negotiated a loan from the local credit union savings bank and issued around 10,000 schillings in scrip notes that had to be stamped each month to retain their validity. The money was used to pay the wages of city employees and was also accepted in payment of local taxes. The money circulated quickly and was actually preferred to the national currency which in any case was in short supply. It has been estimated that each note changed hands 463 times on average as against the average for the national currency of 213 transactions (Douthwaite and Wagman, 1999: 97). There was no risk as the scrip was backed by the national currency loan. Major public works were carried out and unemployment fell by 25 per cent. However, within 13 months the scheme was declared illegal by the national government, fearing the long-term consequences as other towns prepared to follow suit. Yale economist Irving Fisher promoted the scrip idea in the US (1933) and 300–400 experiments were launched. Mary-Beth Raddon points out that most of these were seen as emergency measures which were withdrawn following the influx of New Deal money (2001: 11), while Douthwaite and Wagman record that many were shut down by the federal government in 1933 on the advice of Harvard Professor Russell Sprague who claimed that the US monetary system was being 'democratised out of its hands' (1999: 100).

The late twentieth century saw a resurgence in monetary experiments and various 'green dollar' schemes often based more on social or environmental commitment than direct financial need. A well-known example is the Ithaca hours scheme. Ithaca hours are a paper currency issued in 1992 by Paul Glover, a community activist in a small university town in New York state. Printed notes are denominated in one hour, two hour, half and quarter hour. One hour is roughly worth $10. Ithaca hours are issued as loans or grants to charities, and payments to those who advertise in 'Ithaca Money'. They are accepted by nearly 400 businesses operating within the conventional financial system (Boyle, nd). The system now operates in 39 communities in the US (Lietaer, 2001: 188).

Time Dollars, a more strictly hours-based system, was devised in 1986 by Edgar Cahn, a Washington civil rights lawyer and professor. Hours are earned by giving a timed service to another person, so as with a mutual credit scheme the money is created by activity, but the hours can then be transferred or saved. Value is, however, limited to time-based activities; there is no monetary equivalence. The popularity of time dollars has been increased by the decision of the US Inland Revenue System in 1991 not to count the hours for tax purposes. In the UK time-dollar work does not affect income-support payments. Time dollars are now used in many communities worldwide, with a particularly effective version being used for care of the elderly in Japan. Jan Hureau Kippu (caring relationship tickets) are denoted in hours of service. Care-givers can accumulate credits in a health-care time savings account for their own use, or they can transfer their credit to others, for example relatives living in another part of the country (Douthwaite, 1999). While examples from the US and Japan have raised much interest, it should be remembered that Curitiba in Brazil with 2.3 million inhabitants has used complementary currencies for 25 years. In 1992 Curitiba, with its innovative transport system, was voted by the UN as the most ecological city in the world.

Raddon sees a resemblance between the various currency/hours initiatives and Robert Owen's National Equitable Labour Exchange scheme of 1832–34; the local money movement reclaims the 'spirit of Owenism' (2001: 13). She records that Paul Glover was initially planning a LETS scheme while exploring other community economic ideas. He sketched a cartoon Ithaca note for a child and then saw an example of an 'Hour' note issued by Robert Owen. Shortly afterwards he conceived the Ithaca hours plan (Raddon, 2001: 11).

The limitations of alternative currencies as a radical alternative is revealed in the use of descriptions such as complementary, auxiliary or parallel currencies, indicating that such schemes are seen as augmenting the existing money system. This is certainly true of Lietaer who sees community currencies as a complement to national currency systems (2001). Like Huber and Robertson (c.2000) he argues for multi-level currencies, at local, national and international level. Lietaer sees these currencies as being converted through a growing 'cyber-economy' (2001: 266). Lietaer's reliance on the existing framework of economics is shown by his view of complementary currencies as playing a role in economic development which he defines as 'the capacity to transform resources into capital' (2001: 278). For Lietaer, auxiliary currencies address the limitations of the market by balancing communal yin to the market yang. The yin (feminine, caring, community) approach will complement the market yang (2001: 285). It seems as if once more, as in many of the yin–yang analogies, the feminine is left to pick up the pieces. The limitations of such auxiliary currency proposals is that they are not framed within a fundamental criticism of mainstream economic theory and practice. While problems are identified, the global economy is seen as in need of reform rather than reconstruction. The capitalist market economy is not perceived as a mechanism that actually exists to destroy utility by converting it to worthless money. Also, auxiliary money systems do not address the need for democratic control of property and resource access.

The use of 'auxiliary currencies' is seen by Douthwaite and Wagman as 'an important step in the democratisation of money creation' (1999: 6). Bernard Lietaer, on the other hand, fears that the main area of growth will be corporate currencies which will only be issued to the rich, such as frequent fliers or web surfers. Meanwhile national currency authorities may stamp out local currencies as they did in the 1930s. While acknowledging the success of the scrip issues in the 1930s and the very real commitment of organisations such as the New Economics Foundation to these initiatives, these ideas will not present a fundamental challenge to the money/market system unless they are seen in a wider theoretical context.

Mutual credit systems

A mutual credit system operates not through money as the initiator of exchange but through exchange as the creator of a debt or credit. Value is thus brought into the system through an interaction. Effectively, however, mutual credit systems are still a money system; they are not barter (Raddon, 2001: 9). A long-standing example of a mutual credit system is the Swiss WIR. WIR (the acronym is German for 'we') is the Wirtschaftsring-Genossenschaft (Economic Mutual Support Circle) formed in 1934 in Zurich and still in existence. Over the years it has grown from 3,000 to 80,000 members with a turnover of $2 billion. It is made up of individuals and small businesses mainly in the building trades and food sectors. Large businesses cannot join. The circle provides new entrants with credits for working capital. Goods and services are exchanged within the circle.

WIR's founders were Werner Zimmerman and Paul Enz. Inspired by the ideas of Silvio Gesell, they also espoused ecological and feminist issues. Apart from the ideological commitment, WIR was set up to overcome a currency shortage. The starting capital raised to back the circle was 140,000 Swiss francs (a large amount at the time). The aim of WIR was to find satisfying work, fair earnings and secured prosperity. There is a very low charge for credit, and business is based largely on trust. Entry is gained by selling into the WIR system or applying for credit into the system. The WIR unit of account is equivalent to a Swiss franc although WIR currency is not convertible. Total loans are restricted to one-third of annual turnover and secured on a legal basis with a franc-based collateral. WIR service charges are paid in francs. The WIR is therefore an insulated system of mutual services and credit secured on the Swiss franc. As a mutual credit system the organisation is only as effective as the dynamism of its trading. It can also go out of balance if members accumulate excessive debt or credit.

In 1998 the European Commission (DGV) sponsored four Barataria initiatives (named for Gesell's imaginary island), based loosely on the WIR system. These were located in Scotland, Ireland, Holland (Amstelnet in Amsterdam) and Spain (La Kalle in the Vallecas district of Madrid). The Scottish SOCS (Scottish Organisational Currency System) project had 80 members including

Gordonstoun school. All the projects were electronic apart from the ROMA project, Connaught Ireland which used paper scrip (Douthwaite and Wagman, 1999).

LETS schemes

LETS, the Local Exchange Trading System (there now are various versions of the acronym), was devised by a Canadian, Michael Linton in the early 1980s. Linton developed LETS to deal with problems of rural unemployment in Victoria, British Columbia, during the early 1980s recession. His ideas built on those of David Weston who had developed the green dollar scheme in Vancouver (Dauncey, 1988). A LETS is a mutual-services membership organisation which does not issue a currency but keeps a record of debits and credits on computer. Members are generally charged an entrance fee and annual administration fee. Contact is made through a register of member skills. People trade their skills (hairdressing, growing vegetables, baking bread, household repairs) using a local 'currency' such as the 'bobbin' in Manchester, 'readies' in Reading and 'dons' in Swindon. The value of goods or services are negotiated face to face. Credits or debits incur no interest or charge. The exchange itself creates the debit/credit. Balances are public so that people are encouraged not to exploit.

LETS have been developed in the UK through a very active network, LETSLink. There are around 400 LETS with around 40,000 people involved. LETS have become a virtually universal phenomenon, with highly professional training and start-up packs being made available to most countries through the Internet. To the extent that conventional small businesses and local authorities participate in schemes, payments may be made in combinations of LETS credits and conventional money. The UK Government, particularly its Social Exclusion Unit as well as agencies concerned with community regeneration, is keen to encourage such activities. There is some evidence that the New Zealand government has acknowledged the economic benefit of local currencies in economic development. Time dollars and LETS schemes are being seen as a solution to problems of poverty and the failure to fund public services properly. To the extent that LETS schemes mop up symptomatic problems thrown up by conventional finance, they are tolerated by governments. If they became more successful, however, governments may act to suppress or control them.

LETS schemes do have some limitations. One problem is that there is no regulation of debt or credit. Regulation relies on the system being small enough so that people do not interact with those who are already overspent. At the same time there can be a problem of too little use. Because a LETS scheme only generates value through use, failure to interact undermines the system as does building up too many credits or debits. Ironically this is what Michael Linton did to his own local LETS by building up too much debt (Douthwaite and Wagman, 1999: 18). Ideally LETS need to have everyone highly active with balances hovering around zero. One solution adopted by LETS in Germany is to issue credit–debit books to members so that they can see if someone has too much credit/debit before they trade (Douthwaite, 1999: 40). Another problem is when there is a disparity of skills. How does a gardener interact or make exchanges of labour with a lawyer? Raddon also found that the activities of LETS schemes tended to be gendered, which she sees as a pattern for community currencies generally:

> community currencies have always been hampered by features of the gendered economy. This is true of their effectiveness as consumption-based movements, and also of their ability to reconnect consumption and production in more co-operative and self-reliant communities rather than in individual 'homestead' livestyles. (2001: 190)

To be truly radical, she argues, the re-localisation of livelihoods (which she sees as the aim of local currency movements) needs to be widespread and at the level of the collectivity, not an individual or family lifestyle choice.

The relationship between the social and economic role of LETS is also an issue. Within communities there is often an informal exchange network as neighbours and family help each other out. Setting up a formal system hovers somewhere between bringing together people who know each other, and expanding new connections. LETS systems can bring together people in atomised communities and are therefore social as much as economic. In areas where people are in work LETS can be set up to express a political commitment rather than economic need. However, once established, as people get to know each other, personal friendships often render the exchange of services for 'currency' unnecessary. There is therefore a tendency for LETS-style schemes to dissolve into community reciprocity or disuse over time. On the whole, LETS-style schemes are valuable consciousness-raisers and often develop alongside other routes to economic democracy. For a full range of 'home grown' economies rooted in local ecosystems and cultures see Barbara Brandt (1995) and Susan Meeker-Lowry (1995).

No alternative system can exist as an 'economy' unless it is bringing in basic means of provisioning. This raises problems for local schemes and their communities if they have to obtain (earn) external currencies in order to access goods/services that they do not have themselves (resources, knowledge, technology) and the necessities of life generally. If LETS are not about basic provisioning, they are really about discretionary production and consumption and could perhaps be thought of in more conventional terms as use of leisure. LETS are caught in a dilemma. Operating face to face means that they are generally quite small, but being too small can also mean that the system is not large enough to offer the range of skills necessary to enable substantial numbers of people to live entirely in a LETS economy. There is, however, evidence of how important exchange schemes can become when the formal economy collapses, as in the Argentinian crisis and the post-USSR economies.

While local currencies and mutual credit systems are important initiatives they can only tinker at the edges of the money/market economy unless taken on board by the state. Even then the situation is problematic. In the Argentinian crisis of early 2002 one of the many short-lived presidents taking office attempted to introduce a new 'third' currency. It failed, however, to gain credibility with the population. This illustrates the central fact about money. It is social in creation and social in its value. As Raddon argues, 'community currencies demonstrate that collective belief is the basis for all money. They also make it clear that the issue of how conditions of faith in the monetary system are established and maintained is a political process' (2001: 10). To be truly radical, reform of the money system cannot be piecemeal. It has to address what money is and the role it plays in the economic form in which it is located. Capitalised money will produce a capitalist economy. As we have noted, many of the writers in this area remain within the theoretical framework of capitalist finance, merely seeking to iron out symptoms of malaise. We adopt the opposite view, arguing that money/market systems must become socialised. However, if societies are not to return to a very localised form of self-provisioning, some form of money system remains necessary for a complex society. A possible solution is state provision of a basic or citizen's income as an expression of the right to livelihood for every individual.

Basic (or citizen's) income

The case for a basic income has come from several quarters, including Green parties within the European Union and voluntary organisations concerned with inner-city and rural poverty, such as the UK Citizen's Income Research Group, CIRG (formerly Basic Income Research Group) and the Europe-wide Basic Income European Network (BIEN). The radical case for a basic income is that there should be a fundamental human right to provisioning and development of potential that does not depend on waged work. This would end the necessity for over-production, excessive transportation and other ecologically unsound attempts to maintain production in order to maintain incomes-through-employment.

Secondary arguments are that BI would eradicate poverty, reduce income differentials and end the degrading and frustrating means-tested benefits system. It would end the poverty and unemployment traps, whereby people taking low-waged work lose benefits and pay taxes, thereby becoming poorer (Parker, 1989). Furthermore, it would end the workfare approach to poverty, which merely produces a pool of low-paid workers to be exploited by the capitalist system. A BI would improve the distribution of work through an improved labour market system, education and training. Young people could linger in training and education, developing their talents without loss of income. People would have some choice about whether or not to take paid work, while the potential for culture, arts, education, family life, personal development and scope to experiment with eco-logically sound local systems of food production would be greatly extended. With increased scope to re-think existing socio-economic relationships, the necessity to work long hours under stressful conditions in order to achieve income security would be less obviously a fact of life. Under these conditions, gardening, making music, reading, caring and many other 'leisure' activities which place little strain on the environment could replace work concerned with the production and distribution of consumer products. There would be more time for social and community life, while the care of dependants could be shared more equitably. BI would offer women greater economic independence, regardless of their household status.

In arguing for an independent income for everyone, it is important to remember that the benefits of an unearned income through claims to a part-share in the overall sum of financial capital have long been appreciated by the well-off classes. The principle of an unearned income is well-established, and is seen by the wealthy as the means to an active personal, social and public life. This was certainly the case for Virginia Woolf, who celebrated the benefits for a woman of an independent income. Her 'five hundred pounds' meant that she was not reliant on a male income and that no man could hurt her (1927). We would argue that the benefits that the wealthy have received and the creativity that this has unleashed should be open to all members of a society.

Most arguments for a BI are presented on the basis of a rolling up of other benefits and rerouting of taxes. In the UK various forms of universal child benefits or state retirement pensions have been regarded as precursors to a universal BI (Twine, 1992). It is argued that a Basic Income has many advantages. It is simple, easy to understand and to access. It offers income security without the stress and anxiety of means testing. The freedom to earn, or not to earn, to study, to train, to care and to a guaranteed pension in old age are guaranteed, giving autonomy and freedom of choice to individuals and families. All citizens are subject to the same ground rules. The Citizens' Income Study Centre has argued that savings in the administration of the present complex system of benefits, coupled with the unification of cash benefits with tax allowances and other forms of relief, would contribute substantially towards the costs of a CI for all citizens. Nevertheless, extensive work on comparative costings for a BI/CI, assuming continuation of waged labour in its present form, have tended to conclude that a full basic income would require an intolerably high level of income tax for its implementation. The greatest weakness in the case for BI is that under capitalist finance the BI would have to be paid for out of taxation. Each form of taxation, including increased income tax, VAT, taxes on fuel, or other ecological taxes would have unhelpful (and unpredictable) effects upon the economy and would meet powerful political resistance. It could also be seen in waged-based capitalist economies as a means to supply capitalists with cheap labour. Feminists are equally concerned that it may prove to be a back-door 'wages for housework' which would be used to 'encourage' women back into the home. However, the latter argument assumes a degree of independence denied to the bulk of women under the existing system.

For women in low-paid work or living in poverty it would give them a choice between work and home.

The concept of a guaranteed income regardless of work status has never been acceptable to the conventional left. The freedom from the *necessity* to work for a money income has been viewed with a not altogether unfounded suspicion. Under the system of capitalist finance of production, a guaranteed income paid for through transfer taxation would have the effect of subsidising the capitalist employer, especially when coupled with a workfare element. It is for this reason we argue the case for the development of a socialist economics based on the non-equilibrium Marxist theory as developed by Veblen and Douglas. It is only possible to understand the claim for a democratic right to income when seen in the context of the fact that money is issued as of right in any case, but to a privatised section of the community, who then go on to claim they have 'earned' it through their 'investments'. A basic income would be financially and politically feasible if based on non-capitalist, social credit principles of finance, paid in the form of a National Dividend.

The most important change from issuing money-as-of-right to the commercial community to issuing money to the community as a whole would be the extension of provisioning choices to all. This would inevitably mean giving priority to basic needs. It would no longer be necessary to produce armaments for export in order to have bread on the tables, nor would it be necessary to build a car factory before a hospital could be 'afforded'. The reform would encourage local production for local needs. Furthermore, there would be every incentive for money to circulate efficiently if it were meeting immediate needs within each locality. For this to happen, however, it would be necessary to adapt the mechanisms whereby availability of finance currently regulates production. While a BI based on social credit principles would put money in the hands of the citizens, it would have the limitation of not being available at the point of production rather than consumption. For this reason Douglas saw the importance of issuing credit through producer/consumer banks, thus introducing the principles of guild socialism and producer co-operation.

For economic democracy on the social credit model to be realised, all *new* investment would be created by decentralised producers' banks, linked through a national accounting system in which statistics were collected and collated. Money coming into existence as producers' credits and consumers' credits would operate as a tool for economic democracy. This type of proposal is not entirely foreign to the economics profession, and was addressed by the Nobel Prize-winning economist James Meade (Hutchinson and Burkitt, 1997: 89–93). The proposals for democratic control of finance and investment contain nothing foreign to the present system, except in so far as financial *profitability* would cease to be the dominant criteria for investment and income distribution. Vastly complicated calculations occur every minute of the day throughout business, commerce and the institutions of finance. The major change is that individuals, co-operating within identifiable local communities, can become proactive, both as producers and consumers, rather than reactive to an alienating economic system. Once more the key factor is finance.

Producer banks – the example of Mondragon

There is a long history in many societies of co-operative economic structures. The UK was the home of the consumer co-operative movement, while France and Italy could have more claim to being the home of producer co-operatives (Mellor *et al.*, 1988). Many forms of co-operation and mutuality exist: credit unions, agricultural co-operatives, building societies, friendly societies. However, most suffer from one of two problems. They are either small and vulnerable, unless in a specialist niche market, or large and driven to behave like other large-scale commercial organisations for financial reasons. In these circumstances meaningful membership involvement and participation has given way to large bureaucracies indistinguishable from their commercial counterparts. Even more menacing is the fact that democratic structures have been used by 'carpet-baggers', people joining only to seek an immediate financial return through privatisation of the collective savings of generations of working-class people. Recent years have seen increasing pressure to de-mutualise successful building and insurance societies and even consumer co-operatives (Mathews, 1999).

Despite these difficulties, there is evidence within the co-operative movement of the type of financial structure that Douglas was advocating. The importance of a producer bank in the successful development of co-operatives is demonstrated by the famous example of the Mondragon worker co-operatives in the Basque Country in Spain. Originally established during the 1950s, the brainchildren of local priest José Maria Arizmediarrieta, the worker co-operatives provided incomes through the manufacture and sale of paraffin stoves and electrical equipment. Although the co-operatives were locally financed from the outset, the creation of the Lankide Aurrezkia (Working People's Bank) was crucial to the financial survival of small production units intent upon providing a range of social and economic benefits, not only to the workers but also to the local community (Douthwaite, 1996: 160–71). Under Spanish law 10 per cent of profits ('net surplus') went into a social fund to finance schools and community training. For most of their existence, virtually until the advent of the Single European Market in 1993, and its removal of protective tariffs, the worker-controlled and worker-owned Mondragon co-operatives and their co-operative bank, run by representatives of its own staff and that of its member co-operatives, survived commercially as a series of small, egalitarian, democratically run organisations. The co-operatives and their bank were founded on the identical principles as outlined in Douglas' Draft Mining Scheme (Douglas, 1920: Appendix), save that they remained subject to the national and international institutions of finance.

The Lankide Aurrezkia operated very much like an industrial holding company, requiring regular financial data, with full accounts and detailed future plans every four years, from each worker co-operative. New workers bought shares related to the bank's own joining fee, roughly equivalent to a year's wages, for which they could obtain an interest-free loan, deductible from wages. The *individualised internalised capital accounts* (IICA) created in this way gave the workers part ownership of the firm, so that they received an annual percentage of the profits, in effect a dividend. The bank provided capital at low interest to supplement the savings/capital of the members of each worker co-operative, capital without which the co-operatives could not have survived. Equally valuable to the co-operatives was the bank's consultancy division, providing advice and guidance on marketing, exporting, production techniques, industrial buildings, personal and legal affairs, and audit and management control systems.

The Mondragon experiment provides the most extensive example of a working model of a decentralised, community enterprise loan fund with striking similarities to the Draft Mining Scheme proposed under the theoretical framework of social credit. For details of the Mondragon experiment see Douthwaite (1996), Mathews (1999), Daly and Cobb Jr. (1990) and Lutz and Lux (1988). The conceptual roots of the Mondragon experiment have been traced to Distributism, an economic reform movement of the early twentieth century, and one which was very closely allied to social credit (see Mathews, 1999). Furthermore, many accounts of Mondragon Co-operatives explore the management structure in great detail. The potential for non-hierarchical management structures has been considerably understated in conventional literature, and merits detailed study. However, in this work we focus upon the financial constraints on socialist forms of production and income distribution. The early success of the Mondragon experiment in setting up worker-co-operatives lay in the support of the bank and its protected status under Spanish financial independence. A full social credit analysis of the history of Mondragon/Lankide Aurrezkia and its relationship to national and international finance (beyond the scope of this work) will provide the basis for future development of economic democracy. The limits of the Mondragon experiment is that it has not disentangled itself from the market economy or from industrial production. Its main products have been white goods such as refrigerators and cookers. A sustainable economic democracy would need to combine producer banks with sufficiency provisioning.

Sufficiency and financial independence

The 1990s saw the growth of movements that went by several names, including 'simple living', 'voluntary simplicity', 'new frugality' and 'financial independence'. Books such as Duane Elgin's *Voluntary Simplicity* (1981), and Joe Dominguez and Vicki Robin's *Your Money or Your Life* (1992) appeared in the last decade of the twentieth century. During 1996 sales figures for *Your Money or Your Life* reached 20,000 per month in the US, resulting in the book being on the Business Week Best Seller List, reaching Number 1 in December. It has been translated into French, Dutch, German, Korean, Thai, Japanese and Swedish. Dominguez and Robin formed the New Road Map Foundation, supported by other leading environmentalists such as Thomas Berry, Donella Meadows and Juliet Schor (author of *The Overworked American: The Unexpected Decline of Leisure*). The New Road Map Foundation has set out to create 'a regionally dispersed, all-volunteer, self-organising and empowered network' designed to impact upon the way people think about, spend and earn money.

The Foundation aimed to bring together leading thinkers on the ecological and cultural limits to growth. Echoing social credit, their main thesis was that what the worker seeks is not *work* but an *income*, two very different things. Most people can find plenty of work to do, professional, artistic, creative, technical, medical, productive, agricultural in all manner of combinations. The problem is to move from the financially powerless status of wage or salary dependence in order to achieve financial independence (FI). Once FI is achieved, the tasks the individual selects as their life goals, as scientist, engineer, agriculturalist, educationalist, medical practitioner, trader or artist, can be pursued independently of an employing organisation. As work and income are de-linked, individuals become 'knowledgeable stewards' of their own life energy, able to work for socially just and environmentally sustainable projects without the need to consider where the money is to come from or to sustain the social and environmental disintegration of the capitalist system of production and distribution. Those working for a wage or salary are asked to answer three questions:

1. If it wasn't for the money would I be doing the work I'm doing?
2. If it wasn't for the money, would I tolerate the conditions under which I work?
3. If the answer to either of the first two questions is 'no', what action can I take?

The aim is to move from a position of debt-ridden powerlessness, where income getting and spending dominates virtually the whole of life, to the situation where income is secure and money becomes a useful tool to secure the chosen requirements of life. Dominguez and Robin (1992: 329–37) suggest a route as follows:

1. The first step is to evaluate what money can buy – and what it cannot.
2. Work out total earning and spending.
3. Work out net hourly earnings. To do this it is necessary to work out the job-related expenses, including the cost of running a car, travel, work clothing, meals out, convenience foods, health care and holidays necessary to recuperate from work. In so far as these do not provide intrinsic satisfaction, they are deducted.
4. At the end of the month expenditure is recorded and divided into clothes, food, mortgage and so on.

5. Each expense is translated into hours of work. The question then arises – was each one worthwhile?
6. Which expenses could be cut? Money can be well spent, e.g. on certain luxuries and cultural activities. The aim is to achieve stress-free comfort, not permanent misery.
7. After the evaluation stage it is possible to start cutting *unnecessary* expenditure, including moving nearer to work, to a smaller house, growing and preparing more own food, sharing meals with friends, buying fewer compensatory goods and getting rid of clutter. The expenditure of *time* is a vital consideration.
8. Once financial expenditure is reduced by 20 per cent it becomes possible to pay off debts, start saving, and to earn interest from the savings.

The final stage is to invest the savings so as to receive a secure income sufficient to cover all eventualities within the sufficiency lifestyle. The lifestyle change would result in reduced consumerism, travel and other forms of consumption which lead to environmental degradation. Furthermore, it would free time and energy for the pursuit of sustainable activities such as preventative medicine, urban renewal, organic agriculture and subscription farming. These measures would in turn reduce the drain on agricultural products and labour of the majority world imported to the 'developed' world by multinational corporations.

Dominguez and Robin recommend the purchase of national government bonds as an investment. This is, in effect, a route to a basic income or national dividend by the back door. The route is open to all citizens under western democracy. Dominguez and Robin point out that a government has two basic ways of raising money – taxation and borrowing. When government expenditure exceeds its cash income, it may increase its taxes or borrow more through treasury securities (or agency bonds). Every few months a new bond is issued, with maturity dates ten, twenty or thirty years into the future. The first task of each new issue is to pay off the holders of old issues becoming due, with the remaining money being spent on the government budget. For the US, they argue, the national debt is the 'most senior obligation' of the government, so that payment of the principal and interest take priority over other expenditures to maintain the 'credit rating' of the federal government (1992: 312). Hence they are a secure investment.

The bond issues are bought by banks, insurance companies, brokers, mutual funds, credit unions, large and small companies, and individuals, all dealing in society's credit. Only the money paid for the original treasury bond goes to the government. For the rest of its life the bond is sold on the 'secondary market', with the government continuing to pay the interest to the holder of the bond. Dominguez and Robin argue that buying government bonds does not endorse the government's spending policy. On the contrary, by reducing the need to raise interest rates to attract foreign investment, individuals help to minimise the outflow of interest payments. Also, since taxes finance the major part of government spending, the more people earn the more they are supporting the current pattern of expenditure. However, the more money invested in government bonds by individuals, the more individuals are, in effect, being paid by the government to undertake voluntary activities of their choice while minimising environmentally destructive consumerism (1992: 312–27). FI provides individuals with a basic income or national dividend under their own control and without the necessity for political campaigning.

The most obvious problem with the financial independence movement is that it assumes a level of income that can be aggregated and invested. The Simple Living Network does offer programmes specially designed for low-income groups but it is argued that it is up to the individual to determine their level of sufficiency and the balance between material and non-material satisfactions. From a socialist perspective we would wish to see much more political commitment to a spread of income availability. However what we can take from the FI movement is the possibility of those with economic choice taking a route towards *collective* financial independence. The movement has enormous potential. The sums of money passing through a school, hospital, university, town or city being *controlled from outside* are vast and available for diversion to the service of those producing and consuming the services they provide if they can be made the basis of community investment.

Financial independence seeks to gain control of personal time and subsistence resources through manipulation of existing finance streams. The final part of this chapter reviews two further categories of financial schemes designed to lighten the oppression of the poor. However, neither Jubilee 2000 nor the various micro-credit schemes tackle the root causes of poverty itself. Those root causes are inherent in the capitalist financial system.

Jubilee 2000

In the final years of the twentieth century a number of national and international voluntary organisations formed a coalition, seeking to celebrate the Millennium by cancelling the unpayable debts of the world's poorest countries. Leading members of the UK Coalition included the African Liberation Solidarity Campaign CAFOD, Christian Action on Third World Debt, Christian Aid, Comic Relief, Evangelical Alliance, International Confederation of Free Trade Unions, Jubilee Centre, LAMB, Medical Action for Global Security, Mothers Union, National Black Alliance, National Federation of Women's Institutes, New Economics Foundation, Oxfam, Reform Judaism, SCIAF, Tear Fund, Third World First, TUC, UNISON, UNA, USPG, WDM, VSO, World Vision, YWCA, and all major Christian denominations. The Coalition sought to work with economists, business people, politicians and aid agencies to find practical proposals to relieve the oppressive debt, taking account of the interests of both creditors and debtors.

In the Judeo-Christian Bible and several other ancient traditions, the 'jubilee' principle provided for periodic restoration of economic order. Rituals of social renewal offered periodic cancellations of debt and restoration of access to self-support on the land through renewal of customary land tenure rights (Hudson, 1993: 5). The Jubilee 2000 Coalition focused upon financial debt, arguing that in many of the world's poorest countries debt repayments to rich countries and international financial institutions take priority over the lives and prospects of millions of people. The debts of these countries have grown so huge that the interest payments often amount to far more than they can afford to spend on health care and education combined. Although the original loans, dating from the 1970s, had already been repaid many times over, the total owed continues to grow, locking the poor into a cycle of poverty from which they can never escape. On the whole, the major part of the debt of the poorest countries is bilateral debt owed to governments (50 per cent) and multilateral debt owed to international financial institutions (35 per cent). The rest (15 per cent), the so-called 'private' debt, is owed largely and directly to commercial banks. At the start of the twenty-first century Jubilee 2000 was replaced by Jubilee +. Details of the work of Jubilee + and many similar organisations now circulate on the Web.

Freedom from the debt would, it is argued, enable the poorest countries to develop and so overcome poverty. While the breadth of the Jubilee Coalition is impressive, it ignores the broader issues and fails to engage in joined-up thinking. Freed from debt, a country could build more roads, hospitals and schools, could export more cash crops and could build up their tourism industries. But are these sustainable ends? Are these actually the ways in which the *people* of a particular country, as opposed to their western-educated elites, wish to see their resources used? How far would remittance of the money debt facilitate the second (but major) plank of the Biblical jubilee notion of return of customary land-tenure rights of subsistence? The campaign to relieve one symptom of the malaise of capitalism, that of Third World debt and the hardships imposed on the peoples of debtor countries by structural adjustment programmes, has undoubtedly raised awareness of the issues involved. The proposed solutions, however, would at best secure a return to 'business as usual' expansion of unsustainable economic growth. Further exploration of international debt is beyond the scope of this book. We note, however, that the US is the most heavily indebted nation in the world, while Cuba has benefited ecologically and culturally through exclusion from the international debt and 'development' scene. Capitalism has been equally successful in obscuring the issues surrounding another tool for 'development': micro-finance.

Micro-credit

Micro-credit initiatives grew rapidly in the last decade of the twentieth century, becoming central to 'development' policy. In general terms, micro-credit makes small-scale loans available to individuals, enabling them to set up or support a micro-enterprise. The basic idea spread from Mohammad Yunus's initial 1976 loan of £17 to 42 very poor people in Bangladesh, leading to the founding of the Grameen Bank in 1982. As Yunus described it, he was not trying to set up as a money lender. Rather, he sought a solution to the immediate problem of poverty, with all its humiliation and degradation of human life. He found 42 very poor people working independently at various crafts, forced to borrow small sums from traders and money lenders at extortionate rates in order to buy their working materials. With a student, he set out to create a bank for the poor, learning from scratch. They sought to cover all aspects of rural economic life, including trade, small manufacturing and retailing. Contrary to normal banking practice, the clients were not required to demonstrate possession of large savings or securities. On the contrary, they had to prove poverty and negligibility of savings. The experiment threw up a surprising fact. Repayment of loans borrowed by people without collateral proved far better than those whose borrowings were secured by vast assets. More than 98 per cent of the loans of the Grameen Bank are repaid. According to Yunus, this is because borrowers recognise that it is their only route out of poverty. By 1998 1,112 branches in Bangladesh were employing 12,000 people and lending to 2.3 million borrowers, each month lending $35,000 in tiny loans. They found that over the same period, a similar amount came back in repayments. From the outset, the Grameen Bank focused almost exclusively on loans to women entrepreneurs (Stretton, 1999: 92–3). Micro-finance schemes combining savings activity with lending activity now exist in both state-sponsored forms and as part of the work of non-governmental organisations in nearly every country of the world (Hulme and Mosley, 1996).

The notion of micro-credit has overtaken a previous generation of analyses which focused on the role of state banking, the question of de-nationalising or liberalising banking, and on banks supplying subsidised credit to specific categories of borrower. Earlier analyses in the 1970s and 1980s saw bank credit as affecting informal-sector lending arrangements, such as borrowing from a money-lender or pawning goods at a pawn shop. However in the 1990s a trend toward ignoring the informal sector and paying close attention to the institutional and organisation aspects of micro-finance was visible both in the NGO community and among major aid donors. As a result, privatisation and liberalisation of banking now get little public attention. Meanwhile, banks remain central in Structural Adjustment programmes (as recommended by the World Bank in 1989). In Sri Lanka, for example, the 2001 IMF adjustment package included specific components aimed at commercialisation and de-nationalisation of the two major national banks, the People's Bank and the Bank of Ceylon. Micro-finance programmes remain relatively small in scope compared with the main banking system in nearly every country. However, they have come to play a large part in aid discourse and in donor strategies for the poverty-alleviating impact of the aid packages.

Micro-finance schemes have evolved from a credit focus toward a savings focus, serving to draw into capitalism previously non-monetised labour and resources. In ideological terms micro-credit is said to be able to help alleviate poverty by helping members of poor households to make investments. It is also said to make poor people's livelihoods more sustainable by encouraging thrifty habits, while facilitating the growth of a small-business sector capable of responding to, and able to cope with, the changing employment needs of entrepreneurs who are shifting upward (expanding) from micro-proprietors to small capitalist businesses. Otero and Rhyne (1994) begin their book on micro-finance with the argument that millions of small entrepreneurs *lack* credit. This sense of the shortage of capital has a subjective aspect to it and is actively encouraged by the micro-finance literature. Micro-finance does have one special aspect that is new in banking practice. People are encouraged to form small groups which offer a peer guarantee if any individual is unable to repay their loan. These groups, called 'social collateral', 'thrift groups', or 'joint liability groups', are intrinsically a way to offload the costs of avoiding default onto the borrowers themselves. Borrowers may also be obliged to save a minimum amount each week, making a series of vows or 'promises', such as 'I will not pay dowry for daughters at the time of marriage' at every weekly meeting (Holcombe, 1995). Attendance at meetings may be obligatory, as in the Grameen Bank, but in other schemes the rules and conditions may vary.

The micro-finance debate illustrates one way that capitalist ideology encourages people, in this case often women and especially poor people, to discipline themselves and yet to partake of the emulative and status-seeking behaviours of capitalism. Linda Mayoux (1998a, 1998b) has described three approaches toward micro-finance. One approach, often taken by donor agencies like the UK's Department for International Development, is a neo-liberal pro-poor view that sees micro-finance as potentially reducing poverty. Within this approach gender-sensitive generalisations are sometimes made about women, but these remain within neo-liberal feminism, assuming that women's primary role is to service children. For instance, the claim that investment in women is likely to increase children's health because women generally spend more of the additional income on children is rooted in a stereotype of women as sacrificing their own needs or their personal development in favour of developing the capacity of their children. Husbands and fathers are ignored in this neo-liberal, women-oriented discourse. It is deemed to be more efficient to lend money to women, or better yet to encourage them to save money and thus require fewer loans. This approach would seem to promote neo-liberal notions of 'freedom' through market-oriented production and 'equal' opportunities.

The second viewpoint is the communitarian view of people empowering themselves, not individually but in groups, through the processes linked to micro-finance. This viewpoint is often found in the policy documents of non-governmental organisations, particularly where these have grass-roots origins and are small scale with representative links between members and leaders. The third viewpoint stressed by Mayoux is a feminist empowerment view, overlapping with the second view and sharing some points in common with the neo-liberal optimism about micro-finance. This third view stresses the need to recognise constraints and then deal with them, and their causes. These views get progressively less optimistic about poverty reduction and more concerned about the class locations of women (i.e. women's heterogeneity), a classic debate among feminists.

The micro-finance debate fails to tackle the fundamental question of whether under the private property system poverty can ever be alleviated. It fails to differentiate between money capital and physical capital, the real capacity for investment in capacity, training and apprenticeship. Furthermore, the necessity to employ and exploit waged labour in order to repay the borrowed finance remains. Evidence from urban India demonstrated that profits were only earned if a woman hired others. Women working as sole operators, as in Ahmedabad's cloth industry, have no profits to report (Kantor, 2001). Furthermore, as in all attempts to 'free' women by drawing them into the money economy, the necessity to provide the cooking/cleaning/education/social-reproduction services essential to the maintenance of monetised economic activity remains firmly outside the terms of debate.

Bill Cooke, a development management specialist, has argued that participation in development processes is conditioned by the powers that manage the processes themselves. Within modern capitalism, participation cannot occur on terms as idealistic as Habermas's ideal speech acts or on a 'level playing field' as claimed by neo-liberals (Cooke and Kothari, eds, 2001). Rather, there is a specific and historically traceable origin of development 'fashions', including the fashion for participatory development and for empowerment as an outcome of money-related initiatives. Furthermore, this origin is colonial/imperial in nature. As Cooke observes, development managers, such as the staff of major aid donors' local bureaux, even use the term 'empowerment' as part of an instrumental process, regardless of the fact that it remains dominated by (and specified by) first-world industrial countries' agendas.

> This is not to say that the dynamics of the relationship between First World agendas and what actually takes place as 'development' are complex and cannot be negotiated and even subverted. However, participation and empowerment cannot be in the gift of the First World, nor a requirement it makes of the Third, unless there is some imbalance of power between First and Third to begin with. This imbalanced power relationship means that any negotiation or subversion [and] participation in practice ... always takes place within First World boundaries ... (e.g. unconditional Third World Debt relief). (Cooke, 2001: 19)

Cooke goes on to analyse how discourses glorifying ownership have seeped into the donor community and even grass-roots NGOs' talk. This analysis coincides with our view that both in terms of discursive infection and of ignoring or masking real social inequalities of capitalism, the neo-liberal discourse is dangerous, domineering and subtly colonising the remnants of non-capitalist culture. It can ruin the best intentions concerning innovations in the money arena. Although this is not the place to explore these issues further, our framework creates a platform for further empirical research about how the processes work and how people resist neo-liberalism in practice. We argue the necessity to look beyond monetary innovation as a means to commandeer labour and resources to the service of capitalism, turning instead to forms of reform bringing social control over money.

Linking practice with theory

Proposals for monetary reform, basic income and the other reforms we have discussed would need to be endorsed by local if not national legislation. This will not be achieved while the present domination of mainstream economic thinking prevails. Meanwhile, small-scale experiments in worker control or co-operation, micro-credit and so on survive only so long as they remain *financially* viable under the system of capitalist financing, i.e. they must continue to provide *workers* with *incomes*. Other experiments, including LETS and 'downsizing' remain questionable as challenges to the *status quo*, depending as they do on the acquisition of sufficient personal income through co-operation as waged (or salaried) workers. The challenge for the next generation of thinkers is to work out what mechanisms, what mental mindsets and what political system of representations are needed to facilitate the transition from capitalist to post-capitalist social relations. In that post-capitalist vision it is likely that a regular 'basic income' paid to each member of each social unit would give a stable foundation for involvement in the polity. It is also likely that large-scale money movements will be socially debated through accountable institutions. Many other details would need to be addressed. How far should, and can, local initiatives encourage the free movement of goods? How would the free movement of people be enabled? On what basis would new residents in a community become integrated into the local economy?

Without a fundamental criticism of capitalist theory and practice, many innovations are doomed in the long run by the underlying social structure and its political-economic inequalities. The danger is that they will tend to reproduce underlying social inequalities rather than overcoming them. In this sense they may offer false hope. At the same time, people involved in developing new strategies may gain substantial empowerment or heightened awareness, and the value of these achievements must not be neglected. Every attempt to transform lives within capitalism is potentially an attempt to transform capitalism itself.

10 Towards Sustainability and Economic Democracy

It is becoming increasingly clear that to tackle unemployment and rebuild healthy, stable societies can only be done when citizens and nations take back control of their economies. (Hines, 2000: 239)

Historians in the 22nd century will look back in astonishment that people living now were brainwashed into believing the only way to get a satisfactory livelihood was to compete with people on the far side of the world to produce and sell products most of which were not strictly necessary for a decent life. (Robertson, 1998: 67)

We concur with Hines in his view that economic democracy is fundamental to social and ecological sustainability and with Robertson that the present economic system makes no social or environmental sense. Even perishable goods are flown thousands of miles (Paxton, 1994) as transnational corporations 'spin' the world to ecological destruction (Beder, 1997). Despite well-established alternative perspectives, neo-classical economic theory and the capitalist market have captured academic departments and government thinking in the dominant economies. They assert that there is no alternative to the dominance of money/market-oriented economic systems and the theories that sustain them. At the core of our critique of TINA economics is the role of money. What we have offered is a review of theories about money and about the operation of capitalised money economies together with alternative theories and practices. What we are saying is not new. It has been said many times before but been silenced. The main reason for the silencing is that the theories presented were directly against the interests of dominant groups and their supportive philosophies. A second reason is that within radical circles there has been a lack of 'joined up' thinking and a failure to theorise money adequately.

Money and forms of credit have existed historically but they have played a dominant role in capitalist market society, the money society. What is different about contemporary society is that it is a system based upon a particular kind of money, money created as debt through private banks. This has developed to such an extent that in Britain, for example, only 3 per cent of money is issued without debt by the democratically elected government as notes and coin, and even this is issued into the economy through banks. The second problem with modern society is that people do not have an independent source of provisioning. Without access to money and the market they and their families cannot survive. Therefore, in our view, the functioning of the economy as a provisioning system is of far greater significance than whether individual firms expand or contract, or the balance of payments is positive or negative. This is a fundamental matter for democracy. In a capitalised money society the decisions of private organisations and individuals based on 'economic' calculation decide the whole quality of life or even existence of the majority of people.

In this book we present the case for sustainability (a sufficiency economy) and economic democracy (a socialist economy). While mainstream economics is problematic on both counts, radical schools fail to provide us with a comprehensive answer. For example, while we find institutional/evolutionary economics helpful in re-engaging the economy with society (Hodgson *et al.*, 1994), pressures for economic conformity are still evident. Contemporary institutional economics has much to say about the evolution of specific firms or types of firms, but seems to pay little attention to the ecological sustainability of the economic system. There is a temptation among institutionalist economics to slip back into neo-liberal thinking rather than moving forward with the old-institutionalist (Veblenian) agenda for constructive social change, which sees economics as a political question. In the search for acceptance within the mainstream there is always a danger of being diverted into the paths of neo-classical theorising and the use of optimisation models which are idealist rather than realist.

Meanwhile, fundamental critiques of the terms within which capitalism works are deemed unscientific and beyond the scope of the mainstream economics profession. Central to mainstream economics and neo-liberal thinking is the separation of economics from other related social science disciplines. In opposition to the pretence of 'value-neutral facts' what is needed is holistic thinking across the academic disciplines if a socio-economic theory adequate to the times is to be achieved. Joined-up thinking works because the natural world supports and sustains, surrounds and permeates the social world. Our argument questions the value neutrality of neo-liberalism both as politics and as an academic tradition. While many people are taking the battle to the streets in anti-globalisation struggles or in their daily lives, we see this theoretical critique as part of what Gramsci called the 'war of position' (1996, original 1948; written 1928–35). Gramsci advocated the use of a 'war of position' in the political field rather than just a 'war of manoeuvre' in the military field between socialists and imperial capitalist powers. By a war of position, Gramsci refers to the gradual shifting of hearts, minds, and thought patterns away from the routines conditioned by capital's hegemony. Gramsci's insight is pulled together with the statement: 'In politics the "war of position", once won, is decisive definitely' (1996: 239). This chimes with Foucault's critique of the coercive power of the dominant discourse. Foucault's concept of resistance is consistent with the slogan 'think global, act local' which is commonly found among anti-globalisation protestors. Instead of the rather vague and unclear notion of anti-globalisation, we would describe the vociferous public protests of the years 1995 to 2001 as anti-capitalism protests, which is what they were.

One of the main impacts of the TINA era has been a general co-option or muting of opposition to global capitalism, particularly within the academy. As Alastair McIntosh recalls in his account of the exclusion of the Centre for Human Ecology from the Edinburgh University in 1996, academics who campaign were perceived to be an embarrassment: 'Yes they may do paid work for industry. And yes their reports may be used by industry for lobbying. But that's pro-fessional consultancy, which carries a dignity not shared by campaigning' (2001: 250). As funding regimes have become more and more overtly connected to 'business' requirements, there is little space for the radical or independent voice in modern research and information systems. In money societies even knowledge is a commodity for sale.

In this chapter we first compare our critical approach with some comparable monetary reform ideas. Then we present a summary stressing the links between work and money in a transformed social economy, and finally we survey the disastrous route that the Good Ship TINA (There Is No Alternative) has been following. We begin with money and monetary reform.

Money as a social phenomenon

It has become clear throughout this book that money is not a natural form, although it may exist in many societies. As Marx argued, money has to be a socially recognised form because the value of commodities is also a purely social reality. Neither money nor the good itself has a 'price'. What this means is that money does not have any inherent value even where it appears to be in a commodity form, such as gold. At the same time it is not neutral, just a veil for a real economy that happens in its name. Money is a social phenomenon with real economic effects. In money societies where a great deal of human provisioning and other activities occur via the money system, without it essential goods will not circulate. One key essential for the functioning of a money system is the existence of social trust. If only in this sense, the efficacy of money is a social and political question.

While money systems are not natural, as Marx pointed out, they appear natural to those engaged within them. Participation is also enforced by need, such that people have no choice but to engage with it where they have lost control over resources and even the skills needed to provision themselves. Money societies are also disciplinary societies in the Foucauldian sense. Conformity is taken to represent consent where the vast majority of people appear content to get and spend their money through innumerable transactions recorded daily within the formal economy. The seeming 'naturalness' justifies the 'scientific' study of economics, the seeming consent justifies the rejection of any normative approach to the economy with a view to effecting political change, and the confusion of money making with wealth creation justifies business-as-usual. Economists demand that any interference with the invisible hand must be justified *scientifically* not politically and all economic calculation assumes the neutrality of money. Money cannot be given directly to the people as a whole to whom it rightly belongs: it must be cycled through the productive system to come out as wages and salaries. The more that is produced, the more possible it becomes to distribute wealth (in goods and services through money) more fairly, *as long as* the redistribution process does not affect the ability of firms and individuals to *create* what economists see as wealth in the first place (by borrowing money into circulation). Although people appear to engage voluntarily in the money economy, most certainly they are not driven by the nicety of calculations assumed to embody

Rational Economic Man. Given the social nature of money and value (Zelizer, 1994) there is no logical basis for a 'scientific' study of economic actions. Hence the dependence on modelling.

We would not agree with Dodd that 'money's indeterminacy is its sole distinguishing feature' (1994: 152). Money is a very determinant phenomenon even if its value cannot be fixed. Dodd points to the dilemma of money: it promotes both freedom and inequality. Money appears to empower its holder because of the freedom it represents for the expression of needs and desires.

> Money ... is not defined by its properties as a material object but by symbolic qualities generically linked to the ideal of unfettered empowerment ... of complete freedom to act and assimilate at will ... [linking] the conception of money in general as a transparent symbolic medium ... with the idea of economic empowerment. (Dodd, 1994: 154)

At the same time 'money has been bound up with the unequal distribution of wealth and property whenever and wherever it has been found' (ibid: 159). Hence 'money ... symbolizes and is structurally interconnected with massive conflicts of interest based on the unequal distribution of wealth and power in society' (ibid: 160).

Simmel captures the abstract nature of money and its destructiveness but is also attracted by its seeming freedom. For Simmel 'exchange is the purest and most developed kind of interaction' (1900: 82) and 'money represents pure interaction in its purest form' (1900: 129), where 'the abstract value of wealth ... represented by money is ... the soul and purpose of economic activities' (1900: 511). Although Simmel claims that 'not a single line of these investigations is meant to be a statement about economics' (1900: 54), his view echoes the idea of money as a symbol of modernity and economy. He sees 'money as the incarnation and purest expression of ... economic value' (1900: 101), where 'the ideal purpose of money ... is to be a measure of all things without being measured itself ... it stands as the point of indifference and balance between all other phenomena in the world' (1900: 511) and 'when money stands still, it is no longer money according to its specific value and significance' (1900: 510).

Simmel also captures the dilemma of money systems that seem at one level to enhance human enjoyment. 'We invest economic objects with a quality of value as if it were an inherent quality and then hand them over to a process ... from which they return multiplied and more enjoyable to the final purpose ... subjective experience' (1900: 78), while 'the satisfaction of desire has a price' (1900: 76). Like Marx, Simmel also notes the ability of money to destroy utility: 'money is nothing but the vehicle for a movement in which everything else that is not in motion is completely extinguished ... it lives in continuous self-alienation ... and direct negation of all being in itself' (1900: 511).

As we have seen, capitalised money does not add value to society: it extracts it. It does not create security: it destroys it. The present money system is a mechanism for creating social value through the illusion of economic value. It defines those people and activities that are deemed to be 'valuable' in money terms, but it is only the fact that those people can access money that creates that value. It is a tautology. Money values money-value. At present money creation is largely outside democratic control. Even banks have little grip on circulation. Money is stolen, recycled, counterfeited, replaced. Who gets it and how is a question of power. Therefore, the issue and circulation of money is not neutral, it is not a function of economic exchange or economic logic, it is a matter of social power. As such it is a political question as it always was.

Once money is recognised as society's credit created as debt to be redeemed by those working in the money/market economy, we need look no further to establish the principle of money/credit as social. All economic agents who 'make' money, as bankers, commercial interests, or wage and salary earners, are in debt to society and the natural world for the real goods and services supplied to them by right of their possession of money. Money is the legal endorsement of society's credit. Having established this, the next stage is to examine ways in which individuals and groups have sought to retain and regain control over their own work and the intellectual and natural resources inherited from past generations, through gaining control over their finances. Freedom from wage and debt slavery is an essential first step to regaining the fundamental conditions of economic democracy.

In earlier chapters we have looked at a number of alternative mechanisms, new currency systems, mutual systems, basic income, downshifting. Our argument is that while many of these point to ways forward they will not provide the kind of radical shift that is needed unless they are framed within a holistic theoretical critique. As Bernard Lietaer has argued, monetary practice is well ahead of money theory and 'money is too important to be left only to bankers and economists' (preface to Douthwaite, 1999: 6–7). While we would concur with these sentiments about mainstream economic theory, there are also limits within the monetary reform perspective that Lietaer represents.

Monetary reform

Following the upsurge in the monetary reform debate during the 1930s, interest was not rekindled until the latter part of the twentieth century. In the UK the resurgence has been led by organisations such as the New Economics Foundation and by theorists such as Richard Douthwaite, James Robertson, Bernard Lietaer and Michael Rowbotham. Calls for monetary reform are based on a range of motives, but most commonly offer a basic criticism of debt-based money and a call for more democratic or local control of money creation.

Criticism of debt-created money rests on its propensity to drive the economy into continual expansion, risking environmental damage as well as pressure to overwork and over-consume. Interest payments and fractional reserve banking demand continued economic activity to maintain the circulation of debt-based finance. Money paid at interest must always expand earning power to cover the interest payment: production and circulation must take place if money is to circulate at all as it is borrowed into existence. This is the basis of Douglas' A+B theorem: there must always be new borrowings to cover the shortfall in the purchasing power of the current period, because some of the purchasing power of the product must have been spent in its creation. As Douglas observed, a debt-based economy will face continual crises of purchasing power, requiring new forms of debt-created finance. The late-twentieth-century solution has been the creation of private purchasing power through credit. Mortgages are particularly important, with the same houses being bought over and over again for ever-increasing prices. Mortgage borrowing in the UK counts for around 60 per cent of credit money and in the US 80 per cent. There is, however, always a limit to individuals, companies or countries borrowing money into existence. The system goes into decline as soon as potential new borrowers will not, or cannot, take on debt.

Monetary reform is the vital element in the creation of a sufficiency steady-state economy. As Douthwaite points out 'sustainability requires a money supply system that can run satisfactorily if growth stops' (1999: 27). Lietaer sees debt-based money as causing a scarcity of currency, while the market system based on 'scarce competitive fiat (hierarchy) money' (2001: 273) does not allow for the development of full human potential (2001: 265). He argues for new money systems based on sufficiency, co-operative and mutual credit principles (2001: 273), claiming that the opposite to scarcity is not abundance but sufficiency. For Lietaer, monetary specialists and greens alike typically see no connection between the money system and sustainability (2001: 242). However, Lietaer's own views are limited by his lack of attention to economic conflict. As Douthwaite observes, treating money as a scarce or problematic resource is a relic of the days of a limited supply of gold or silver. Monies based on limited currencies such as gold were certainly problematic, since they restricted trade. Douthwaite sees the laws on usury as being linked to the shortage of specie (1999: 33). If gold has to be paid back with additional gold, this must be achieved by extracting gold from someone else. With non-commodity money this problem appeared to be solved, offering the illusion that everyone could win, with interest and profits being extracted from an ever-growing cake.

The case for public (state) or people's control of money systems can be traced at least as far back as Abraham Lincoln and Thomas Jefferson. Both thought that money creation should be government-based. For Jefferson:

> If the American people ever allow the banks to control the issuance of their currency, first by inflation and then by deflation, the banks and the corporations that grow up around them will deprive the people of all property *until their children will wake up homeless on the continent their fathers occupied.* The issuing power of money should be taken from the banks and restored to Congress and the people to whom it belongs. I sincerely believe the banking institutions having the issuing power of money are more dangerous to liberty than standing armies. (Jefferson quoted by Rowbotham 1998: 34–5, emphasis in original)

Abraham Lincoln set out his ideas on monetary policy in a Senate document in 1865 just weeks before he was assassinated:

> Money is the creature of law, and the creation of the original issue of money should be maintained as the exclusive monopoly of

national government ... [which] possessing the power to create and issue currency and credit as money ... should create, issue and circulate all the currency and credit needed to satisfy the spending power of the government and the buying power of consumers ... the people can and will be furnished with a currency as safe as their own government. Money will cease to be the master and become the servant of humanity. Democracy will rise superior to the money power. (Lincoln quoted by Rowbotham, 1998: 220–1)

Neither got their way.

As many money reformers point out, who issues money has seigniorage – the ability to buy for 'free' in the economy. This is what kings did when issuing currency. The National Debt reflects the military and political ambitions or the personal extravagance of the rulers. Countries able to issue world currencies can consume vast amounts of resources. In 1998 the US had 57 per cent of the world foreign exchange reserves which effectively enabled it to 'tax' the world of billion of dollars through the operation of its banking system (Douthwaite, 1999: 54). Banks effectively have seignorage when they receive interest payments or when debts repaid are loaned out again as the 'bank's money'. When loans are paid back they do not cancel out the debt and return to zero. Money created into existence by the repayment of debt remains tangible: the bank has got 'its' money back. As lenders to owners and investors, banks have become major owners and investors themselves in modern society. When Enron collapses and major banks are 'exposed', what does this mean? Are they investor or lender?

If money issue produces seigniorage, this would suggest that the use of that money should be decided by the people as a whole, rather than by powerful interests represented by the monarch, the banks or even the state. In *Creating New Money* James Huber and James Robertson (*c*.2000) call on the UK and other national governments to restore seigniorage, thereby ending the creation of money by the banks. To do this, they argue, it would be necessary to declare sight deposits as legal tender, requiring a 'simple but fundamental' change in the law. This, the authors maintain, would be an uncontroversial reform, having virtually no effect on the everyday routines of banks and financial markets. They take as an example Article 16 of the Statute of the European System of Central Banks and the European Central Bank. The Article, entitled 'Banknotes', reads:

The Governing Council shall have the exclusive right to authorise the issue of banknotes within the Community. The ECB and the national central banks may issue such notes. The banknotes issued by the ECB and the national central banks shall be the only such notes to have the status of legal tender within the Community. (Quoted in Huber and Robertson, c.2000: 21)

By changing the title of Article 16 to 'Legal Tender' it could now read as follows:

The Governing Council shall have the exclusive right to authorise the issue of legal tender within the Community. Legal tender includes coin, banknotes, and sight deposits. The ECB and the national central banks may issue such means of payment. Coin, banknotes and sight deposits issued by the ECB and the national central banks shall be the only means of payment to have the status of legal tender within the Community. (Huber and Robertson, c.2000: 21)

Huber and Robertson claim that reform would merely give recognition to the *status quo*: central banks are public authorities 'central to the monetary system, responsible for creating and regulating the stock of all official money within their territory' (c.2000: 21). While traditionally the state prerogative has been limited to coins and banknotes, sight deposits have been regarded as legal tender, i.e. as a legally recognisable form of payment of debt or wages. Seigniorage reform would restore the prerogative of the state to issue legal tender while capturing as public revenue the seigniorage income that arises from issuing it. Commercial banks would no longer be able to create new credit. Instead they would adopt the role they are commonly assumed to hold, as mere credit-broking financial intermediaries.

The suggestion that governments be empowered to spend new money into circulation while reaping the financial benefits of doing so, holds much in common with social credit as a route to economic democracy. Like Douglas, Huber and Robertson suggest that central monetary authorities should be legally accountable to elected governments but independent of party political control, creating new money 'in the context of broad policy objectives that have been democratically approved' (c.2000: 18). Although that is as far as Huber and Robertson go, their text provides a valuable guide to the legalities of the money-creation process.

However, if seigniorage reform is not presented within a theoretical and political framework, the question of exactly *how* the new changes would impact on the economic processes of production, distribution and exchange is unclear. Increasing the fiat role of the state neatly sidesteps the fundamental question of what exactly money *is* in the first place. Questions need to be asked about *for and by whom* should monetary reform be undertaken. For these reasons, much excellent work investigating the ills of the unsustainable debt-based economy remains incomplete, with the implicit assumption that the overall aim is rationalisation of existing economic structures. Douthwaite, Robertson and Lietaer, for example, argue for multiple money systems with the implication that at least one of these continues to fund a capitalised market system. Douthwaite sees three main uses for money – store of value, exchange medium and unit of account. The problem is that these uses act against each other. Money used as a store of value can undermine its use as a medium of exchange. He argues for multiple, complementary money systems for store of value, national, international and local trade. However, it is unclear how a local money system, for example, would enhance the local economy if the national or global economy carries on business-as-usual. This would be particularly important where essentials had to be bought in from national/international currency areas.

It is evident from Douthwaite's work that, if anything, he sees an increasing role for private financial activity. He argues for a new international currency, the 'ebcu' (energy-backed currency units) but goes on to say 'the market should solely determine the value of national and regional exchange currencies in relation to the ebcu ... speculators ought to be able to moderate the rate of change of the currencies and prevent them overshooting their new values' (1999: 65). He even refers uncritically to the circular flow (1999: 70). Basically, he sees different currencies as offering 'semi-permeable membranes' protecting local economies and balancing trade for 'stability and sustainability' (1999: 72). Local currencies would be counter-cyclical. When the market economy was going well they would disappear and reappear as they did widely in the 1930s when the formal economy was in depression. For Douthwaite, democratic control of money would support business-as-usual such that 'the allocative function of interest would work properly as the capital market would not be constantly blown hither and thither by control-of-money-supply considerations' (1999: 62).

Lietaer's ideas are equally sanguine about the continued existence of the capitalist economy. He adopts the notion of 'integral economies' based on combining the yang economies of financial and physical capital (i.e. industry) and the yin of natural and social capital. He sees these as both necessary and complementary: 'it is time to recognize that both types of capital – financial and social – are indispensable for human activity to flourish' (2001: 277). He seeks a win-win approach for finance, business and society (2001: 237):

> Social capital is best nurtured by co-operation-inducing Yin currencies, while global industrial trade would be best handled by competition-generating Yang currencies ... currency is always about relationships ... different kinds of currency will tend to induce different kinds of relationships among its users ... where you want to create a cooperative, egalitarian, Yin type of relationship use Yin type currencies ... trading with Yang currencies will tend to shape competitive, hierarchical relationships, perfectly appropriate for certain contexts like business. (Lietaer, 2001: 274)

The use of the term 'capital' here is also indicative. Lietaer talks of natural, social, financial, physical (and knowledge) capital. As we observed in Chapter 8, why use the word 'capital' rather than social relationships, social interactions or social processes? As Ben Fine (1999) has argued, the use of such concepts merely concedes ground to neo-liberal thinking.

Monetary reform is weakened in its demand for 'monetary justice' if it is not linked to a wider critique of the capitalist economy. Although at times insightful and inspired in their chosen field, monetary reformers tend not to be rooted in opposition to waged labour, as social credit money theory is, nor are they grounded more generally in socialist principles. Central to our view of sustainable economic democracy would be a money system created by users within an economic community based on sufficiency. That community may vary in size or origin, but central to its provisioning would be local democratic control over basic resources.

From waged labour to social credit

As Marx observed, a particular form of income distribution, waged labour, linked to production for profitable exchange underlies the economics of capitalism. We have argued that capitalism feeds on human co-operation and the natural world, while basing its dominance on the flimsy theoretical foundations that the economic agent is always and everywhere motivated by greed, competition and self-interest. It is not only debt that creates exploitation: it is the desire of dominant groups in society (which may be within the government itself) to live a privileged life at the expense of others. Resources are enclosed, crippling taxes and tributes are extracted, money is salted away, people are forced by need into bonded or waged labour. As Kovel has argued, waged labour is inherently undemocratic:

> However kindly the face put to it, and however it is rationalised and justified by appeals to necessity and efficiency, the fact remains, that by converting our power to transform nature into a commodity to be exchanged for wages, one reduces human beings to the level of machines. (Kovel, 2000: 11–12)

Like Douglas, we do not attempt to present a blueprint for an alternative to capitalism. Instead, we seek to expose the foundations of the present money system so that available options may emerge. Money is man-made. We use the male pronoun consciously. Society's money is debt-created, to be bought back mainly through waged labour. The way money circulates is determined by institutions created by human beings. It is possible to study those institutions. In particular, it is possible to study the history of the institutions in order to understand how and why they are as they are. In the light of the findings, various possible routes to alternatives may emerge.

Social credit was the economics of guild socialism, a founding strand of the UK Labour party, which came very close to becoming politically dominant in the formation of Labour party policy. It is, perhaps, idle to speculate what *might* have happened to socialism in Europe had the UK Fabians *not* set up the London School of Economics in order to teach aspiring Labour politicians businesslike and politically correct 'marginalist' neo-classical economic theory. As events unfolded, mainstream economic theory held sway over the moulding of Labour's political agenda, while the demand to end capitalism was replaced by the demand for a better deal for the employed (and the unemployed) working class under capitalism (see Hutchinson and Burkitt, 1997). The Labour party in 1922 distanced itself from social credit and guild socialism. It rejected proposals for a 'national dividend', argued from within the social credit context, which opened up the possibility of an unearned income as a right for all citizens regardless of work status in recognition of the right of all to a share in the common cultural inheritance.

Whereas a monetary reformer such as Douthwaite sees three types of currency – people currencies, private banks and governments – Douglas' perspective is much more focused on the role of people's banks, rather than people's currency systems: that is, the creation of money at the local level through producer/consumer banks. The main point would be that a decision to invest would not be based on the concept of profitability or the ability to return the money, but on the needs of the community. Douglas also saw the need for statutory endorsement of any newly evolving economic structures, if they were to do anything more than handle small-scale local exchange. The necessity for state regulation was also recognised by Marx, Veblen, and the guild socialists generally. Social control of money, i.e. social credit, would require statutory endorsement of the money-creation process. This is little different to the position now where the privatised control of the money-creation process is state-sanctioned.

Autonomous local networks or 'free enterprise' creation of money on the Hayekian model would not resolve the inequalities inherent in a capitalised money system. Production, distribution and exchange between freely associated producers would need to be guaranteed and protected within a framework of law devised within a democratic process. The essence of the social credit system was, therefore, the issue of a national dividend as a basic income and the organisation of provisioning through local co-operatives. The key to their interaction would be the producer/consumer banks.

As Rowbotham observes: 'Douglas pointed out that in a modern industrial society there was potentially enough for everyone and that included a share of the leisure bound up in unemployment and progress' (1998: 235). He argues that Douglas bridged the 'divide of jealousy' between rich and poor created by scarcity-money and the conflict between the businessman and his (*sic*) employees. Like Douglas, Rowbotham sees class conflict as rooted in the money system. For him, the main problem of the 'exploitable status of a wage dependent population' would be resolved by a basic income and a 'decentralisation and balance of financial power'. Furthermore, as Rowbotham rightly indicates, neither capitalists nor socialists have paid attention to the role of the financial system, although we would argue that Marx did. To focus only on the financial system could lead to a simplistic and negative 'blame the bankers' approach. Douglas' ideas must be set within the context of the work of Veblen and Marx if they are not to be distorted into nationalistic or authoritarian politics. However, if we leave money and banking untheorised, or ignore a rich mine of radical thought that had its origins in egalitarian politics, whenever banking crises emerge the forces of reaction can once more step in to 'save' the people from their 'enemies' within or without.

Debt-based money has played a particular role in the construction of inequality in modern society. That should not, however, imply that those who developed the credit-banking system foresaw the outcome. They may have developed fractional reserve banking to make extra profit, but it did also aid trade. What has happened in practice is that money has been used to accumulate real resources and to force the majority of people into waged labour. It has also become clear that money, which has no intrinsic value, is destroying the value of everything else. From within money-valuing systems it is perfectly logical to destroy every square inch of the planet, turning it into money while declaring the world to have maximised its value. However, wealth is created by society as a whole: individuals and firms make very little contribution *as individuals*. Douglas, like Marx and Veblen, argued for the right of all members of society to share in the benefits of their shared heritage of knowledge, skill and resources.

In this book we are not advocating the implementation of the ideas of Douglas or social credit solutions. We are exploring their theoretical framework and their critique of debt-based money systems as the basis for new forms of socio-economic theorisation that will not confuse wealth creation with money-making, nor commodity production and exchange with the provisioning of human societies. We are looking towards a politics capable of accepting the functioning of money systems as a political question. Such a politics will see money as the servant of mutual socio-economic arrangements and not the master. We are looking towards a system of provisioning that will enhance human potential without destroying the life of the planet.

Sufficiency and subsistence

While democratic control of money issue and provisioning systems have been central to this book, ecological sustainability is equally vital. Arguably, if there were no limits to growth an expansionary capitalist system could continue provided it could solve its problems of business cycles and inequality. However, as we have argued, there are two problems. First, the issue of money under debt-creation has the inherent problem of a shortage of money in any time period where there is no investment for the future or further debt-created money. The capitalised money system can only deal with both cir-culation and inequality through constant growth, and the consequences of economic growth and externalised ecological costs have become increasingly obvious. Second, with debt-based money there is no direct link between production and provisioning: what is profitable is not necessarily socially useful or egalitarian. For ecological sustainability, therefore, it would be necessary to link economic activity directly to provisioning and to internalise all ecological costs. What is needed is a steady-state economy with as far as possible a circular metabolism through recycling, reuse and non-use. A sustainable economy cannot run on the linear capitalist principles that result from debt-based money issue. Democratic par-ticipation is central:

> Bringing economic decision-making close to the people who are not only going to pay for the decision but live with the conse-quences of it makes it more likely that the decision will be a good one – for the environment and for people. (Group of Green Economists, 1992: xiii)

From a green perspective the key to sustainability is sufficiency. The current competitive system is destructive not only for the envi-ronment, but for people (Lane, 2000). It is argued that many people would willingly adopt a mode of voluntary simplicity (Elgin, 1981) and that in production terms 'small is beautiful' (Schumacher, 1973). The green economy is seen as a local economy, meeting local needs from the local environment with local labour. Veronika Bennholdt-Thomsen and Maria Mies argue that ecological sustainability must begin from a subsistence perspective (1999). They claim that the conditions for subsistence already exist, or can be rekindled, in both the North and the South. Retention of the remaining 'commons' must be the first priority together with a rejection of the global market economy and the western way of life that underpins it.

Certainly our critique of the destruction and expropriation of the means of subsistence in the formation of capitalist market systems would lead us to have great sympathy with these ideas. Often within green thought there is a confusion between subsistence as sufficiency and as self-reliance. Subsistence economies are generally taken to be those that have existed before industrialisation, the tribal or peasant economy. Bennholdt-Thomsen and Mies are using the idea in the sense of reclaiming an independent means of livelihood by disengaging from money/market economies. Wolfgang Sachs, one of the founders of the Wuppertal Institute, writes on similar lines:

> Local self-reliance has long been perceived solely in terms of conservation of resources. But it should be viewed more broadly as an inversion of market relations on two levels: first, to downscale the range of exchange relations so as to strengthen the local economy, closing more economic circuits within the regional space; and second to stimulate unpaid work and a whole new variety of non-economic activities. In other words, a different model of economic security is proposed, one where wealth is not derived from specialising in export for distant markets, and sending the earned money to distant producers in order to import a large percentage of food, energy, materials, insurance, health care, but rather from reducing people's involvement in the national and international economy and providing more locally. In the long run, what we might call a market-enhanced self-reliant economy should enable people to live gracefully with less money, less consumption and less wage labour, because an infrastructure which is geared towards self-sufficiency will compensate for losses in income. (1986: 333)

Sachs attacks the 'smoke stack economy' of 'super-industrialism', which plunders resources and inflates administration, transforming resources into wastes and ecological destruction.

Hines also sees the contemporary political battle as not being between left and right but between the localists and globalists. His call is 'Localists of the world unite – there is an Alternative' (2000: 241). Crucially, Hines insists that localism should not be interpreted as narrow nationalism, protectionism or beggar my neighbour. It would be a global manifesto that is a 'supportive internationalism of localisation' (2000: 245). As he indicates, the most likely source of reactionary nationalism are communities suffering economically under the pressures of the globalised, competitive capitalist market. In this observation, Hines joins Gandhi, Douglas and many others in making the links between trade and warfare. Marshall Sahlins has also demonstrated a link between warfare and peaceful exchange between factions or nations (1974). Global economic competition continues to operate under thinly veiled threats of military warfare.

At the local level a provisioning economy based on sufficiency would be defined and organised in many different ways and on different technological and cultural bases. What would no longer exist would be the globalisation of commodity production based on the 'comparative advantage' of cheaper wages and resource costs in money terms. This would not preclude trade in exotics, meaning literally those things that are not obtained locally, but this would be based on fair trade. With no accumulation of riches in particular economies there would be no pressure for economic migration, although cultural exchange and movement of peoples between communities would still occur. There may well still be need for mass production of some sorts of provisioning and for specialisation in some areas. That is something that needs to be debated in terms of resource use and appropriateness, not on the basis of a monetary calculation.

What is important is that the economic myth that people's wants are insatiable needs to be challenged. We are arguing that in money/market systems people are not driven by greed but by need and insecurity. What people do not have in modern commodified economies is any direct access to their means of sustenance, of livelihood. Before any sufficiency system can be devised, natural resources and provisioning decisions would need to be placed in the hands of democratically controlled communities. One of the greatest difficulties in reclaiming democratic control over basic subsistence needs is the confusion of needs and wants under capitalism. In its search for capital accumulation, the capitalist economy has incorporated both wants and needs. However, its ability to meet needs is not equitable or systematic. Meeting needs is not its prime function. Prioritisation of needs over wants can only be achieved if consumption demand and supply decisions are brought together. This, of course, is what classical economic theory claims happens, but in practice consumption is aggressively supply-led where richer communities are bombarded with pressures to consume. Putting demand and supply in the hands of people collectively as envisaged by social credit would solve this problem.

The good ship TINA

We liken the capitalist economy to an ancient galley ship (Hutchinson and Olsen, 2001), an analogy that has also appealed to other critics (Hines, 2000). Designed and developed to meet the unsustainable aspirations of a bygone era, the ship draws its energy through monetary mechanisms which now require a thorough overhaul if social and environmental sustainability is to be achieved. We argue that attempts to achieve *economic* sustainability are analogous to the maintenance of a sinking ship whose captain and crew imagine they can pilot the ship to safe waters. Twenty-first century attempts to maintain the ship/economy are placing unsustainable strains upon the planet's own life-support systems. As we show in Figure 10.1, the ship/economy is embedded in the social and natural economy (compare Figure 8.1 where the real economy was discussed).

Economic theorists have spent their lives analysing the activity on the ship without looking at what lies beyond. The maintenance of equilibrium within the circular flow of the ship-based money economy has remained the focus of mainstream economic theorising throughout the twentieth century. However, although the formal money economy (the central section of Figure 8.1) *measures* wealth in money terms, it does not *create* wealth: that is done with resources provided by human society and its natural environment. While the formal economy can put a money value on 'wealth', creating such measures as GNP, it fails to measure the degradation and depreciation of social and natural capital.

In consequence, with unnerving speed, the ship/economy is heading towards a series of icebergs. Suggestions that the ship be slowed down at least until a safe route forward is discovered are met with blank incomprehension by the crew (policy-makers, leading politicians, academics and financiers) and passengers (top business management). Meanwhile wage-slaves and non-ship (unpaid social reproduction and self-provisioning) labour lack the knowledge and power to gain control of the ship and route it into safer waters.

Until very recently, most people spent most of their lives off the 'ship', supplying almost all their needs and pleasures from their own land, within local communities. As traditional resources, knowledge and skills have been plundered by ship culture, the natural resources of the earth have been despoiled. The main problem is that the passengers and crew have no conception of the true extent of their dependence upon, and desecration of, 'non-ship' labour and the fertility of the land. It is difficult to visualise the conditions of virtual

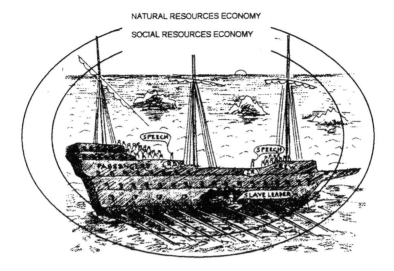

Figure 10.1   The Sinking of TINA

slave labour which produced the chips for our computers, and the distant chemical factory which manufactured the ink you are now reading. As the ship grew in proportion to the social and material resources available to communities on the land, questions were raised from different quarters about the advisability and desirability of its growth. However, since most unease was expressed on land, i.e. by non-ship labour, it had no effect whatsoever on the crew of the ship. They had their own agenda: they sought to enable the ship/economy to grow and continue moving forwards. They simply took. There was no other agenda on the agenda. Of course the ship must grow, and it needed resources to do so.

Note that this analogy, like all analogies, is only useful up to a point. All agents on the 'ship', i.e. in the formal economy, relate to each other through the money system. They are paid to do things, or pay for things, in money. One problem is that many tasks are undertaken from mixed motives: a nurse is paid to care, but does not *only* care because s/he is paid. Furthermore, people cannot be classed as *either* passengers *or* crew *or* slaves *or* non-ship labour. Individuals play more than one role at a time. Passengers, wealthy business people, often work very hard within the system in managerial roles; they are certainly not the 'idle rich'. The crew, leading politicians, academics, bankers and professional salary earners generally work with the 'passengers' to devise ways to keep the ship moving forward. The slaves, waged workers below senior management level, follow orders for money rewards. Most of the *essential* work necessary to keep the ship afloat is done by non-ship labour. *All* on board the ship are at some time in their lives, often for much of their lives, part of the pool of non-ship labour (working in their homes and in voluntary work in the community). The amount of non-ship labour necessary to keep the ship going is vast. Without it the ship would sink without a trace.

However, if the ship does crash into an iceberg, the survivors (crew, passengers or slaves) will not survive for long because there is nowhere else for them to go. The ship has grown so large that it has drained the land and its peoples of the ability to survive outside the ship. Although the Good Ship TINA (There Is No Alternative), the money economy of western capitalism, is an artificial construction, made entirely from non-ship materials and non-ship labour, it has been around so long that it seems to be a natural phenomenon. Nobody, whether crew, passengers, slaves or non-ship labour, absolutely nobody can imagine life without the ship. Since the possibility of TINA running into an iceberg is unthinkable, discussion of alternatives does not even appear on the agenda. Debt-fuelled economic growth is left to continue unabated, and the ship sails on, devouring the very resources upon which its existence depends.

A new vision

The case for sufficiency and democratic control of the means of subsistence lies in the fact that in an ecologically finite and interconnected world freedom cannot be defined by consumption and the mainstream utopian idea of economic 'autonomy'. Instead, freedom must be defined by the right to sufficiency on an egalitarian and democratic basis. Our first task has been to undertake the necessary critique of male-dominated/capitalist economic thought and in particular the real and ideological role that money plays. Secondly, we have sought to envision enlightened change to the basic financial institutions of society, that is, to the money and banking system. We have also suggested some movements or organisations that seem to embody some of the principles we are discussing. It remains beyond the scope of this book to map out a detailed blueprint for the adaptation of the present system to meet future needs. Nevertheless, the mere envisioning of the possibility of change is in itself revolutionary. It facilitates consideration of change on personal and community levels. Once individuals question their own relationship with money by reviewing the ways they obtain and spend their incomes, new vistas are opened up. Changing the conceptualisation of the income/work relationship is at once liberating and revolutionary. Economic orthodoxy can be critiqued and challenged on theoretical grounds, but it requires a judicious mix of theory and practice to mount a meaningful challenge to the *status quo*.

Radical socio-economic change can only be achieved in the context of a clear understanding of the nature of the money society. Small-scale monetary experiments will not overthrow capitalism, nor will isolated examples of small-scale localisation or socialisation. What is needed, as Hines argues is localisation (and we would add socialisation) at a global scale (2000) – that is, a global commitment to the local, everybody's local, which would also embrace the habitat of non-human species. Exposing the real nature of monetary systems and their destructive role together with feasible proposals for new forms of socio-economic organisations and statutory instruments can provide us with at least a pathway to that vision.

Bibliography

Adams, W.M. (1993) *Green Development*, London: Routledge.

Adams, John (1995) *Risk*, London: University College London Press.

Alier, Joan Martinez (1987) *Ecological Economics*, London: Macmillan.

Alier, Joan Martinez (2000) 'International Biopiracy versus the Value of Local Knowledge', *Capitalism, Nature, Socialism*, 11:2, pp. 59–66.

Athanasiou, Tom (1997) *Slow Reckoning: The Ecology of a Divided Planet*, London: Secker and Warburg.

Bakker, Isabella, ed. (1994) *The Strategic Silence: Gender and Economic Policy*, London: Zed Books, and Ottawa: The North-South Institute.

Becker, Gary (1976) *The Economic Approach to Human Behaviour*, Chicago: University of Chicago Press.

Beder, Sharon (1997) *Global Spin: The Corporate Assault on Environmentalism*, Totnes and Vermont: Green Books and Chelsea Green Publishing.

Bennholdt-Thomsen, Veronika and Maria Mies (1999) *The Subsistence Perspective: Beyond the Globalised Economy*, London and New York: Zed Books. Australia: Spinifex.

Bhaduri, Amit (1973) 'A Study in Agricultural Backwardness Under Semi-Feudalism', *Economic Journal*, March, pp. 120–37.

Bhaduri, Amit (1977) 'On the Formation of Usurious Interest Rates in Backward Agriculture', *Cambridge Journal of Economics*, 1, pp. 341–52.

Bhaduri, Amit (1983) *The Economic Structure of Backward Agriculture*, London: Academic Press.

Bhaduri, Amit (1986) 'Forced Commerce and Agrarian Growth', *World Development*, 14:2, pp. 267–72.

Bhaskar, Roy (1993) *Dialectic and the Pulse of Freedom*, London: Verso.

Blaug, Mark (2000) 'Henry George: Rebel with a Cause', *European Journal History of Economic Thought*, 7:2 (Summer), pp. 270–88.

Booth, David (1998) *The Environmental Consequences of Growth*, London: Routledge.

Boserup, Ester (1970) *Women's Role in Economic Development*, New York: St Martin's Press.

Boyle, David (no date) *Why London Needs its Own Currency*, London: New Economic Foundation.

Braidotti, Rosi, Ewa Charkiewicz, Sabine Hausler and Saskia Wieringa (1994) *Women, the Environment and Sustainable Development*, London: Zed Press.

Brandt, Barbara (1995) *Whole Life Economics: Revaluing Daily Life*, Philadelphia: New Society Publishers.

Brass, Tom, and Marcel van der Linden, eds (1997) *Free and Unfree Labour: The Debate Continues*, Berlin and Paris: Peter Lang AG.

Brennan, Teresa (1997) 'Economy for the Earth: The Labour Theory of Value Without the Subject/Object Distinction', *Ecological Economics*, 20:2, pp. 175–85.

Brohman, John (1995) 'Economism and Critical Silences in Development Studies: A Theoretical Critique of Neoliberalism', *Third World Quarterly*, 16:2, pp. 297–318.

Bromley, Daniel W. (1991) *Environment and Economy: Property Rights and Public Policy*, Oxford: Blackwell.

Buchan, James (1997) *Frozen Desire*, London: Picador.

Buck, Nick, Jonathan Gershuny, David Rose, and Jacqueline Scott, eds (1994) *Changing Households: The British Household Panel Survey 1990–1992*, ESRC Research Centre On Micro-Social Change, Univ. of Essex.

Bujra, Janet (2000) 'Diversity in Pre-Capitalist Societies', Ch. 10 in Tim Allen and Alan Thomas, eds, *Poverty and development into the 21st century*, Oxford: Oxford University Press.

Bullard, Robert D. (1990) *Dumping in Dixie: Race, Class and Environmental Equality*, Boulder, CO: Westview.

Burkitt, Brian (1984) *Radical Political Economy*, Brighton: Harvester.

Cameron, Sam (1995) 'A Review of Economic Research into Determinants of Divorce', *British Review of Economic Issues*, 17:41, Feb. 1–22.

Carley, Michael, and Ian Christie (2000) *Managing Sustainable Development*, London: Earthscan.

Carney, Diana (2000) 'Implementing the Sustainable Livelihoods Approach', Ch. 1 in Diana Carney, ed., *Sustainable Rural Livelihoods: What Contribution Can We Make?*, London: Department for International Development (DFID).

Carson, Rachel (1962) *Silent Spring*, London: Hamish Hamilton (1964 edn).

CGAP (Consultative Group to Assist the Poorest) (1995) 'Micro-Finance for Poverty Alleviation and Private Sector Development', *Focus*, Note No. 1, Oct., <cproject@worldbank.org>.

Chomsky, Noam (2002) *Understanding Power: The Indispensable Chomsky* (ed. Peter R. Mitchell and John Schoeffel), New York: The New Press.

Chossudovsky, Michel (1997) *The Globalisation of Poverty: Impacts of IMF and World Bank Reforms*, London/Penang: Zed Books/Third World Network.

Cole, G.D.H. (1919) *Self-Government in Industry*, London: Bell.

Cooke, Bill (2001) 'From Colonial Administration to Development Management', IDPM Working Paper No. 63, Institute for Development Policy and Management, March.

Cooke, Bill, and Uma Kothari, eds (2001) *The Tyranny of Participation*, London: Zed Books.

Crow, Ben (1999) 'Researching the Market System in Bangladesh', Ch. 5 in Harriss-White, ed., *Agricultural Markets From Theory to Practice: Field Experience in Developing Countries*, London, Macmillan.

Crow, Ben, and K.A.S. Murshid (1994) 'Economic Returns to Social Power: Merchants' Finance and Interlinkage in the Grain Markets of Bangladesh', *World Development*, 22:7.

Da Corta, Lucia, and Davuluri Venkateswarlu (1999) 'Unfree Relations and the Feminisation of Agricultural Labour in Andhra Pradesh, 1970–1995', *Journal of Peasant Studies*, 26:2&3, pp. 71–139.

Da Corta, Lucia, and Davuluri Venkateswarlu (2001) 'Transformations in the Age and Gender of Unfree Workers on Hybrid Cotton Seed Farms in Andhra Pradesh', *Journal of Peasant Studies*, 28:3, April, pp. 1–36.

Daly, Herman, ed. (1973) *Towards a Steady-State Economy*, San Francisco: W.H. Freeman.

Daly, Herman (2001a) *The Feasta Lecture* 1999, *Feasta Review*, No. 1, pp. 15–27.

Daly, Herman (2001b) 'Five Policy Recommendations for a Sustainable Economy', *Feasta Review*, No. 1, pp. 28–35.

Daly, Herman, and John B. Cobb Jr. (1990) *For the Common Good: Redirecting the Economy Toward Community, the Environment, and a Sustainable Future*, London: Green Print. (NB: another edition is published by Beacon Press, 1994.)

Dauncey, Guy (1988) *After the Crash: The Emergence of the Rainbow Economy*, London: Greenprint.

Davies, Glyn (1994) *A History of Money: From Ancient Times to the Present Day*, Cardiff: University of Wales (1996 edn).

De Angelis, Massimo (1996) 'Social Relations, Commodity-Fetishism and Marx's Critique of Political Economy', *Review of Radical Economics*, 28:4, pp. 1–29.

Dodd, Nigel (1994) *The Sociology of Money*, Cambridge: Polity.

Dominguez, Joe and Vicki Robin (1992) *Your Money or Your Life*, New York: Penguin.

Dordoy, Alan and Mary Mellor (2000) 'Ecosocialism and Feminism: Deep Materialism and the Contradictions of Capitalism', *Capitalism, Nature, Socialism*, 11:3, pp. 41–61.

Douglas, Clifford Hugh (1918) 'The Delusion of Super-Production', *English Review*, Dec. 1918, pp. 428–32.

Douglas, Clifford Hugh (1919a) 'The Pyramid of Power' pp. 49–58, 100–7: 'What is Capitalism?' pp. 166–9: 'Exchange and Exports' pp. 368–70, *English Review*.

Douglas, Clifford Hugh (1919b) *Economic Democracy*, Sudbury: Bloomfield (1974 reprint).

Douglas, Clifford Hugh (1920) *Credit-Power and Democracy*, London: Cecil Palmer.

Douglas, Clifford Hugh (1922) *The Control and Distribution of Production*, London: Stanley Nott (1934 edn).

Douglas, Clifford Hugh (1924) *Social Credit*, Vancouver: Institute of Economic Democracy (1979 reprint).

Douglas, Clifford Hugh (1934) 'Major Douglas at Aberdeen', *The New Age* (11 October), pp. 271–2.

Douthwaite, Richard (1996) *Short Circuit: Strengthening Local Economies for Security in an Unstable World*, Totnes, UK: Green Books.

Douthwaite, Richard (1999) *The Ecology of Money*, Totnes, UK: Greenbooks.

Douthwaite, Richard and Dan Wagman (1999) *Barataria: A Community Exchange Network for the Third System*, Utrecht: Strohalm.

Dow, Shiela (2000) 'Prospects for the Progress of Heterodox Economics', *Journal of the History of Economic Thought*, 22:2, pp. 157–70.

Dugger, William M. (2000) 'Deception and Inequality: The Enabling Myth Concept' in Robert Pollin, ed., *Capitalism, Socialism, and Radical Political Economy*, Cheltenham: Edward Elgar.

Dupré, John and Regina Gagnier (1999) 'The Ends of Economics' in Martha Woodmansee and Mark Osteen, eds, *The New Economic Criticism: Studies at the Intersection of Literature and Economics*, London and New York: Routledge.

Ecologist, The (1993) *Whose Common Future? Reclaiming the Commons*, London: Earthscan.

Egan, Beth (2001) *The Widow's Mite: How Charities Depend on the Poor*, London: Social Market Foundation.

Ehrlich, Paul (1968) *The Population Bomb*, London: Pan/Ballantyne.

Ekins, Paul (2000) *Economic Growth and Environmental Sustainability*, London: Routledge.

Ekins, Paul and Manfred Max-Neef (1992) *Real Life Economics*, London: Routledge.

Elgin, Duane (1981) *Voluntary Simplicity*, New York: William Morrow.

Emeagwali, Gloria Thomas, ed. (1995) *Women Pay the Price: Gender and Structural Adjustment in Africa*, London: Africa World Press.

Epstein, Edwin M. (1969) *The Corporation in American Politics*, New Jersey: Prentice-Hall.

Esping-Anderson, Gøsta (1996) *Welfare States in Transition: National Adaptions in Global Economies*, London: Sage.

Fairclough, Norman (2000) *New Labour, New Language*, London: Routledge.

Feiner, Susan (1995) 'Reading Neo-classical Economics: Towards an Erotic Economy of Sharing', in Edith Kuiper and Yolande Sap, eds, *Out of the Margin: Feminist Perspectives on Economics*, London and New York: Routledge.

Feiner, Susan (1999) 'Portrait of Homo Economicus as a Young Man', in Martha Woodmansee and Mark Osteen, eds, *The New Economic Criticism: Studies at the Intersection of Literature and Economics*, London: Routledge.

Ferber, Marianne A. and Julie A. Nelson (1993) *Beyond Economic Man*, Chicago: University Press.

Fine, Ben (1999) 'The Developmental State is Dead – Long Live Social Capital?', *Development and Change*, 30:1, pp. 1–19.

Fine, Ben (2001) *Social Capital Versus Social Theory: Political Economy and Social Science at the Turn of the Millennium*, London: Routledge.

Fisher, Irving (1933) *Stamp Scrip*, New York: Adelphi Company.

Folbre, Nancy (1982) 'Exploitation Comes Home: A Critique of the Marxian Theory of Family Labour', *Cambridge Journal of Economics*, 6, pp. 317–29.

Folbre, Nancy (1993) *Who Pays for the Kids? Gender and the Structures of Constraint*, London: Routledge.

Folbre, Nancy (2001) *The Invisible Heart: Economics and Family Values*, NY: The New Press.

Frank, Thomas (2001) *One Market Under God: Extreme Capitalism, Market Populism and the End of Economic Democracy*, London: Secker and Warburg.

Freeman, Alan (1995) 'Marx Without Equilibrium', *Capital and Class*, 56, pp. 49–90.

Freeman, Alan (1996) 'The Psychopathology of Walrasian Marxism', in Alan Freeman and Guglielmo Carchedi, eds, *Marx and Non-Equilibrium Economics*, Cheltenham: Edward Elgar.

Freeman, Alan, and Guglielmo Carchedi, eds (1996) *Marx and Non-Equilibrium Economics*, Cheltenham: Edward Elgar.

Friedmann, Harriet (2000) 'What on Earth is the Modern World-system? Foodgetting and Territory in the Modern Era and Beyond', *Journal of World-systems Research*, 1:2 (Summer/Fall), pp. 480–515.

Fukuyama (1992) *The End of History and the Last Man*, London: Hamish Hamilton.

Funtowicz, Silvio and J. Ravetz (1994) 'Emergent Complex Systems', *Futures* 26:6, pp. 568–82.

Galbraith, John K. (1975) *Money: Whence It Came and Where It Went*, London: Penguin.

George, Susan (1988) *A Fate Worse Than Debt*, London: Penguin.

Georgescu-Roegen, Nicolai (1971) *The Entropy Law and the Economic Process*, Cambridge, MA: Harvard University Press.

Gibson-Graham, J.K. (1996) *The End of Capitalism (as we knew it)*, Oxford: Blackwell.

Giddens, Tony (1998) *The Third Way*, Oxford: Blackwell.

Goldman, Michael (1998) *Privatizing Nature: Political Struggles for the Global Commons*, New Jersey: Rutgers University Press.

Gramsci, Antonio (1996) *Selections From the Prison Notebooks of Antonio Gramsci*, ed. and transl. Quintin Hoare and Geoffrey Nowell Smith, Madras: Orient Longman.

Granovetter, Mark S. (1985) 'Economic Action and Social Structure', *American Journal of Sociology*, 91, pp. 481–510.

Gray, John (1998) *False Dawn: The Delusions of Global Capitalism*, London: Granta Books.

Groh, Trauger M. and Steven S.H. McFadden (1990) *Farms of Tomorrow*, Kimberton, PA: Biodynamic Farming.

Group of Green Economists (1992) *Ecological Economics*, London: Zed Books.

Halsey, A.H. (1992) *Decline of Donnish Dominion: The British Academic Professions in the Twentieth Century*, Oxford: Clarendon Press.

Hammond, J.L. and Barbara Hammond (1911, 1917, 1919) *The Village Labourer 1760–1832*, Stroud: Allan Sutton (1995 edn).

Harcourt, Wendy, ed., (1994) *Feminist Perspectives on Sustainable Development*, London: Zed Press.

Hardin, Garrett (1968) 'The Tragedy of the Commons', *Science*, 162, December, pp. 1243–8.

Hardin, Garrett (1973) 'The Tragedy of the Commons', in Herman Daly, ed. *Toward a Steady-State Economy*, San Francisco: W.H. Freeman.

Harding, Sandra (1986) *The Science Question in Feminism*, Milton Keynes: Open University.

Hargrave, J. (1945) *Social Credit Clearly Explained*, London: SCP Publishing House.

Harriss, Barbara (1989) 'Organised Power of Grain Merchants in Dhaka Region of Bangladesh: Comparison with Indian Cases', *Economic and Political Weekly*, 24 March 1989, pp. A39–A44.

Harriss-White, Barbara (1999) 'Introduction: Visible Hands', Ch. 1 in Harriss-White, ed. (1999).

Harriss-White, Barbara, ed. (1999) *Agricultural Markets From Theory to Practice: Field Experience in Developing Countries*, London: Macmillan.

Hartmann, Heidi I. (1979) 'The Unhappy Marriage of Marxism and Feminism: Towards a More Progressive Union', *Capital & Class*, 8, Summer, pp. 1–33.

Harvey, Graham (1998) *The Killing of the Countryside*, London: Vintage.

Hayek, F. (1976) *Denationalisation of Money*, London, Institute of Economic Affairs.

Heilbroner, Robert L. (1988) *Behind the Veil of Economics: Essays in the Worldly Philosophies*, New York, London: W.W. Norton.

Helleiner, Eric (1999) 'Denationalising Money?: Economic Liberalism and the "National Question" in Currency Affairs', in Emily Gilbert and Eric Helleiner, eds, *Nation-States and Money*, Routledge: London.

Henderson, Hazel (1988) *The Politics of the Solar Age*, New York: Knowledge Systems Inc.

Hewitson, Gillian J. (1999) *Feminist Economics: Interrogating the Masculinity of Rational Economic Man*, Cheltenham: Edward Elgar.

Himmelweit, Susan (1995) 'The Discovery of "Unpaid Work"', *Feminist Economics*, 1:2, pp. 1–19.

Himmelweit, Susan, ed. (2000) *Inside the Household*, London: Macmillan.

Hines, Colin (2000) *Localization: A Global Manifesto*, Earthscan: London.

Ho, Mae-Wan (1999) *Genetic Engineering: Dream or Nightmare?*, Dublin: Gateway and Third World Network.

Hodgson, Geoffrey M. (1988) *Economics and Institutions: A Manifesto for Modern Institutional Economics*, Cambridge: Polity Press.

Hodgson, Geoffrey M. (2001) *How Economics Forgot History: The Problem of Historical Specificity in Social Science*, Routledge: London.

Hodgson, Geoffrey M., Warren J. Samuels and Marc R. Tool, eds (1994) *The Elgar Companion to Institutional and Evolutionary Economics*, Aldershot: Edward Elgar.

Hofrichter, Richard (1993) *Toxic Struggles*, Philadelphia: New Society Press.

Holcombe, Susan (1995) *Managing to Empower: The Grameen Bank's Experience of Poverty Alleviation*, London: Zed Press and Dhaka: University Press.

Huber, Joseph and James Robertson (*c*.2000) *Creating New Money: A Monetary Reform for the Information Age*, London: New Economics Foundation.

Hudson, Michael (1993) *The Lost Tradition of Biblical Debt Cancellations*, New York: Henry George School of Social Science.

Hulme, David and Paul Mosley (1996) *Finance Against Poverty*, London: Routledge.

Hunt, E.K. (1994) 'Class, Social, in Institutional Economics' in Geoffrey M. Hodgson, Warren J. Samuels and Marc R. Tool, eds, *The Elgar Companion to Institutional and Evolutionary Economics*, Aldershot: Edward Elgar.

Hunt, E.K. and Howard J. Sherman (1990) *Economics: An Introduction to Traditional and Radical Views*, New York: Harper Collins.

Hutchinson, Andrew and Frances Hutchinson (1997) *Environmental Business Management: Sustainable Development in the New Millennium*, London and New York: McGraw-Hill.

Hutchinson, Frances (1995) 'A Heretical View of Economic Growth and Income Distribution' in Edith Kuiper and Jolande Sap, eds, *Out of the Margin: Feminist Perspectives on Economics*, London: Routledge.

Hutchinson, Frances (1998) *What Everybody Really Wants to Know About Money*, Charlbury: Jon Carpenter Publishing.

Hutchinson, Frances and Brian Burkitt (1997) *The Political Economy of Social Credit and Guild Socialism*, London and New York: Routledge.

Hutchinson, Frances, and Wendy Olsen (2001) 'The Unsustainable Ship of Capitalist Money Management', Conference Proceedings, International Sustainable Development Research Conference, University of Manchester, 5–6 April.

Hynes, H. Patricia (1989) *The Recurring Silent Spring*, New York: Pergamon.

Ingham, Geoffrey (1984) *Capitalism Divided? The City and Industry in British Social Development*, London: Macmillan.

Ingham, Geoffrey (2000) 'Babylonian Madness: Or the Historical and Sociological Origins of Money' in John Smithhin, ed., *What is Money*, London: Routledge.

Jacobs, Michael (1991) *The Green Economy*, London: Pluto.

Kabeer, Naila (1994) *Reversed Realities*, London: Verso.

Kantor, Paula (2001) 'Female Mobility in India: Its Determinants and Influence on Economic Outcomes', Conference of the International Association for Feminist Economics, Oslo, Norway.

Kennedy, Margrit (1995) *Interest and Inflation Free Money*, Philadelphia and Gabriola Island: New Society Publishers.

Keynes, John M. (1919) *The Economic Consequences of the Peace*, London: Macmillan.

King, John E. (1988) *Economic Exiles*, London: Macmillan.

Klein, Naomi (2000) *No Logo*, London: Flamingo.

Korten, David C. (1995) *When Corporations Rule the World*, NY: Kumarian Press.

Kovel, Joel (2000) 'The Struggle for Use Value: Thoughts about the Transition', *Capitalism Nature Socialism*, 11:2, pp. 3–22.

Kuiper, E. and J. Sap, eds (1995) *Out of the Margin: Feminist Perspectives on Economics*, London: Routledge.

Lane, Robert (2000) *The Loss of Happiness in Market Democracies*, New Haven: Yale University Press.

Lang, Tim and Colin Hines (1993) *The New Protectionism: Protecting the Future Against Free Trade*, London: Earthscan.

Langley, Paul and Mary Mellor (2002) '"Economy" Sustainability and Sites of Transformative Space', *New Political Economy*, 7:1.

Latouche, Serge (1993) *In the Wake of the Affluent Society: An Exploration of Post Development*, London: Zed Press.

Lawson, Tony (1997) *Economics and Reality*, London: Routledge.

Lee, Keekok (1989) *Social Philosophy and Ecological Scarcity*, London and New York: Routledge.

Leyshon, Andrew and Nigel Thrift (1997) *MoneySpace: Geographies of Monetary Transformation*, London: Routledge.

Lietaer, Bernard (2001) *The Future of Money*, London: Century.

Lowenstein, Roger (2001) *When Genius Failed: The Rise and Fall of Long Term Capital Management*, London: Fourth Estate.

Lutz, Mark A. (1999) *Economics for the Common Good*, London: Routledge.

Lutz, Mark A. and Kenneth Lux (1988) *Humanistic Economics: The New Challenge*, New York: Bootstrap Press.

Mabey, Richard (1980) *The Common Ground: The History, Evolution and Future of the English Countryside*, London: Dent.

Macintosh, Maureen (2000) 'The Contingent Household: Gender Relations and the Economics of Unpaid Labour', in Susan Himmelweit, ed., *Inside the Household: From Labour to Care*, London: Macmillan.

Marx, Karl (1865/1898) *Wages, Price and Profit*, Peking: Foreign Language Press. (1975 edn).

Marx, Karl (1962) *Capital, Vol. III*, London: Lawrence Wishart.

Marx, Karl (1962) *Capital, Vol. III*, Moscow: Foreign Languages Publishing House.

Marx, Karl (1974) *Capital, Vol. I*, London: Lawrence Wishart.

Marx, Karl (1975) *Wages, Price and Profit*, Peking: Foreign Language Press.

Massingham, H.J. (1942) *The English Countryman: A Study of the English Tradition*, London: Batsford.

Mathews, Race (1999) *Jobs of Our Own: Building a Stakeholder Society, Alternatives to the Market and the State*, London and Sydney: Pluto Press/ Comerford and Mitchell.

Mayhew, Nicholas (2000) *Sterling: The Rise and Fall of a Currency*, Allen Lane, the Penguin Press.

Mayoux, Linda (1998a) 'Women's Empowerment and Micro-Finance Programmes: Approaches, Evidence and Ways Forward', DPP Working Paper no. 41, Open University, Development Policy and Practice Research Group.

Mayoux, Linda (1998b) 'Participatory Learning for Women's Empowerment in Micro-Finance Programmes: Negotiating Complexity, Conflict, and Change', *Bulletin of the Institute of Development Studies*, 29:4, pp. 39–50.

McCain, Marian von Eyk (2001) 'Time Bargains', *Resurgence*, 205, p. 53.

McCloskey, Donald N. (1994) *Knowledge and Persuasion in Economics*, Cambridge and New York: Cambridge University Press.

McEwan, Arthur (1999) *Neo-Liberalism or Democracy?*, London: Zed Press.

McIntosh, Alastair (2001) *Soil and South: People versus Corporate Power*, London: Aurum Press.

McMurtry, John (1999) *The Cancer Stage of Capitalism*, London: Pluto.

Meadows, Donella, J. Randers and W.W. Behrens (1972) *The Limits to Growth*, New York: Universe Books.

Meeker-Lowry, Susan (1995) *Invested in the Common Good*, Philadelphia: New Society Publishers.

Mellor, Mary (1992) *Breaking the Boundaries: Towards a Feminist Green Socialism*, London: Virago.

Mellor, Mary (1997a) *Feminism and Ecology*, Cambridge: Polity.

Mellor, Mary (1997b) 'Women, Nature and the Social Construction of "Economic Man"', *Ecological Economics* 20:2, pp. 129–40.

Mellor, Mary (1999) 'Ecofeminist Economics: Women, Work and the Environment', public lecture presented to Economia Ecologica 1998–99 sponsored by Fundacio Bancaixa Spain, Valencia, May 1999.

Mellor, Mary (2000a) 'Nature (Re) Production and Power: A Materialist Ecofeminist Perspective', in Fred P. Gale and R. Michael M'Gonigle, eds,

Nature, Production, Power: Toward an Ecological Political Economy, Edward Elgar: Cheltenham.

Mellor, Mary (2000b) 'Challenging the New World (Dis)Order: Feminist Green Socialism', in Sue Himmelweit, ed., *Inside the Household: From Labour to Care*, London: Macmillan.

Mellor, Mary, Janet Hannah and John Stirling (1988) *Worker Co-operatives in Theory and Practice*, Milton Keynes: Open University Press.

Merricks, Linda (1996) 'Frederick Soddy: Scientist, Economist and Environmentalist – An Examination of his Politics', *Capitalism, Nature, Socialism*, 7:4, pp. 59–78.

Mies, Maria (1986) *Patriarchy and Accumulation on a World Scale: Women in the International Division of Labour*, London: Zed Books.

Mitra, Ashok (1977) *Terms of Trade and Class Relations*, London: Frank Cass.

Monbiot, George (2000) *Captive State: The Corporate Takeover of Britain*, London: Macmillan.

Morris, William (1944) *Selected Works*, London: Cassell.

Nelson, Julie (1993) 'Gender and Economic Ideologies', *Review of Social Economy*, LI:3, pp. 287–301.

Nelson, Julie (1996) *Feminism, Objectivity, and Economics*, London: Routledge.

Nelson, Julie (1997) 'Feminism, Ecology and the Philosophy of Economics', *Ecological Economics*, 20:2, pp. 155–62.

Niggle, Christopher J. (1990) 'The Evolution of Money, Financial Institutions, and Monetary Economies', *Journal of Economic Issues*, XXIV:2, June, pp. 443–50.

Norberg-Hodge, Helena, Todd Merrifield and Steven Gorelick (2000) *Bringing the Food Economy Home: The Social, Ecological and Economic Benefits of Local Food*, Dartington, Devon: International Society for Ecology and Culture.

O'Connor, James (1973) *The Fiscal Crisis of the State*, New York: St. Martin's Press.

O'Connor, James (1988) 'Capitalism, Nature, Socialism: A Theoretical Introduction', *Capitalism, Nature, Socialism*, Issue 1, Fall, pp. 11–38.

O'Connor, James (1996) 'The Second Contradiction of Capital' in Ted Benton, ed., *The Greening of Marxism*, London and New York: The Guilford Press.

O'Hara, Phillip Anthony (2000) *Marx, Veblen, and Contemporary Institutional Political Economy: Principles and Unstable Dynamics of Capitalism*, Cheltenham: Edward Elgar.

Olsen, Wendy Kay (1998) 'Paradigms in the Analysis of Credit: Structures and Discourses in South Indian Banking', University of Bradford, Graduate School of Social Sciences and Humanities, Working Paper No. 5, September.

Olsen, Wendy Kay (2001) 'Stereotypical and Traditional Views About the Gender Division of Labour in Indian Labour Markets', *Journal of Critical Realism*, 4:1, pp. 4–12.

Olsen, Wendy Kay, and Lucia DaCorta (1990) 'On the Road to Nimmanapalle: An Empirical Analysis of Labour Relations in Drought-Prone Villages in South India', Discussion Paper No. 66, Department of Economics, University of Manchester, March.

Olsen, Wendy Kay and R.V. Ramanamurthy (1998) 'Contract Labour and Bondage in Andhra Pradesh (India)', *Journal of Social and Political Thought*, July, 1:2, <www.yorku.ca/jspot>.

Orage, Alfred R. (1926) 'An Editor's Progress Parts 1, 2 and 3', *The Commonweal*, pp. 376–9, 402–4, 434–7.

Otero, M. and E. Rhyne, eds (1994) *The New World of MicroEnterprise Finance*, London: IT Publications.

Parker, Hermione (1989) *Instead of the Dole: An Enquiry into Integration of the Tax and Benefit System*, London: Routledge.

Patnaik, Utsa (1987) *Peasant Class Differentiation: A Study in Method with Reference to Haryana*, Bombay: Oxford University Press.

Patnaik, Utsa (1988) 'Ascertaining the Economic Characteristics of Peasant Classes-in-Themselves in Rural India: A Methodological and Empirical Exercise', *Journal of Peasant Studies*, 15:3, April.

Patnaik, Utsa, and Manjari Dingwaney, eds (1985) *Chains of Servitude: Bondage and Slavery In India*, New Delhi: Sangam Pub.

Paxton, Angela (1994) *The Food Miles Report: The Dangers of Long Distance Food Transport*, SAFE Alliance.

Pearson, Ruth, and Cecile Jackson, eds (1998) *Feminist Visions of Development*, London: Routledge.

Penty, Arthur J. (1921) *Guilds, Trade and Agriculture*, London: Allen and Unwin.

Perkins, Patricia E. (Ellie) (2001) 'Discourse-based Valuation: Toward a Green Feminist Alternative to Globalized Markets', paper presented at the International Association for Feminist Economics Conference, June, Oslo.

Pinchbeck, Ivy and M. Hewitt (1969) *Children in English Society Vols I & II*, London: Routledge and Kegan Paul.

Polanyi, Karl (1944) *The Great Transformation*, Boston: Beacon Press (1957 edn).

Pretty, Jules (2001) 'The Real Costs of Modern Farming', *Resurgence*, 205, pp. 6–9.

Raddon, Mary-Beth (2001) 'Toward a New Harmony of Money and Reciprocity: Community Currencies in a Gendered Economy', PhD Thesis, University of Toronto.

Ramage Andrew and Paul Croaddock (2001) *King Croesus' Gold*, London: British Museum Press.

Robertson, James (1998) *Transforming Economic Life*, London: Schumacher Society and New Economics Foundation.

Robertson, James (2001) 'Sharing the Value of Common Resources Through Taxation and Public Expenditure', *Feasta Review*, 1, pp. 77–87.

Rowbotham, Michael (1998) *The Grip of Death: A Study of Modern Money, Debt Slavery and Destructive Economics*, Concord, MA and Charlbury: Jon Carpenter Press.

Rowe, Dorothy (1997) *The Real Meaning Of Money*, London: Harper Collins.

Rowell, Andrew (1996) *Green Backlash: Global Subversion of the Environment Movement*, London and New York: Routledge.

Sachs, Carolyn (1996) *Gendered Fields: Rural Women, Agriculture and Environment*, Boulder, CO: Westview.

Sachs, Wolfgang (1986) 'Delinking from the World Market', in Paul Ekins, ed., *The Living Economy: A New Economics in the Making*, London: Routledge and Keegan Paul.

Sahlins, Marshall (1974) *Stone Age Economics*, London: Tavistock.

Sayer, Andrew (1992) *Method in Social Science: A Realist Approach* (second edn), London: Routledge.

Schor, Juliet B. (1991) *The Overworked American: The Unexpected Decline of Leisure*, New York: Basic Books.

Schumacher, Fritz (1973) *Small is Beautiful*, London: Blond and Briggs.

Schumpeter, Joseph A. (1934) *The Theory of Economic Development: An Inquiry into Profits, Capital, Credit, Interest and the Business Cycle*, Oxford and New York: Oxford University Press (1961 edn).

Schumpeter, Joseph A. (1954) *History of Economic Analysis*, London and New York: Routledge (1994 edn).

Seers, Dudley (1983) *The Political Economy of Nationalism*, Oxford: Oxford University Press.

Sen, Amartya (2000) 'A Decade of Human Development', *Human Development*, 1:1, February.

Sherman, Howard J. (1993) 'The Historical Approach to Political Economy', *Review of Social Economy*, Fall, LI:3, pp. 302–22.

Shiva, Vandana (1988) *Staying Alive: Women, Ecology and Development*, London: Zed Books.

Simmel, Georg (1900) *The Philosophy of Money*, ed. David Frisby (1990), London: Routledge and Kegan Paul.

Simon, J. and H. Kahn, (1984) *The Resourceful Earth*, Oxford: Blackwell.

Smith, Adam (1776), *The Wealth of Nations*.

Smith, Mark J. (1998) *Social Science in Question*, London: Oxford University Press in association with the Open University.

Steingraber, Sandra (1998) *Living Downstream: An Ecologist Looks at Cancer and the Environment*, London: Virago.

Street, A.G. (1933) *Farmer's Glory*, London: Faber and Faber.

Stretton, Hugh (1999) *Economics: A New Introduction*, London: Pluto.

Thompson, E.P. (1991) *Customs in Common*, London: Penguin (1993 edn).

Thrift, Nigel and Andrew Leyshon (1999) 'Moral Geographies of Money', in Gilbert, Emily and Eric Helleiner, eds, *Nation-States and Money*, London: Routledge.

Twine, Fred (1992) 'Citizenship: Opportunities, Rights and Routes to Welfare in Old Age', *Journal of Social Policy*, vol. 21:2, pp. 161–75.

Veblen, Thorstein (1899) *The Theory of the Leisure Class*, New York: Mentor Books (1953 edn).

Veblen, Thorstein (1904) *The Theory of Business Enterprise*, New York: Mentor (1932 edn).

Veblen, Thorstein (1914) 'The Instinct of Workmanship and the State of the Industrial Arts' in Thorstein Veblen, *The Portable Veblen*, New York: Viking Press.

Veblen, Thorstein (1921) 'The Engineers and the Price System' in Thorstein Veblen, *The Portable Veblen*, New York: Viking Press.

Veblen, Thorstein (1923) *Absentee Ownership and Business Enterprise in Recent Times*, London: George Allen and Unwin (1924 edn).

Veblen, Thorstein (1948) *The Portable Veblen*, New York: Viking Press.

Veblen, Thorstein (1990) *The Place of Science in Modern Civilization*, New Brunswick and London: Transactions (First published 1919).

Veblen, Thorstein (1998) *Essays in Our Changing Order*, New Brunswick and London: Transactions (originally published 1934).

Vilar, Pierre (1991) *A History of Gold and Money 1450–1920*, London: Verso.

Wackernagel, Mathis and William Rees (1996) *Our Ecological Footprint*, Gabriola Is: New Society Publishers.

Walters, William (1999) 'Decentring the Economy', *Economy and Society*, 28:2, (May), pp. 312–23.

Warburton, Peter (1999) *Debt and Delusion: Central Bank Follies that Threaten Economic Disaster*, London: Allen Lane/Penguin.

Waring, Marilyn (1989) *If Women Counted*, London: Macmillan.

Weisacker E., A. Lovins and L. Lovins (1997) *Factor Four: Double in Wealth, Halving Resource Use*, London: Earthscan.

White, Gordon, ed. (1993) *The Political Analysis of Markets*, Special Issue of the *IDS Bulletin*, 24:4, Sussex: Institute of Development Studies.

Wood, Ellen Meiksins (1999) *The Origin of Capitalism*, New York: Monthly Review Press.

Woolf, Virginia (1927) *A Room of My Own*, London: Hogarth Press.

World Bank (1989) *World Development Report 1989*, Washington, DC: International Bank for Reconstruction and Development.

Worldwatch Institute (2000) *State of the World 2000*, New York: W.W. Norton & Co.

Wright, Lesley and Marti Smye (1997) *Corporate Abuse*, London: Simon and Schuster.

Zelizer, V.A. (1994) *The Social Meaning of Money*, New York: Basic Books.

Index

Compiled by Sue Carlton